Unexplained Mysteries
of World War II

Also by William B. Breuer

An American Saga
Bloody Clash at Sadzot
Captain Cool
They Jumped at Midnight
Drop Zone Sicily
Agony at Anzio
Hitler's Fortress Cherbourg
Death of a Nazi Army
Operation Torch
Storming Hitler's Rhine
Retaking the Philippines
Devil Boats
Operation Dragoon
The Secret War with Germany
Hitler's Undercover War
Sea Wolf
Geronimo!
Hoodwinking Hitler
Race to the Moon
J. Edgar Hoover and His G-Men
The Great Raid on Cabanatuan
MacArthur's Undercover War
Feuding Allies
Shadow Warriors
War and American Women

Unexplained Mysteries
of World War II

William B. Breuer

CASTLE BOOKS

This edition published in 2006 by

Castle Books ®

A division of Book Sales, Inc.
276 Fifth Ave., Suite 206
New York, NY 10001

This edition published by arrangement with and permission of
John Wiley & Sons, Inc.
111 River Street
Hoboken, New Jersey 07030

This publication is designed to provide accurate and authoritative information in regard to the subject matter covered. It is sold with the understanding that the publisher is not engaged in rendering professional services. If professional advice or other expert assistance is required, the services of a competent professional person should be sought.

ISBN-13: 978-0-7858-2253-0
ISBN-10: 0-7858-2253-4

Printed in the United States of America

Dedicated to
RICHARD J. SEITZ
Lieutenant General, U.S. Army (Ret.),
a young paratroop battalion leader
in World War II who earned the
respect and admiration of his
fighting men and later rose to the
top in his profession

Contents

Part Three—Curious Happenings

Part Four—Uncanny Riddles

Part Five—People Who Vanished

Part Six—Peculiar Premonitions

Part Seven—Strange Encounters

Acknowledgments

Many books have been written about the great campaigns, strategic designs, high-level decisions, incidents of battles, and scenes of heroism and daring that occurred during World War II. Absent has been a comprehensive focus on the vast and intriguing arena of the mysterious, baffling, oddly coincidental, and inexplicable. This volume helps fill that reportorial void.

There has never been, nor is there ever likely to be, a shortage of "scholarly experts" without personal experience in war who scoff at episodes that defy the accepted terms of logic. However, as nearly all combat veterans and high commanders know, logic is often a stranger in wartime.

The accounts in this book have been painstakingly collected over a period of years from newspapers, magazines, and other publications of the World War II era; military reports stored in various archives; books by authors of integrity who participated in or had intimate knowledge of the events they described; and interviews or correspondence with participants. In the last category, I have scrupulously guarded against inadvertent bias or exaggeration by requiring corroboration by two or more persons directly involved in an incident.

With regard to premonitions, I have used only episodes in which a person had either voiced an omen to at least two other individuals prior to the incident, had entered the foreboding in a diary, or if the person survived the event, had promptly told at least two others about the presentiment.

Many persons played roles in the creation of this book. My wife, Vivien, a skilled writer, was of enormous help in researching, coordinating interviews, and providing pertinent observations and suggestions on the manuscript. Others who have assisted significantly include:

Pierre Gosset, Battle of the Bulge Foundation, Liege, Belgium; Hilary Roberts, Imperial War Museum, London; Dr. Richard J. Sommers, U.S. Army Military History Institute, Carlisle, Pennsylvania; Alyce Mary Guthrie, executive director, PT Boats, Inc., Memphis, Tennessee; Henry J. Shaw, Jr., chief historian, Marine Corps Headquarters, Washington, D.C.; Colonel Lyman F. Hammond (Ret.), director, Douglas MacArthur Memorial, Norfolk, Virginia.

Professor Reginald V. Jones, Prime Minister Winston Churchill's World War II scientific adviser, Aberdeen, Scotland; Dr. William F. Atwater, Don F. Pratt Museum, Fort Campbell, Kentucky; Major Keith O'Kelly (Ret.), Queen's Messenger, Hampshire, England; Dr. John Duvall, 82nd Airborne War Memorial Museum, Fort Bragg, North Carolina; Dr. Dean C. Allard, senior historian, and B. F. Cavalcante, archivist, Naval Historical Center, Washington, D.C.; Dr. Dan Holt, director, Dwight D. Eisenhower Library, Abilene, Kansas; Charles Steinhice, reference librarian, Chattanooga Public Library, Chattanooga, Tennessee; and the staff at the Modern Military Records, National Archives, Washington, D.C.

WILLIAM B. BREUER

Chilhowee Mountain
Tennessee
July 1996

It is a riddle wrapped in a mystery inside an enigma.
—Winston S. Churchill

Part One

Puzzling Events

Dress Rehearsal
for Pearl Harbor?

LIEUTENANT MASTAKE OKUYAMA was leading a squadron of Japanese Imperial Navy bombers on a sweep up China's broad Yangtze River, known to the Chinese as Ch'ang Chiang (Long River), for it flows for thirty-one hundred miles from deep within the country and empties into the Yellow Sea. Among the great cities on the Yangtze's banks are Shanghai and Nanking. It was the morning of December 12, 1937.

At the same time that Lieutenant Okuyama and his squadron were winging up the rich valley of the Yangtze, keeping a sharp eye below for vessels plying up and down the river, the USS *Panay*, a 450-ton gunboat, was heading downriver. Especially built in Shanghai for service on China's rivers, the *Panay* was built to protect American shipping from the bands of cutthroat pirates that infested those waters.

In charge of the *Panay* was Lieutenant Commander James J. Hughes, a Naval Academy graduate, who had held the post since the previous year. His gunboat was 191 feet overall, and its arms included a main battery of two three-inch guns, a battery of .50-caliber antiaircraft machine guns, and ten standard .30-caliber machine guns for use against pirate attacks at close quarters.

Her twin buff funnels and awning-rigged upper walls identified the *Panay* as a shallow-draft boat, and the huge American flags billowing from her bow and stern staffs could be seen at a great distance by even the most myopic individual.

The *Panay*, which had a crew of fifty-five, was on a "mercy mission," having evacuated from Nanking, which was under siege by the Japanese army, four U.S. Embassy officials, five refugees, and a bevy of western journalists. Now, just before noon, Commander Hughes's boat had churned for thirty miles, and he radioed his position to Shanghai, reporting that he was anchoring the craft.

A savage war had been raging in China since the sultry night of July 1, 1937, when an "incident" occurred near Peking's (Beijing's) historic Marco Polo Bridge. A jittery unit of the Kwantung Army, which the warlords in control of the Japanese government had sent to "guard" their interests in the city, opened fire on a nearby encampment of Generalissimo Chiang Kai-shek's Nationalist Chinese Army after one of the latter's soldiers suddenly vanished into the darkness.

It was later discovered that the Chinese soldier had been struck with a sudden need to heed the call of nature, but shots rang out and the two sides began a firefight. Using that pretext ("wanton aggression against Imperial Japan") Japanese warlords poured troops, tanks, and airplanes into China, and a full-scale conflict erupted.

Japan was fully mobilized. Printed government pamphlets exhorted the home front and the military to "self-sacrifice" for the beginning of "a crusade to liberate Asia and the western Pacific from imperialism." Actually, that "liberation crusade" had its origins ten years earlier. In 1927, Japanese generals and admirals held that an armed conflict with the United States was inevitable. So they drew up a top-secret plan called the Tanaka Memorial—a blueprint for military conquest of China and vast expanses of Asia and for war with the United States.

Now, a decade later on the Yangtze River near Nanking, all hands on the gunboat *Panay* were enjoying a leisurely lunch when they were interrupted at 1:30 P.M. by a shout from Chief Quartermaster Lang: "The Japs are letting bombs go!"

Roaring down on the anchored *Panay* was Lieutenant Mastake Okuyama's squadron, which would later be described as having eight to fifteen aircraft. Commander Jim Hughes rushed to the pilothouse, which was then ripped apart by an explosion that broke the skipper's leg.

On deck, Universal News's Norman Alley grabbed his motion-picture camera and started filming. The planes zoomed in so low that he could easily make out the faces of the pilots. Alley was dumbfounded over the fact that they continued to bomb the *Panay* when they no doubt could clearly see the huge American flags fore and aft, waving in the breeze.

At the same time, crewmen on the *Panay* leaped to their machine guns and sent bursts in the direction of the diving Japanese planes. Jim Marshall, Far East correspondent of *Collier's* magazine, was watching in amazement. The attackers were so low that it was impossible for them not to know they were bombing an American ship, he reflected. Moments later, Marshall was seriously wounded by bomb fragments that struck him in the neck, shoulder, stomach, and chest.

Meanwhile, Lieutenant Arthur F. Anders, the executive officer, took command from the badly injured skipper, Jim Hughes. While directing the futile machine-gun fire against the swooping Japanese aircraft, Anders, of Vallejo, California, tumbled over with jagged wounds in the throat.

Twenty minutes after the first explosion, the *Panay*, riddled by machine-gun bullets and bomb fragments, began to sink. Lieutenant Anders, sprawled on deck, bleeding profusely and unable to speak because of his neck wound, took a piece of white chalk and scribbled on the bulkhead: "Take to [life] boats. Stay as close to shore as possible. Then send the boats back."

Crewmen and passengers scrambled over the side, climbed into the lifeboats, and paddled madly for shore. Others jumped off the side and began

USS Panay *sinking in the Yangtze River. (U.S. Navy)*

swimming. Suddenly, they heard the terrifying noise of Japanese planes diving once again, and then there was the angry hissing of machine-gun bullets pelting the water around them.

Just as the survivors reached the shelter of the reeds along the bank, a Japanese launch raced up and rained bursts of machine-gun fire toward the huddled men. Then the launch turned and raked the sinking *Panay*. But before the gunboat went under, the launch pulled up to it and a few Japanese officers scrambled aboard, perhaps in a search for secret codes or new devices.

For several days, the survivors' ordeal continued as they trudged inland for twenty miles to seek haven within Chinese lines. All the while, bands of Japanese soldiers stalked the countryside in an effort to hunt them down.

Once the *Panay* survivors reached safety, they took stock of their losses. Two American sailors and an Italian newspaper reporter, Sandro Sandini, had been killed, and seventeen crewmen and U.S. Embassy officials had been wounded, some of them seriously.

In the meantime, the day after the *Panay* was sunk, Japanese General Iwane Matsui, a squat figure with horn-rimmed glasses who rode astride a symbolic white horse, led his victorious troops into Nanking on the heels of Chiang Kai-Shek's retreating forces. Matsui proclaimed that the "Japanese Imperial way is shining through."

With that, Japanese troops launched a bloodbath in Nanking, the likes of which had been unknown since the days of the barbaric Attila the Hun. An estimated 250,000 Chinese civilians—men, women, and children—were murdered, mainly by beheading with samurai swords or bayoneting. The carnage came to be known as the Rape of Nanking. Even hardened German army observers were shocked by what they reported to Berlin as systematic butchery.

When word of the *Panay* episode reached the United States, there were strident cries of outrage. Usually reserved Cordell Hull, the white-haired, soft-spoken secretary of state, denounced the *Panay* sinking as the handiwork of "wild, half-insane" Japanese admirals and generals.

American anger intensified a few days later, when Colonel Kingero Hashimoto, the senior Japanese officer in the region, who hated the United States with a passion, was quoted in newspapers as declaring, "I had orders to fire [on the *Panay*]."

In the White House, President Franklin D. Roosevelt viewed the newsreel film shot from the deck of the *Panay* by Universal News's Norman Alley. Then, exercising presidential power, Roosevelt ordered the censoring of the close-ups of Japanese pilots' faces before the newsreel was released to American theaters. This selective film editing was intended to calm the public's outrage and avoid war with the powerful Japanese military machine.

Had the *Panay* attack really been an accident? Or had it been a sort of dress rehearsal for the sneak raid on Pearl Harbor, Hawaii, that would be launched nearly four years later? Did the Japanese warlords want to test American will and fiber by their deadly attack? Far from being a "tragic case of mistaken identity," as the Japanese later claimed, many American military leaders privately were convinced that the assault had been a planned, finely tuned operation, a joint venture involving dive bombers, a heavily armed launch, and foot soldiers.

Perhaps the Japanese warlords had many questions that could be answered by the *Panay* attack. Just how strong—or weak—would be the official American reaction to the bloodletting and property destruction? How strong and well-trained was the United States military establishment? There were a few thousand American marines stationed in nearby Shanghai. Would they be rushed to the scene of the *Panay* attack to confront possible follow-up assaults?

Seeking not to be plunged into direct confrontation in the Far East, the Roosevelt administration, after expressing a proper amount of public indignation, couched their official protests to the Japanese government in delicately worded phrases, charging that the Japanese pilots had been guilty of "reckless flying."

Possibly in a bid to cloak their real future intentions against the United States, the Japanese government apologized for the Yangtze River violence and handed over a compensation check in the amount of $2,214,007.36. However, the stark question remains: Had the Japanese warlords become so emboldened by America's wishy-washy response to the unprovoked attack on the *Panay* that they considered the United States to be a paper tiger and continued with their plans for the sneak raid on the U.S. Pacific Fleet at Pearl Harbor?[1]

Shadowy German Scientist

EARLY IN 1939, war clouds were gathering over Europe, but most of the German *Herrenvolk* (people) wanted peace. In late August, William L. Shirer, an American correspondent for CBS radio, strolled the streets of Berlin and talked with scores of ordinary citizens. That night, he wrote in his diary: "Everybody here is against the war. How can a country get into a major war with a population so dead against it?"

Adolf Hitler had already pondered that question. At a conference in his Bavarian mountaintop retreat on August 22, the führer told his top generals and admirals: "I shall give a propaganda cause for starting the war. Never mind if it is plausible or not. The victor will not be asked afterward if he told the truth. In starting and waging a war, it is not right that matters, but victory!"

At dawn on September 1, 1939, five German armies, paced by swarms of shrieking Stuka dive-bombers, poured over the Polish frontier and began to converge on Warsaw from three sides. The speed, power, and finesse of the German juggernaut, the most powerful that history had known, created a new word in the languages of many nations: *Blitzkrieg.*

On September 3, after the German führer had curtly rejected an ultimatum by British Prime Minister Neville Chamberlain to withdraw from Poland, England and France declared war on Germany. Woefully unprepared for a major conflict, Great Britain and France could only sit on the sidelines and watch the far-outnumbered, undertrained, and ill-equipped Polish army be smashed in only twenty-seven days.

Then, on October 17, three weeks after the Nazi swastika was hoisted over Warsaw, Vice Admiral Hector Boyes, the Royal Navy attaché at the British Embassy in Oslo, Norway, ripped open the envelope he had just been handed by an aide and began reading the anonymous letter enclosed. Written in longhand, the source said that if the British wanted highly important information on German technical and weapons developments, it should indicate an affirmative answer by altering the beginning of the regular BBC (British Broadcasting Company) German Service broadcast to insert the words: "*Hullo, hier ist London*" (Hello, here is London).

Intrigued and mystified by the curious letter from an unknown yet seemingly authoritative source, Admiral Boyes rushed the missive to his government in England.

In that late autumn of 1939, London was gripped by a climate of foreboding. There had been plenty of war news—all of it bad. In an atmosphere of gloom, Stewart Menzies, chief of MI-6 (Great Britain's secret service), and his top officials gathered in his headquarters on Broadway, a quiet side street near Parliament Square and Westminster Abbey.

Menzies and his aides discussed intensely the significance of the anonymous letter that Admiral Boyes had received in Oslo. Was it the handiwork of a crackpot? Several felt that it might be some sort of psychological warfare gambit perpetrated by the Abwehr, the Third Reich's secret service, a clandestine apparatus with some sixteen thousand agents on seven continents.

Finally, the MI-6 hierarchy, at Menzies's urging, decided to follow up on the Oslo letter and authorized changing the BBC broadcast preamble to "Hullo, hier ist London."

Thus began one of the most intriguing and complex mysteries of World War II.

On November 4, 1939, a week after the BBC broadcast, a guard at the British Embassy in Oslo, six hundred miles from London, was making his rounds in a heavy snowstorm when he spotted a parcel on a stone ledge. Wrapped in kraft paper and bound by sturdy string, the container was roughly three inches thick, twelve inches wide, and fifteen inches long. It was half covered by snow, and had it not been found at the time, the package might have been buried in the white stuff, undetected for weeks.

The parcel was addressed to Admiral Hector Boyes, and the guard rushed it to the naval attaché. When Boyes opened the package—very gingerly, for it might have contained a bomb—he found eight pages of typewritten text detailing German technical innovations under development and a number of sketches of what appeared to be revolutionary new weaponry, including huge rockets. Boyes rushed the parcel to London.

Thirty-six hours later, copies of the mystery package contents were distributed to several British scientists and intelligence experts for their analyses and conclusions. Most of the experts were skeptical. A few of them considered the documents to be fakes, a devious scheme by the Germans to cause the British to waste valuable time pursuing technological developments that didn't exist.

However, twenty-eight-year-old Reginald V. Jones, who was on the staff of the British secret intelligence service, was startled by the extent of the technical disclosures. It seemed logical that the Germans were developing an entirely new dimension of warfare. Chief among these haunting new German weapons were a radio-controlled glide-bomb, a pilotless aircraft called the V-1 (later known to the Allies as a buzz bomb), and massive long-range rockets labeled V-2s.

While British scientists used the detailed drawings and text to develop countermeasures, the identity of the person responsible for the Oslo mystery package remained a subject of heavy debate among the British privy to its secrets. How had one individual (presumably a German) been able to collect so many Third Reich top secrets—including detailed drawings—and have the means and the ingenuity to get the priceless data to British leaders?

It was clear that the individual had an extensive technical and scientific background and direct access to weapons developments in the Third Reich. It was also obvious that the Oslo-packet author was a staunch anti-Nazi, one who desperately wanted Adolf Hitler's dreams of conquest stifled and who would risk death for the cause.

Professor Reginald V. Jones of British intelligence was startled by the contents of the Oslo package. (Courtesy R. V. Jones)

There were countless conjectures over the identity of the conspirator. Whomever he or she may have been, the unknown person played an unheralded but major role in Britain's thwarting Adolf Hitler's plans for the future. Perhaps MI-6 chief Stewart Menzies, who had numerous clandestine contacts within the Third Reich, had known. If so, he took the puzzling secret to his grave.[2]

Spy in the War Cabinet?

IN EARLY AUGUST 1940, England braced for an invasion by the German Wehrmacht, which was coiled across the channel and ready to spring. Within ten months after war had broken out, Adolf Hitler reigned as the absolute ruler of most of western Europe.

"If the Boche [Germans] come," Winston Churchill confided to an aide, "We'll have to hit them on their heads with beer bottles—we've got no other weapons!"

However, Hitler decided he would never have to launch Operation Sea Lion, a cross-channel invasion. On August 1, he signed General Order No. 17, which directed Hermann Goering, who had been recently elevated to the specially created post of Reichsmarschall, to bring England to its knees with air power alone.

Arrayed along the channel coast and on up into Norway were 3,358 Junkers, Dorniers, Heinkels, Stukas, and Messerschmitt 109s and 110s—a force of unprecedented numbers. All across southern England, a few hundred Royal Air Force (RAF) fighter pilots, flying Spitfires and Hurricanes, grimly prepared to confront this mighty challenge.

These RAF fighter pilots were a breed apart—brash, scrappy, and courageous. A few years earlier, many had been avowed pacifists. Some had signed the controversial Oxford Pledge, in which they swore that they would never fight "for King and Country." But now, with the survival of England at stake, they would fight and give their lives if need be.

Air Marshal Hugh Dowding, chief of the RAF Fighter Command, had been forewarned by electronic intercepts (code-named Ultra) that Goering was unleashing an all-out onslaught. Armed with this knowledge, the revolutionary miracle of radar, and an excellent radio-control system, the fifty-eight-year-old Dowding would direct what Churchill called the Battle of Britain from an underground chamber (known as The Hole) at Fighter Command headquarters at Bentley Prior in Middlesex.

For four weeks, fierce, murderous clashes raged over the skies of England and the channel. Through Ultra, Dowding knew in advance the Luftwaffe's targets and tactics, permitting RAF tactical officers to gather their squadrons at the right places, times, and altitudes, concentrating British power against the main assaults, rather than frittering away the slender RAF air reserves by chasing madly across the skies after secondary or decoy flights.

But, while Air Marshal Dowding had a figurative ear planted in Hermann Goering's Luftwaffe headquarters, the Germans apparently had a pipeline directly into the British War Cabinet. Although Goering and his commanders were not privy to detailed RAF tactics, the enormous advantage that Dowding enjoyed, Adolf Hitler and the German high command were learning of top-level British governmental decisions within hours after they were made.

At this time, with Britain in its greatest peril since the Spanish Armada sailed into the English Channel in 1588, United States Naval Intelligence in Washington, D.C., and Hawaii was intercepting and decoding top-secret wireless messages transmitted by the Japanese naval attaché in Berlin to the chief of the Third Section, Naval Staff, at Imperial General Headquarters outside Tokyo. In part, one signal read: "I have received from the German navy minutes of a meeting held by the British War Cabinet on 15 August (1944). . . ."

Unfortunately for Great Britain, this telltale Japanese communication, and many others in a similar vein, would not be known until late in the war in Europe. In 1940, American Naval Signals Intelligence was staffed by only a handful of men, and only a few of them were capable of translating Japanese into English. So tremendous was the flood of intercepted Japanese communications that it took three and a half years before hard-pressed American naval men reached the stack of accumulated intercepts that revealed the Nazis seemed to have had a pipeline into the British War Cabinet.

Who was this Nazi mole in the highest councils of the British government? At a time when the Battle of Britain was raging in 1940, how had this person managed to slip long and detailed War Cabinet minutes involving the most crucial decisions to Berlin?

What were the informant's motives? Was he or she planning on not only providing the Nazis with high-grade intelligence, but also trying to undermine the Winston Churchill government and have it replaced by another that would be receptive to surrendering when the Germans leaped the channel and invaded Great Britain?

Could this person have been an associate of the notorious Tyler Gatesworth Kent, a twenty-nine-year-old American who had been destined for high places in the U.S. State Department? A tall and personable young man, Kent had come to the American Embassy in London in October 1939 (a month after war broke out). Well-educated, studious, and a speaker of five languages, Kent had developed a firm belief in the Nazi line that international Jewry had propelled the world into war in order to gain influence and authority over the ruins.

Despite his drastic theories, Tyler Kent was trusted completely and assigned to the top-secret embassy code room by Ambassador Joseph P. Kennedy, Sr. (whose son John would one day be president of the United States). There, Kent had access to the most highly confidential communications between Ambassador Kennedy and U.S. Secretary of State Cordell Hull. Also available to the young embassy official were dispatches by other American envoys in Europe who used the London facility as a message center.

What's more, Tyler Kent handled the Gray Code, a cipher system that the State Department thought to be unbreakable. It was the Gray Code that Winston Churchill and President Roosevelt used for their most secret communications.

In early 1940, it became clear to British security agencies that secret information was finding its way to Berlin and Rome, the Axis partners aligned against Great Britain. A complicated trail led to Tyler Kent, and at 10:00 A.M. on May 20, Kent was arrested by Scotland Yard detectives. Found in his possession was a set of keys that enabled Kent to get into the safe where Ambassador Kennedy kept his secret papers.

Tyler Kent denied that he was a spy, although raiding detectives had found some fifteen hundred secret embassy documents hidden in his apartment. He was dismissed from the State Department and, with his immunity gone, was tried, convicted, and sentenced to seven years in Dartmoor, the harshest of British prisons.

Since Kent had been arrested on May 20, 1940—some three months prior to the beginning of the Battle of Britain—he could not have committed the treachery of furnishing secret War Cabinet proceedings to Berlin. But had he left behind in the government a fellow traveler who carried on in his place? Either way, the traitor who provided Adolf Hitler with a pipeline into a crucial British agency remains an unknown figure.[3]

Phantom of Scapa Flow

UNDER A BRILLIANT DISPLAY of northern lights that illuminated the region, a German U-boat commanded by Lieutenant Günther Prien, a bold and dashing skipper, slipped through the maze of channels and currents girdling the stronghold of the British Home Fleet—Scapa Flow, the vast anchorage in the Orkney Islands of northeast Scotland. Prien headed for his target, the old battleship *Royal Oak*. It was nearing midnight on October 13, 1939—six weeks since Great Britain went to war with the Third Reich.

The British admiralty was not too concerned about the safety of its warships. Scapa Flow was considered to be impenetrable to submarines. On the *Royal Oak*, most of the 1,146 members of the crew were sleeping peacefully, secure in the knowledge that German U-boats could not get to them.

Suddenly, the stillness over Scapa Flow was shattered by three tremendous explosions, one right after the other. Lieutenant Prien had fired three torpedoes, all of which crashed into the battleship. Mortally wounded, the *Royal Oak* capsized in only thirteen minutes, taking to a watery grave 832 crewmen and the ship's skipper, Rear Admiral H. F. C. Blagrove. Meanwhile, the U-boat sneaked back out of Scapa Flow along the same route it had entered, undetected and unscathed.

It was a stupendous maritime feat and a colossal propaganda victory for the Third Reich. Günther Prien and his crew were received as heroes in Berlin, and the U-boat skipper was decorated with the Knight's Cross by Adolf Hitler himself.

In London, the admiralty, deeply embarrassed and humiliated by the *Royal Oak*'s demise while in its own anchorage, assumed that the U-boat had been guided to its target by a spy in the Orkneys. MI-5, the British counterintelligence service, was promptly blamed by the admiralty for failing to flush out this Nazi spy.

MI-5 agents descended en masse on the Orkneys to find the elusive spy who had made this German exploit possible. The search failed. Spy mania gripped the people of the Orkneys: Clearly, a highly dangerous Nazi was loose in their midst.

Sixteen months later, in the spring of 1942, a popular American magazine, the *Saturday Evening Post*, published an article identifying the Scapa Flow spy as a former officer in the German Imperial Navy, Captain Alfred Wehring.

U-boat skipper Günther Prien, hero of Scapa Flow. (Captured German painting, National Archives)

According to the *Post* account, Wehring had been recruited in 1928 by German intelligence to be its man at Scapa Flow, which, it was believed, would be a crucial location in any coming war against the British. Wehring adopted the fictitious name Albert Oertel, posed as a Swiss watchmaker, and opened a small shop in the village of Kirkwall in the Orkneys.

Twelve years later, Wehring emerged from deep undercover and signaled to Captain Karl Doenitz of the U-boat command detailed intelligence about Scapa Flow's defenses, its unpredictable currents, and its navigation obstacles.

Authored by Curt Reiss, an American journalist and espionage scholar, the *Saturday Evening Post* blockbuster article said that, acting upon this A-1 intelligence from Wehring, Doenitz sent Lieutenant Prien, guided by Alfred Wehring (Albert Oertel), into Scapa Flow to attack the *Royal Oak*. Wehring boarded the U-47 at the mouth of the flow, acted as pilot-navigator, then returned to the fatherland in triumph after twelve years of deep undercover in Scotland.

Almost imperceptibly, the "Phantom of Scapa Flow" entered the hallowed halls of espionage lore. Even the top Nazis were impressed by Wehring's spy feat. SS General Walther Schellenberg, chief of the Sicherheitsdienst (SD), the intelligence branch of the Schutzstaffel (SS), pointed to the Scapa Flow episode as a prime example of the importance of "intelligently planned co-operation between [spies in the field] and military operations."

After the war, Major General Vernon G. W. Kell, the MI-5 chief, wrote that "the Germans had been supplied with up-to-date information by a spy." In England, with peace coming nearly six years after the *Royal Oak* had been sunk, controversy continued to swirl around the event. The admiralty clung to its strong contention that Wehring (Oertel) had been the culprit.

However, a number of British journalists, probing into the affair, descended on the Orkneys and failed to locate anyone who had ever known of, much less seen, Alfred Wehring, who for twelve years was said to have been masquerading in Kirkwall as Albert Oertel, a Swiss watchmaker.

Lieutenant Günther Prien, the one man who could have provided precise information, died in mid-1941, when the U-boat was sunk in the Atlantic Ocean. Word of his demise was withheld from the German people for six months.

So the question remains: Had there really been a Nazi undercover spy long embedded in the fabric of life in the Orkneys, a German who performed one of history's boldest espionage feats, or had it simply been the Phantom of Scapa Flow, who had become quite real?[4]

Bewildered Allied Generals

UNITED STATES SENATOR William Borah dubbed it "The Phony War." British Prime Minister Neville Chamberlain called it "The Twilight War." To the Germans, it was a *Sitzkreig* (sitting war). Since Adolf Hitler's high-octane military machine had crushed Poland in September 1939, the British and French in the Maginot Line and the Wehrmacht in the Seigfried Line had been idling the time away, trying to keep from shooting one another.

Newspaper editorial writers in Britain and the United States put on their sharpest hue of rose-colored glasses. The Phony War, they wrote, would eventually fade away, with each combatant returning home with no further loss of life or destruction of property.

Against this heady climate of optimism, on January 10, 1940, a light aircraft winging along Belgium's border developed engine trouble and had to make an emergency landing. The plane's wings were ripped off as it crashed through the trees. From a nearby guard post along the frontier with Germany, several Belgian soldiers dashed to the scene to help.

The two men who had been in the plane had survived the crash. Although wearing civilian clothes, both men were officers in the German army. One was the pilot and the other was Major Helmuth Reinberger, thirty-two years of age. Neither man was injured. The two Germans were taken to a nearby Belgian army headquarters, from where they demanded to be allowed to telephone their ambassador or the German military attaché in neutral Belgium.

A small, but exceedingly hot, potbellied stove warmed the command post. Seated on a chair, Major Reinberger seemed to be dozing. Elsewhere in the room, two Belgian soldiers were relaxing. Suddenly, Reinberger leaped to his feet and bolted to the stove. He flung open the door of the stove, burning his hands painfully, and crammed a batch of papers that had been concealed under his long, gray greatcoat into the fire.

At that moment, Captain Emilio Rodrigue, the Belgian area commander, was just entering the room to interrogate the Germans. He rushed to the stove and reached in and pulled out the papers, which had started to burn briskly. His hands, too, became badly burned.

Without a word, Reinberger made a lunge for the Belgian captain's revolver, and the two men went down in a heap and rolled back and forth on the floor. Other Belgian soldiers rushed to help subdue the German officer.

"I'm finished!" Reinberger declared. "I'll never be forgiven for what I've done! I didn't want your revolver to kill you, I wanted it to kill myself!"

Although Reinberger's papers had been damaged in the fire, Belgian intelligence pieced together fragments and were greeted by the heading "General Order of Operations." The order began: "The German Army in the West will take the offensive between the North Sea and the Moselle River. . . ." There were words such as Festung Holland (Fortress Holland), VII Fliegerkorps (Seventh Flying Corps), and Panzergruppe (tank group). The Belgian generals could not believe their eyes: Here was almost the entire operational plan for Case Yellow, the pending German invasion of France and the Low Countries.

Had Reinberger's papers been a "plant," one to get the Western Allies chasing their tails indefinitely? Belgian intelligence was determined to find the answer. When Major General Wernher Wenninger, German military attaché in Brussels, asked permission to talk with Major Reinberger, approval was granted quickly and the two Germans were ushered into a comfortable room where they could speak confidentially. However, unbeknown to the Wehrmacht officers, the Belgians had bugged the room.

Belgian electronic eavesdroppers situated down the hall heard Reinberger explain to the general that he had succeeded in burning all of the Case Yellow operations plan—a bald-faced lie, but one that seemed to bring relief to the worried Wenninger. The courier's remark proved to the Belgians that the papers were genuine, not a plant.

In Berlin, Adolf Hitler didn't believe Reinberger's tale and flew into a towering rage. "It was the greatest storm I had ever seen," Colonel General Wilhelm Keitel, the führer's military confidant, later declared. "The führer was possessed, foaming at the mouth, pounding the wall with his fists, and hurling insults at 'the incompetents and traitors of the general staff,' " whom he threatened with execution for their involvement in the seeming fiasco that had unveiled to the enemy his plans for imminent conquest in the West.

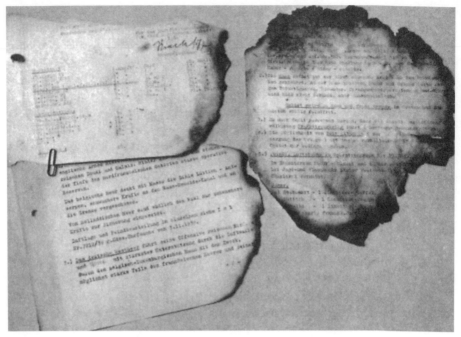

Burned fragments of the German plan for Case Yellow. (National Archives)

Hitler and his generals presumed that the Case Yellow plan would be smuggled to the Allied high command. But when German intelligence reported no changes in British and French troop dispositions, the führer ordered Case Yellow to proceed as planned, with minor alterations.

Throughout the early months of 1940, a mountain of other evidence became available to the Allies pointing toward Hitler's plan for a full-blooded offensive in the West.

In Rome, on January 12, 1940, Princess Marie-José of Piedmont, the wife of the Italian crown prince, paid a call on Count Galeazzo Ciano, dictator Benito Mussolini's son-in-law and the Italian foreign minister. Ciano, a tall, handsome chap, secretly hated "that Nazi gang" with a passion. He especially loathed Hermann Goering and Gestapo chief Heinrich Himmler. Almost in tears, Princess Marie-José expressed the fear that the German army was on the brink of charging into Belgium, her native country.

That night Count Ciano penned in his diary: "I told her that in the light of our latest information, it now seems very probable. She no doubt will immediately inform [Belgian] King Leopold." Ciano then, in essence, made a mighty effort to derail the conquest train of "that Nazi gang."

Elsewhere during prior weeks, "turned" spies working for the French had pilfered documents that designated the objectives of Case Yellow. French and British reconnaissance flights had reported heavy concentrations of German troops and panzers just behind the Reich frontier. And, most significant of all, Ultra, the top-secret British deciphering service, had intercepted and decoded hundreds of Wehrmacht wireless signals that indicated Case Yellow was nearly ready to go.

On April 30, 1940, Dr. Josef Mueller, a prominent lawyer from Munich, landed in a Lufthansa civilian airliner at the Rome airport and caught a taxi to his hotel. Mueller, a devout Catholic, was on the most crucial mission of his life: He would try to warn the British and French that Adolf Hitler was preparing to launch Case Yellow.

Dr. Mueller was a leader in the Schwarze Kapelle (Black Orchestra), a tight-knit conspiracy of prominent German generals and government leaders, whose aim was to get rid of the führer—one way or another. The conspirators were convinced that Hitler was taking the fatherland recklessly down the road to total destruction.

Mueller had been picked for this vital assignment because he had numerous contacts in the Vatican and was well liked by Pope Pius XII. Among the lawyer's other friends at the Holy See was Father Robert Leiber, a Jesuit who was a confidant of the Pope.

In an earlier mission in October 1939, Mueller had met secretly with the Pope, who had agreed to become an intermediary between the Schwarze Kapelle and the British government. The Pope's contact would be D'Arcy Osborne, the British ambassador to the Vatican. The Pope stressed that his motive was peace based on the assurances of France and England that they would not take advantage of any inner turmoil that might erupt following the "disposition" of Adolf Hitler and invade and occupy Germany. Neither the British nor French governments were willing to make that concession.

Josef Mueller was in anguish about his task. He considered himself to be a loyal German. If his mission succeeded and Case Yellow was repulsed by an alerted British and French army, how many of the flower of German youth would fall due to his action?

Mueller carried with him a carefully worded statement that had been drawn up by Schwarze Kapelle leaders before he left. Its main theme was that Adolf Hitler was preparing to attack in the West—and soon. Mueller handed the statement to his old friend Father Leiber, who, presumably, passed it on to the Pope and to Ambassador Osborne.

Father Leiber then rushed to inform his former college classmate, the Jesuit priest Reverend Theodor Monnens, and Monnens, in turn, took the alarming message to Adrien Nieuwenhuys, the Belgian ambassador in Rome. Nieuwenhuys scoffed at its contents, but changed his mind a day later when Abbot General Hubert Noots, a Belgian who was the head of the Premonstratensian Order, told Nieuwenhuys that the Wehrmacht would soon invade the Low Countries and France with swarms of panzers, infantry, Fallschirmjäger (paratroops), and airplanes. Ambassador Nieuwenhuys became deeply alarmed, and he fired off a warning to his government in Brussels. It was May 2.

A week later on the night of May 9, old friends Colonel Hans Oster, deputy chief of the Abwehr, and the Dutch military attaché, Major Gijsbertus Sas, were dining at Oster's home on the outskirts of blacked-out Berlin. Oster, who had long been a member of the Schwarze Kapelle, was both depressed and furious. Bitterly, he told Major Sas that earlier that evening, the führer had given the final order to kick off Case Yellow.

At that moment, there were 2.5 million German troops, formed into 102 divisions, 9 of them armored and 6 motorized, massed along the French, Belgian, and Dutch borders. Zero hour would be 3:30 A.M. the next day, May 10, 1940.

After dinner, Colonel Oster drove to the German high command to see if there had been a change in plans. There had been none: The attack was on. Returning to his home, Oster exclaimed to Sas, "The swine has gone to the Western Front." The "swine" was Adolf Hitler.

Sas telephoned the Belgian military attaché in Berlin, then rushed to his own embassy. He placed a call to Dutch military headquarters in The Hague, and by means of a prearranged code, told his superiors, "Tomorrow at dawn! Hold tight!"

A few hours after Major Sas had spread the alarm, a cavalcade of blacked-out vehicles rolled up to a huge concrete bunker located in a heavily forested mountaintop south of the ancient German city of Aachen. It was 3:00 A.M. on Y day (assault day) for Case Yellow. Code-named Felsennest (Aerie on the Cliffs), the bunker would be Adolf Hitler's command post for directing the offensive.

Only thirty minutes after the Nazi warlord had arrived, swarms of screeching Stukas began pounding targets in neutral Belgium and The Netherlands. Two hours later, German infantry and panzers charged over the frontiers. Despite the colossal amount of high-grade evidence, much of it from within the higher councils of the enemy camp, the bewildered Allied generals were taken by total surprise. Even the führer's commanders were astonished by the speed and extent of their own victories.

Within an incredible six weeks, the surging Wehrmacht conquered France, Belgium, Luxembourg, and The Netherlands, and drove the British army off the Continent. Left behind in the channel port of Dunkirk were nearly all of England's tanks, artillery pieces, vehicles, and ammunition.

Why the Allied high command, which became paralyzed when Case Yellow struck, had been so remarkably unprepared for the onslaught remains one of the most baffling mysteries of the war.[5]

Hitler Scuttles Operation Felix

IN THE WAKE of the fall of France in mid-1940, Adolf Hitler was enraged by British Prime Minister Winston Churchill's snubbing of the "peace" overtures the führer had issued and of England's obvious bulldog determination to con-

A British soldier stands guard on Gibraltar to warn of possible German assault.
(National Archives)

tinue the war single-handedly. So while Hitler's generals were drawing up detailed plans for Sea Lion, the looming cross-channel invasion of England from northern France and Belgium, Hitler decided to "drive the Anglo-Saxons [as he always called the British] out of the western Mediterranean." The fuhrer's goal could be achieved by capturing the Rock of Gibraltar, a British crown colony occupying a peninsula on the southern coast of Spain. A limestone mass which rises 1,408 feet above the water, the fortress is separated from the African coast by the narrow Strait of Gibraltar.

Gibraltar is connected with the Spanish mainland by a low, sandy isthmus a mile and a half long. This strip forms a heavily guarded "neutral zone" between Spain and Gibraltar. If the Germans were to seize the huge rock, the narrow passage linking the Atlantic Ocean and the Mediterranean would be closed to Allied ships.

An ambitious plan code-named Felix was drawn up by the German high command. Gibraltar would be attacked in late November 1940. Because of his long-standing close relationship with Generalissimo Francisco Franco, the

Spanish dictator, Admiral Wilhelm Canaris, the Abwehr (German secret service) boss, was assigned by Hitler to do the spadework for Felix. Canaris's mission was primarily to reconnoiter "The Rock," long a British bastion, prior to the attack and to coerce Franco into joining the venture. Spain had been neutral during the war, but far more neutral toward Nazi Germany than toward the Western Allies.

Suddenly, Canaris, who had for a lifetime been willing to remain in the shadowy background, became smitten with delusions of Napoleonic grandeur. Not only did he make plans to carry out the spying aspect of Felix, but he embarked on a grandiose plot to have himself designated controller of the entire operation.

In his self-appointed role as a sort of "super field marshal," Canaris led a star-studded intelligence team to the Spanish mainland just across the water from Gibraltar to study the terrain and to develop a basic attack plan. Perhaps never in the history of espionage had a mission involved such a galaxy of distinguished spies—the chief of German intelligence himself (Canaris); his top aide, Colonel Hans Piekenbrock; and Commander Wilhelm Leissner, the Abwehr chief in Spain (who was deep in undercover as Gustav Lenz, a respected businessman of Madrid).

Fired up by his self-instigated role, Canaris launched an avalanche of reconnaissance ventures around Gibraltar and infiltrated a bevy of spies into Spain, which, as a result, became a popular tourist attraction of the Abwehr. In order to get himself a free vacation at an ornate Spanish resort, all an Abwehr man had to do was to hatch some scheme that had even a remote bearing on Felix.

By the end of 1940, the entire Gibraltar area had been charted in detail and the defenses had been mapped, down to machine-gun posts and minefields. However, it had all been a monumental waste of time and effort, because Hitler suddenly scuttled his chance to capture the crucial bastion of Gibraltar. No explanation for his decision has ever come forth.[6]

Japanese Spies in Washington

IN THE SPRING OF 1941, with the war clouds spreading over the Pacific, Japanese warlords at the Imperial General Headquarters outside Tokyo were totally unaware that U.S. Army and Navy cryptologists had broken the warlords' secret codes and were eavesdropping on their wireless messages. Operation Magic was the cover name that American intelligence used to protect the source and circulation of the inside information from within the highest councils in Tokyo.

Collaborating on unmasking and deciphering the Japanese signals were the Navy's Combat Intelligence Unit, set up in Hawaii under the command of Lieutenant Joseph J. Rochefort, and the Army's Special Intelligence Service, led by a brilliant young cryptologist, Colonel William Friedman.

Intercepting and deciphering the avalanche of Japanese wireless messages was a gargantuan task for the undermanned American intelligence units, but large numbers of the intercepts disclosed clues to an alarming situation in officially neutral United States: This country, especially Washington, D.C., had become the focus of widespread Japanese and German conspiracies and espionage. Intercepts also indicated that an undetermined number of Americans in high-level positions in the Roosevelt Administration were, knowingly or otherwise, providing highly valuable intelligence to Tokyo and Berlin.

Who were the mysterious "J—— and W——" that the Japanese ambassador in Washington informed Tokyo were reliable information sources because they "are in close touch with the president and his wife Eleanor?" Were these two mystery persons social acquaintances? Political contacts? Or did they hold sensitive posts in the Roosevelt Administration?

In May 1941, the cagey Japanese spymaster in Washington, Taro Terasaki, who, from the sanctuary of his embassy in the capital, directed the entire Japanese espionage apparatus in the Western Hemisphere, wired Tokyo that the half-million dollars for "the development of intelligence" had been received by him. Who were the sources in Washington receiving payments from this hefty chunk of spy money?

On May 19, Taro Terasaki, who had attended Brown University in Rhode Island years earlier, identified two of his classmates: W—— of the U.S. State Department's European section and a prominent senator. The Japanese spymaster indicated that these two cronies had been "helpful" to him. "Helpful" consciously or unconsciously?

Was J. Edgar Hoover's highly efficient but undermanned Federal Bureau of Investigation, along with Army and Navy intelligence, aware of and keeping a close watch on the high-level Washington officials who, knowingly or otherwise, appeared to be aiding the German and Japanese cause? These questions have never been satisfactorily answered.[7]

Stalin: An Outwitted Bungler

FOR TWO DAYS, in excess of 3 million men of the German army had been lying in the dark woods with their tanks and other vehicles along a two thousand mile stretch of the Soviet Union frontier. They had arrived, driving with masked headlights, during the night of June 19 to the twentieth, 1941.

During the day, they had lain silent, forbidden to make a sound. At a mere rattle of a hatch cover on a panzer, Wehrmacht commanders had tossed fits. Only when darkness fell were the Feldgrau (field gray, the average German soldier) allowed to steal to nearby streams or other watering holes to wash, a few at a time.

Each panzer—there were thousands of them—was in full battle order, carrying ten jerrycans of fuel strapped to its turret, and each had a trailer in tow with even more drums. These were the preparations for a long journey. And indeed one was envisioned—all the way to Moscow, one thousand miles to the east.

Within hours, Adolf Hitler's war juggernaut would be unleashed in Operation Barbarossa, the mightiest offensive that history had yet known. The führer himself, from a new command post hidden in a thick forest near Rastenberg in East Prussia, would be calling the shots. As H-hour (attack hour) approached, Hitler grew increasingly excited. "When Barbarossa commences, the world will hold its breath!" he told his generals.

Far to the east, in the Kremlin in Moscow, Soviet dictator Josef Stalin, customarily one of the most suspicious members of the human species, seemed to be ignoring the stark fact that a colossal threat to the existence of the Soviet Union was being mounted along its western frontier, from Finland on the north to the Black Sea on the south. This, despite an avalanche of high-grade intelligence available to him. Never had a leader of a nation in modern times been so deluged with information about a looming invasion by a hostile force.

Less than three months earlier, British Prime Minister Winston Churchill had sought to warn Stalin of imminent danger. The top-secret message sent to the Soviet leader on April 3 had read:

PRIME MINISTER TO SIR STAFFORD CRIPPS [BRITISH AMBASSADOR IN MOSCOW]. FOLLOWING FROM ME TO J. STALIN, PROVIDED THAT IT CAN BE PERSONALLY DELIVERED BY YOU.

"I HAVE SURE INFORMATION FROM A TRUSTED AGENT THAT . . . THE GERMANS ARE GOING TO MOVE FIVE PANZER DIVISIONS FROM ROMANIA TO SOUTHERN POLAND [ALONG THE SOVIET BORDER] . . . YOUR EXCELLENCY WILL READILY APPRECIATE THE SIGNIFICANCE OF THESE FACTS."

Strangely, Commissar of Foreign Affairs Vyacheslav M. Molotov, who had been handed Churchill's signal by Ambassador Cripps, failed to pass the urgent warning along to Stalin until three weeks later, on April 22.

What Churchill had not disclosed to Stalin was that the "trusted agent" was in reality Ultra, which had been intercepting and decoding hundreds of Wehrmacht orders clearly revealing that Hitler was massing huge forces on the Soviet frontier.

For his part, Stalin scoffed at the Churchill warning. Nearly two years earlier, on August 23, 1939, Adolf Hitler and Stalin had signed a German-Soviet nonaggression pact. Stalin was convinced that the wily Churchill, an outspoken foe of Communism, was engaged in a machination to split Berlin and Moscow.

Soon after, alarming information corroborating Churchill's warning began to pour into the Kremlin from around the world. Among the coded signals was one from Richard Sorge, who was stationed in Tokyo as the Far East correspondent of the *Frankfurter Zeitung*, a leading newspaper in the Third Reich. Sorge had long been in the pay of the Soviet secret service.

Josef Stalin. (National Archives)

In Japan, Sorge had cultivated a close friendship with General Eugen Ott, the führer's envoy to the Mikado. Ott was well connected with members of the Imperial General Staff from whom he learned the most secret information and, often as not, Ott passed these disclosures on to his old pal Richard Sorge, who was clearly a loyal German, or so Ott thought.

So on May 19, 1941, Sorge, an old hand at espionage, sent a message to the Kremlin that Hitler was massing nine field armies (a correct total), which included 150 divisions (only 3 divisions too low) along the Soviet frontier. Less than two weeks later, Sorge dispatched to Moscow a detailed account of the strategy the Wehrmacht would use to bring the Soviet Union to its knees. A few days afterward, the *Frankfurter Zeitung* correspondent flashed the precise date of the German attack: June 22, 1941.

Then from Switzerland more danger signals flooded the Kremlin. Soviet spies, headed by Rudolf Roessler, a German émigré who operated a bookstore in Lucerne as a cover, used clandestine transmitters in Geneva and Lausanne to dispatch direct messages to Moscow. These transmitters were known to the German secret service as The Red Trio.

On June 14, then on June 16, 17, and 18, the transmitters sent long, detailed messages, based on high-grade intelligence gathered by the shadowy Rudolf Roessler, code-named Lucy. Not only did the "three musicians," as the Lucy Ring was known in Moscow, supply the Wehrmacht's strategic plan for Barbarossa, the precise number of panzers distributed among the three army groups (North, Center, and South), but they also supplied the date of the invasion. They further radioed the Wehrmacht's precise objectives and even the names of all senior officers down to the corps commanders. After the Lucy Ring radio operator had finished his night-long transmission and had collapsed exhausted on a bed, his only answer from Moscow was a curt: "Understood. Over."

There were other pointed clues that the German armed forces had massed and were about to attack. On June 18, a Wehrmacht deserter slipped across the border into the Soviet Union and reported that the German offensive would hit on June 22. Again, Stalin turned a blind eye to this startling piece of intelligence.

There were other strange happenings that seemed to have mystified Soviet intelligence. During the previous two months, twenty-four Luftwaffe reconnaissance flights had penetrated Soviet air space, even though Berlin and Moscow were supposed to be allies. One plane crashed. Top-quality cameras were found in the wreckage, and they contained film which, when developed, left no doubt that their prime mission had been to photograph Russian military installations along the border.

Moreover, there were economic indicators that could have been interpreted as evidence that Adolf Hitler had his conqueror's eye on the Soviet Union. For the past three months, German firms that had signed a trade-agreement contract with the Kremlin the previous January 10 suddenly stopped sending their goods to Russia.

Now O-Tag (D-day) for Barbarossa was just over the horizon. Hitler's legions, hidden along the border in Poland, were in fine fettle, and hoped to succeed where Napoleon Bonaparte had failed in 1812.

In far-off Washington, D.C., Secretary of State Cordell Hull, a white-haired, courtly Tennesseean, called in the Soviet ambassador, Constantin Umansky, and warned him that American legations in Europe had heard of a planned invasion of Russia by the Wehrmacht.

Finally, Winston Churchill warned Stalin that the British had learned "from unimpeachable sources" (meaning Ultra) the date of the German assault—June 21. Although Churchill had once dismissed Communism as "foul baboonery," he had good reason to alert the man the Western Allies called Uncle Joe.

"If Hitler invaded Hell," the cherubic prime minister remarked to his private secretary, "I would make at least a favorable reference to the Devil in the House of Commons."

In the eerie stillness of the predawn hours on O-Tag, thousands of German artillery pieces roared in a thunderous barrage that struck the Soviet frontier along its entire two thousand miles. German armies totaling 3 million men swept across the border. The Russians were taken by total surprise.

Two hours later, at 6:00 A.M., while panzers were racing into Russia, Count Friedrich von der Schulenburg, the German ambassador in Moscow, handed a document to Commissar of Foreign Affairs Molotov. It was Hitler's cynical declaration of war, reading in part:

> Information received in the past few days by the government of the Reich leaves no doubt as to the aggressive nature of Soviet troop movements . . . The government of the Reich declares in violation of its solemn engagements the Soviet government has been guilty of making preparations, of an obvious kind, and in violations of the German-Russian Non-Aggression Pact, to attack Germany. . . .
>
> As a result, the führer has ordered the armed forces of the Reich to meet such a threat with every means at their disposal.

Pale, tense, silent, Commissar Molotov took the document, spit on it, tore it up, and then rang for Poskrebishev, his confidential secretary. "Show this man out—through the back door!" Molotov barked.

The speed of the Nazi advance was breathtaking. Hundreds of Soviet warplanes were destroyed on the ground. Hordes of dazed Russians surrendered. On the very first day, Brest-Litovsk, key to Soviet central defenses, fell. Confused, cut off, frantic Russian commanders radioed one another: "We are being fired on! What should we do?"

"Fired on? Who by?"

"Hell, the Germans!"

"You must be insane! Why are you sending such a signal uncoded—are you trying to start a war?"

Barbarossa had been a colossal success. In its first phases, perhaps 3 million Soviet soldiers had been killed, wounded, or captured; twenty-two thousand guns, eighteen thousand tanks, and fourteen thousand warplanes were destroyed or seized.

Meanwhile, in London on the morning of June 21, Winston Churchill was given word of the Wehrmacht onslaught. Having been forewarned, he never blinked an eye. Later, he told a confidant, "So far as strategy, foresight, and competence are arbiters, Uncle Joe Stalin and his commissars showed themselves at this moment the most completely outwitted bunglers of the war!"

Bungler that he may have been, how had Joe Stalin been so totally duped as to his old crony Adolf Hitler's malevolent intentions? None of the sources from which he had received high-grade intelligence—Winston Churchill, Richard Sorge, Rudolf Roessler, and Cordell Hull—were in connivance with one another. Indeed, it was doubtful if Sorge and Roessler even knew of the existence of the other.

Had there been a German sympathizer, even a spy, in the Soviet high command? Why had Foreign Affairs Commissar Molotov pigeonholed Churchill's dire warning of April 3 for nearly three weeks before showing it to Stalin? What became of the telltale film that had been taken from the crashed Luftwaffe plane?

These questions may never be answered. All that is certain is that Uncle Joe Stalin had been caught with his epaulets down.[8]

Switzerland: Hitler's Next Conquest?

IN MID-JULY 1941, Brigadier Colonel Roger Masson, the keen-witted 70-year-old chief of Swiss intelligence, was deeply worried. From an A-1 source, he had just received word that Adolf Hitler, who already controlled most of western Europe, was leaning toward invading tiny Switzerland, a neutral country in the war and one that had long been known for its peaceful pursuits.

Masson's pipeline into the Oberkommando der Wehrmacht (German high command) was Rudolf Roessler, a native of Germany who was vehemently anti-Nazi and who operated a small publishing house, the Vita Nova Verlag, in Lucerne, as a cover for his spying activities. Over the years, while living in Berlin, Roessler, a slight, hawk-nosed man who wore horn-rimmed glasses, had cultivated a close friendship with a few generals and colonels on the high command staff. These German officers, at the risk of their own lives, had long been slipping top-secret information to Roessler in Switzerland in order to rid the fatherland of the führer and Nazism.

On receiving the startling news about Hitler's next target being Switzerland, Brigadier Colonel Masson directed his own agents (who had long been living just across the Swiss border in southern Germany) to search for any indication of Wehrmacht concentration in that region. Back came word that six German divisions, two of them mountain troops, were encamped near the border and ready to attack.

For some while, Adolf Hitler's Abwehr had been preparing for eventual war with Switzerland. There were more German spies per square yard in the Swiss Confederation, as the nation is officially called, than in any other country in the world. A German known as Uncle Frank was in charge of the vast espionage network, and he had infiltrated more than one thousand agents into Swiss industrial and political circles. Another Abwehr officer, Major Fritz Heiland, furnished these spies with money, false identification papers, special inks, radios, and cameras.

When a violent deed was required to further Nazi aims, members of Heinrich Himmler's Gestapo or those in the Jagdkommando (hunter commandos) were called on. It was the Jagdkommando that had been designated to inflict the first violent action on peaceful little Switzerland, possibly as a prelude to a Wehrmacht invasion.

In June 1940, a month before master spy Rudolf Roessler warned Swiss intelligence of German intentions, a Swiss railway worker was inspecting tickets on the Romanshorn-Zürich train. When ten male passengers boarded at Weinfelden and took seats in two carriages, the eagle-eyed railway worker became deeply suspicious of a glaring coincidence: All of the ten men were carrying identical brown canvas suitcases.

All the while, the ten passengers had been eyeing the railway worker. Suddenly, as if on cue, all ten leaped up and bolted off the train when it halted momentarily at a village. At Märstetten, the next stop, the railway worker informed Swiss police of his qualms.

Brigadier Colonel Masson, working with the police, organized an intensive search, and two days later, nine of the men with identical brown canvas suitcases were apprehended. Seven were Germans and two were Swiss. Each man had about 500 French francs (115 U.S. dollars) in his pocket. Carried in the various suitcases were an "infernal machine" loaded with six pounds of dynamite, tools, Luger pistols with hundreds of cartridges, and an assortment of vicious-looking daggers.

Under intense interrogation, one of the nine confessed that the sabotage team had been assigned to blow up an ammunition dump at Altdorf and to sabotage the runways of Swiss Air Force airfields at Spreitenbach, Bienne, Lausanne, and Payerne.

Three months later, at dawn on September 4, 1940, a convoy of vehicles bearing the Red Cross emblem halted beside the road near a viaduct over which the Annecy–La Roche-sur-Foron railway crossed a deep ravine. Some men from the convoy got out of their vehicles and began to get busy under the hood of the first vehicle, which appeared to have stalled.

At the same time, several others in the convoy planted nearly two hundred pounds of TNT under a pillar of the bridge; then the convoy drove on. Three hours later, the neighborhood was rocked by an enormous explosion and the bridge collapsed into the ravine. It was over this span that the Swiss would have had to rush troops to repel an invading force.

As one of the fruits of extensive German espionage operations in Switzerland, an area about the combined size of Massachusetts, Connecticut, and Rhode Island, the Wehrmacht was able to publish an eighty-five-page volume entitled *Handbook of the Swiss Army*. It seemed hardly likely that the Germans would have gone to such great effort and expenditure of funds unless Adolf Hitler had planned to invade his southern neighbor, a nation of less than 5 million people.

By early 1941, German espionage agencies were employing against Switzerland the technique of überschwemmung (inundation). For every Nazi spy that disappeared (and the shrewd Roger Masson and his operatives nabbed many of them), five more were sent as replacements. There were now so many Germans living in Switzerland under one cover or another, that they had become almost a state within a state.

Basel, an international juncture between Switzerland, Germany, and France, was the jumping-off spot for Nazi agents being infiltrated into the Swiss Confederation. Disguised as railroad workers, the spies were taken across the border and handed over to accomplices in Switzerland. Over the course of three nights, two members of Swiss counterintelligence counted a total of 348 known German spies sitting quietly in Basel station, waiting for the appropriate time to be slipped into the Swiss Confederation.

This, then, was the situation in mid-July 1941, when six first-rate Wehrmacht divisions were poised across from the northern frontier of Switzerland, and tremendous effort—sabotage, espionage, and industrial infiltration—had been expended to pave the way for an invasion. Why had Adolf Hitler never issued the order to strike, just as he had ordered strikes during the past fifteen months against other small, neutral nations: Denmark, Norway, Luxembourg, The Netherlands, and Belgium?

Perhaps the führer had been hesitant to commit even six divisions, along with numerous Luftwaffe squadrons, at a time when his legions were heavily involved in the Soviet Union, which had been invaded a month earlier on June 21. However, the reason why Switzerland had been spared from almost certain destruction by the Nazi war juggernaut is a question that may never be answered.[9]

Suspicious Advertisement

No sooner had the Japanese bombed a woefully unprepared United States into global war at Pearl Harbor, Hawaii, on December 7, 1941, than the home front became consumed by the specter of a Japanese or Nazi spy, saboteur, or subversive hiding behind every bush, all of these sinister figures boring into the nation's vital core like a worm into a rotten apple.

In that national climate of spy mania, many local law enforcement officers took matters into their own hands. In Norfolk, Virginia, site of a major naval base, the chief of police rounded up and jailed all fourteen Japanese aliens living in that city. In Newark, New Jersey, the public safety director ordered police to board trains and arrest "all suspicious looking Orientals" and "other possible subversives," leaving it up to the individual police officer to figure out who "looked suspicious" and who did not.

In Galveston, Texas, a civilian guard thought a blinking light in a house was flashing signals to unseen enemy ships offshore, so he fired a rifle shot into the structure, barely missing a housewife testing a new lamp. Farmers armed with shotguns and hunting rifles posted themselves at each end of the Missouri town of Rolla and halted each passing vehicle that "looked suspicious." North Carolina's governor ordered state police cars to be painted black (presumably to make them inconspicuous at night and, therefore, difficult targets for armed enemy agents), and he instructed his law officers to make arrests without warrants, otherwise they could not act "even if they saw a spy preparing to blow a bridge."

Oregon's governor promptly proclaimed a state of emergency. When questioned, he admitted that he didn't know what kind of emergency he was heralding. In Denison, Texas, the mayor and city council convened in emergency session and debated buying a machine gun for the police department to use to deal with "gangs of enemy agents." During the session, an excited man burst into the chamber and called out that New York City was being bombed. This action prompted the mayor to propose that instead of one machine gun, the city buy two.

Various local governments organized armed civilian bands to thwart potential saboteurs, and the vigilantes, many of whom did not know which end of a rifle the bullet came out of, stood watch over likely targets: bridges, railroad trestles, water reservoirs, docks, tunnels, dams, and public buildings. Few had any military training. A woman driving across the San Francisco Bay Bridge failed to hear a challenge by a band of armed civilians, one of whom shot at and seriously wounded her. On Lake Michigan, jittery sentries shot and killed a duck hunter and wounded his companion, mistaking the victims for "saboteurs."

Meanwhile, agents of the Federal Bureau of Investigation fanned out across the nation and methodically picked up several thousand persons who were on subversives lists. (By July 1942, the FBI had taken 9,405 loyalty suspects into custody.) Piled on top of that mind-boggling task, the FBI agents had to track down the sources of thousands of rumors that flooded the agency's field offices about enemy spies and saboteurs.

One of the FBI investigations focused on a strangely worded advertisement that appeared in the *New Yorker* magazine sixteen days before Pearl Harbor. The ad promoted a new dice game called The Deadly Double. Hundreds of calls poured into the FBI's Manhattan offices about the advertisement from nervous, even hysterical, citizens.

Actually, it was two ads. A small one near the front of the November 22, 1941, issue—a teaser ad, as it is called in the industry—contained the words: "Achtung! Warning! Alerte!" Below this headline was a pair of dice, one white and the other black, with three faces of each die visible to the reader. The faces of the white die showed the numbers 12 and 24 and an XX (the double-cross sign). On the black die were the numerals 0, 5, and 7. Just above the dice was a solicitation to the curious reader: "See advertisement Page 86."

On page 86, there was a much larger advertisement with a repeat of the blaring headline: "Achtung! Warning! Alerte!" At the bottom of the one-column ad were again the words "The Deadly Double" and below that a stylized drawing of an eagle.

After Pearl Harbor, speculation was rampant about the two ads in the *New Yorker* having been placed by Nazi and/or Japanese spies as a means of notifying their agents in the United States that war was about to erupt.

The numbers 12 and 7 on the dice could have meant the month (December) and the day (the 7th) when the attack would be launched. And the numerals 5 and 0 could have meant the planned time of the assault. The XX (20 in Roman numerals) might have represented the approximate latitude of

the target. No one could come up with a significance for the 24, but it could have been the code designation of the enemy source that had placed the ads.

At the top of the larger ad on page 86 was a drawing that was interpreted by many as depicting the noses of three airplanes (bombers) winging over a large body of water toward their target, presumably Pearl Harbor. Adding credence to this theory was what appeared to be a bomb exploding on the water, antiaircraft shells bursting in the air, and powerful searchlight beams crisscrossing the sky (indicating that the original Japanese plan had called for a night attack, a plan that could have been changed after the advertisement had been submitted to the *New Yorker*).

Many interpreted the words "The Deadly Double" to allude to the war partners, Nazi Germany and the Empire of Japan. The double-headed eagle seemed quite similar to the heraldic symbol of Adolf Hitler's Third Reich.

FBI agents discovered that the advertisement had been placed by the Monarch Trading Company (a dummy corporation). A white male, who had not given his name, had brought the plates for the ad to the *New Yorker* offices and had paid in cash. He had not given his address. Curiously, the man the FBI would identify as the suspect apparently met a sudden, violent death a few weeks later.

Was the *New Yorker* advertisement a sophisticated means for German or Japanese espionage operatives in the United States to warn colleagues and sympathizers that the Japanese were about to launch a sneak attack somewhere in the Pacific? Swamped by a flood of other investigations in the wake of the Pearl Harbor catastrophe, the undermanned FBI was not able to fully explore that possibility.[10]

Operation North Pole

MAJOR HERMANN GISKES, a handsome man with graying hair, who was the Abwehr chief in The Netherlands, was engaged in an ongoing feud with Obersturmbannfiihrer (Lieutenant Colonel) Josef Schreieder of the SD, the security and intelligence branch of the SS, Adolf Hitler's private army. Although Giskes and Schreieder hated one another, they had to collaborate to achieve a common goal—the destruction of the British espionage network in The Netherlands, which had been occupied by the Germans since May 1940.

Major Giskes had code-named his mission Unternehmen Nordpol (Operation North Pole). Schreieder's somewhat overlapping function was to organize "reception committees" for Allied agents and supplies parachuted into Holland, and to arrest and interrogate the captured spies.

In The Netherlands in the spring of 1942 there was no shortage of eager Dutch traitors. The Germans called them Vertauensmann (V-men). These turncoats were greedy scum who were quite willing to send patriotic Dutch citizens to their deaths for relatively small payoffs.

One of these Dutch traitors was George Ridderhof, a sloppy, vulgar creature, a small-time criminal who had been arrested in Amsterdam in November 1942 and convicted for trying to slip illegal diamonds and opium into the country. In prison, he overheard whispered information about a Dutch underground network called Orde Dienst. In charge of the secret organization was a Captain Van den Berg, Ridderhof learned, and Van den Berg was in contact with two agents of the Special Operations Executive (SOE), a British agency whose mission it was to bedevil the Germans in the occupied countries.

Ridderhof contacted the Germans, told them what he had found out about the Dutch underground activities, and offered to work for the occupiers.

Smuggling charges were promptly dropped, and Ridderhof was released from prison and put on the Abwehr payroll at five hundred guilders per month.

Ridderhof was a godsend to Major Giskes and Lieutenant Colonel Schreieder. Although their Funk-Überwachungsstelle (radio surveillance department) already had detected clandestine radio signals from SOE agents in The Netherlands, it could not locate the transmitters. In the weeks that followed, Ridderhof penetrated Captain Van den Berg's underground network and gained information about the location of two transmitters. Within hours, Abwehr and SD men swooped down on the Dutch operators, capturing them and their transmitters.

Van den Berg's operators were told that to avoid execution, they would have to send to London false or misleading messages as compiled by Abwehr men. Most of the captured spies agreed, knowing that they had an ace up their sleeves. Before they had departed from England, their SOE controllers had given the Dutch operators "identity checks" to be used if the spies were captured and forced to send dot-and-dash messages on their wireless sets. Each Dutch agent had been told to make a deliberate mistake after a specified number of letters when sending a message. With this procedure, London would know that the agent had been captured, the transmitter had been "turned," and the messages had been created by the Germans.

One Dutch agent captured after parachuting to the ground was Hubertus Lauwers, a thin, bespectacled man who looked more like a mild-mannered bank clerk or an accountant than a spy. Although a German technician was seated at Lauwers's side when he was forced to send German messages, Lauwers made a deliberate mistake in every sixteenth letter of each message, as he had been instructed by London.

Incredibly, London failed to pick up Lauwers's flaws or those sent out by the other two turned transmitters. Instead, the SOE controllers transmitted to Lauwers the specific drop zones and times when more Dutch agents would land by parachute in The Netherlands. As a result, Abwehr and SD men were on hand to grab the SOE spies when they landed during the following weeks.

By mid-1943, Major Giskes had five turned transmitters pouring false messages into SOE headquarters in London and receiving back secret information. Giskes called it Englandspiel (English talking game). Although delighted to be getting advance notice of SOE plans, Giskes, an espionage operative skilled in cat-and-mouse games, often was puzzled over the subtle duel of wits between the SOE in London and the captured Dutch agents operating the turned transmitters for the Germans. Which adversary was the cat and which the mouse? Why had the British secret service, long recognized for its cleverness and ingenuity, suddenly become stupid?

In early July, a German technician informed Giskes that Lauwers had been adding extra letters to his messages, but that London's suspicions apparently had not been aroused. However, Giskes feared that Lauwers might throw a monkey wrench into his Englandspiel, so he decided to put an end to Lauwers's role.

Over Lauwers's transmitter, London was asked if unnamed "reserve operators" could replace Lauwers. To Giskes's astonishment, approval was received without an inquiry as to the reason for the switch. So Abwehr technicians were put to work operating the turned transmitter, a risky procedure. Each SOE spy's "fist" (everyone has an identifiable way of sending dot-and-dash messages) had been recorded in London before the agent's departure and it was routinely matched with the "fist" being used in The Netherlands. If the "fist" did not match, London would know that the SOE agent was dead or in custody and that the messages coming over the transmitter were false ones from the enemy.

In the predawn hours of June 26, 1943, a radio operator and Professor George L. Jambroes, a Dutchman who before the war had taught physics at Utrecht University, jumped from a Halifax bomber and parachuted into a field near Steenwijk. Jambroes had volunteered to spearhead Plan Holland: the organization of a "secret army," whose function would be to sabotage and disrupt German forces to pave the way for the Allies' cross-channel invasion of north west Europe.

Jambroes was met by the customary reception committee: a contingent of Abwehr and SD men. Amazingly, Jambroes was carrying in his pocket the entire *uncoded* SOE plan for organizing seventeen sabotage and resistance groups of 100 men each throughout The Netherlands. It was an incredible breach of security by the British secret service.

Using the ciphers and other material found on Jambroes, Major Giskes began milking the coup for all it was worth. His German operators reported steadily to London, over Jambroes' transmitter, about the progress of Operation Kern, the buildup of the seventeen sabotage and resistance groups. Jambroes, meanwhile, was ensconced in a prison near The Hague.

Over Jambroes's transmitter, Giskes's operators reported to London that fifteen hundred Dutch resistance fighters had been recruited and were undergoing guerrilla training. But this secret army would need vast quantities of weapons and supplies. A drop zone was specified. A few nights later, hundreds of containers—weighing more than five tons—of the requested items fell from the sky—and were promptly collected by waiting Abwehr men.

It was inconceivable to Giskes that the cagey British secret service would sacrifice such irreplaceable Dutch agents as George Jambroes and others. Why had the sophisticated SOE men in London compliantly fallen into one Abwehr trap after another? Were the British trying to coerce the Abwehr into believing that der Grossinvasion by the Allies would hit in The Netherlands?

Although Giskes had promised the fifty-four Dutch and British agents the Abwehr and SD had seized as a result of Englandspiel that their lives would be spared if they cooperated, matters were taken out of his hands. Reichsführer

Heinrich Himmler's Gestapo took charge of the agents after the Allied invasion of Normandy in June 1944, and forty-seven of them were shot.

In 1945, after the war ended in Europe, there was an uproar in The Netherlands after reports circulated that the British had knowingly sacrificed the Dutch agents as part of a master scheme to hoodwink Adolf Hitler and his generals about the site of the invasion. The Dutch Parliament formed a Commission of Enquiry headed by Dr. L. A. Donker, a judge. Donker requested that the British government allow SOE leaders to testify before his panel, but the request was denied. Then Donker asked permission to conduct further probing in England and approval was granted. However, when the Dutch investigators asked for the records of the Dutch section of the SOE, they were told that the documents had been destroyed in a fire at SOE headquarters on Baker Street.

As time went by, the investigation into Operation North Pole drifted into misty oblivion. Only the SOE leaders and top British officials ever knew if large numbers of Dutch agents had been deliberately sent to their deaths in The Netherlands.[11]

Who Set Fire to the *Normandie*?

IN THE LATE FALL OF 1941, the magnificent French ocean liner *Normandie* was berthed at Pier 88 on the Hudson River, a short distance from bustling Forty-second Street in New York City. Exceeded in length only by Britain's *Queen Elizabeth* (and by only two feet at that), the 1,029-foot *Normandie* had sped safely into New York harbor after being caught in the open ocean while Adolf Hitler's war machine invaded Poland on September 1, 1939.

The *Normandie's* owners were spending one thousand dollars per day in berthing charges, so they kept only a skeleton crew on board to keep her engines from deteriorating. No one seemed concerned about possible sabotage, and there was no worry about fire. Vladimir Yourkevitch, the *Normandie's* designer, had suggested that the vessel was as nearly fireproof as any ship ever built.

In Germany, Hitler's Oberkommando der Wehrmacht had long had a wary eye on the French ship. Two weeks after France surrendered to Germany on June 3, 1940, Admiral Wilhelm Canaris's Abwehr had flashed an order to Nazi spies in the United States: "Observe *Normandie*." The führer and his commanders were well aware that if the United States were drawn into the war against the Third Reich, the monstrous French vessel could be taken over by the United States Navy and quickly converted into a transport that could carry to Europe nearly twelve thousand troops in a single trip.

The New York City waterfront and the port cities of New Jersey were hotbeds of Nazi intrigue. Dingy saloons and flophouses that catered to merchant seamen from all over the world were honeycombed with German agents

Two months after Hitler declared war on the United States, the huge liner Normandie *was destroyed by fire in New York City. (U.S. Navy)*

and Nazi sympathizers. One of the most notorious of these places was the Highway Tavern in New Jersey. Two others were the Old Hamburg in Manhattan and Schmidt's Bar in Bayonne, New Jersey. A bartender at Schmidt's was a Nazi agent, and he regularly plied seamen with drinks on the house, then listened avidly as their tongues loosened and they told tales of their adventures at sea.

Suddenly, on December 7, 1941, the Japanese bombed Pearl Harbor, Hawaii. Four days later, Adolf Hitler called the Reichstag into session to rubber-stamp his declaration of war against the United States. He thundered to the cheering deputies: "We will always strike first! We will always deal the first blow!"

Later that same day, Hitler's crony, the bombastic Italian dictator Benito Mussolini, joined in going to war against the United States.

As Adolf Hitler and his high command had feared, the United States Navy immediately took over the *Normandie* and rechristened her the *Lafayette*.

Feverish efforts were launched to convert the ship into a sorely needed troop transport, and some fifteen hundred civilian workers began swarming, locust-like, over her.

There was a great urgency to complete the conversion task. It was to be finished by February 28, 1942, at which time Captain Robert C. Comand, the *Normandie* skipper, was to sail her from New York to Boston. The transport was to be loaded with some ten thousand troops, plus assorted weapons and equipment, before proceeding into the Atlantic under sealed orders—undoubtedly, the ship would be bound for England.

At 2:34 on the afternoon of February 9, less than three weeks before the *Normandie* was to sail for Europe, shouts of "Fire!" rang out on the ship. Men rushed frantically to put out the blaze, but it was a windy day and they could not get the fire under control. Flames began whipping rapidly through corridors, and within an hour, the ship was a blazing inferno.

As the conflagration spread, civilian workers, crew members, navy and coast guard personnel—some three thousand in all—began clambering over the sides of the *Normandie* and sliding down ropes to the pier, or dashing to safety down gangplanks. New York City firefighters swore that the heat was the most intense that they had known.

Perhaps thirty thousand New Yorkers choked Twelfth Avenue to watch the spectacle. Among them was a small, gray-haired man with agony etched on his face—Vladimir Yourkevitch, who had designed the *Normandie*. Police officers, suspicious of Yourkevitch's heavy accent, refused to let the naval architect through their lines. However, Yourkevitch would have been powerless to save his creation. At 2:32 A.M., the doomed ship, listing heavily from tons of water that had been poured into her by fireboats, rolled over on her side and, like a beached whale, lay in the Hudson's gray ice.

At a time when every ship was crucial, the United States had lost its largest transport vessel. One man was dead. Some 250 others suffered cuts, bruises, burns, or temporary eye or lung irritations.

Several investigating groups tried to pinpoint the blame for this monumental disaster. The FBI and U.S. Attorney Frank S. Hogan grilled more than one hundred witnesses, and a navy court of inquiry was established under Rear Admiral Lamar R. Leahy (Retired). Two months later, a congressional naval affairs subcommittee, which had been set up to probe the *Normandie* debacle, concluded that "the cause and consequences of the fire are directly attributable to carelessness [by civilian workers] and lack of supervision."

However, millions of Americans refused to buy the official government line. How could a huge ocean liner, designed to be virtually fireproof, break out in a conflagration so intense that the ship became a charred ruin in only a couple of hours? Had professional Nazi saboteurs, infiltrated into the United States for the purpose, somehow gotten aboard the guarded *Normandie*? If so, why hadn't some of the fifteen hundred civilian workers who had crammed every nook and cranny of the ship detected the saboteurs igniting the fires? Or had a few members of the civilian workforce on board, harboring Hitler sympathies, conspired to pull off the disastrous arson job?

Nazi skullduggery was suspected, but the fiery destruction of the *Normandie* may forever remain a gigantic enigma.[12]

Convoy SL125:
A Sacrificial Ploy?

ON THE NIGHT OF November 3, 1942, fourteen hundred Allied vessels of all shapes and sizes were knifing through the dark waters of the Atlantic Ocean, bound for an invasion of North Africa. In order to reach their destinations— the major ports of Oran and Algiers—the huge convoy would have to slip through the Strait of Gibraltar, a narrow body of water about thirty-two miles long and from eight to twenty-three miles wide that leads into the Mediterranean Sea. Operation Torch was under way, the first major offensive of the United States since World War I.

For several days, the Luftwaffe and the B-Dienst (German wireless monitoring posts) had been tracking the convoy, which had left from several ports in the British Isles. In Germany, Grand Admiral Erich Raeder, commander in chief of the Kriegsmarine, was not certain about the convoy's precise targets on the Mediterranean coast of North Africa, but he knew that the approaching ships from Britain would have to pass through the Strait of Gibraltar to reach their objectives.

Consequently, nine German and twenty-six Italian submarines were patrolling the sea lanes around the Rock of Gibraltar, and Schnellboot squadrons (swift, heavily armed torpedo boats) in the region had been alerted for action. In essence, a German iron curtain had been pulled over the Strait.

When the Allied convoy from Britain was only about one hundred miles from Gibraltar, a German U-boat wolf pack circling the Rock suddenly sped southward. Twenty-four hours later, the wolf pack was engaged in a running duel with British convoy SL125, commanded by Rear Admiral C. N. Reyne. This second convoy, consisting primarily of empty cargo vessels and a small warship escort, was returning to England from Sierra Leone, a tiny country on the Atlantic seaboard of western Africa.

The running battle between the U-boats and Admiral Reyne's flotilla went on for more than six days, and the German submarines registered thirteen kills, nearly all of them empty cargo vessels. Meanwhile, the precipitate dash by the U-boat pack to chase Reyne's convoy had left the gate to the Strait of Gibraltar wide open. And the sea armada, carrying the Eastern and Central Task Forces bound for Algiers and Oran, slipped through the unprotected Strait unmolested.

It was a curious action by the U-boat wolf pack. Why had it suddenly sprinted to the south to intercept a convoy of empty vessels? And why did the

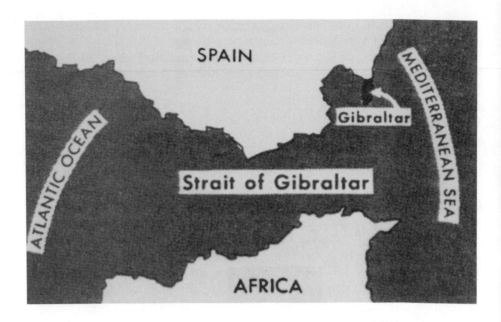

German submarines continue to dog Reyne's convoy for six days and nights? Had the British conducted devious deception practices, possibly through captured and "turned" double agents, to convince the Kriegsmarine that convoy SL125 was carrying a wealth of valuable and important equipment and supplies? Had the artful dodgers of the British deception services covertly arranged to have convoy SL125 come along at the right time, a sacrificial victim to Torch?

Only the Allied brass could provide true answers to those puzzling questions—and they have remained silent. However, years after the war, Admiral Reyne, the luckless commander of convoy SL125, gave a clue that his flotilla may have been the guinea pig in Operation Torch.

Said Reyne: "It was the only time in my career that I had been congratulated by the admiralty for losing a large number of my ships."[13]

Ultimatum: Slipup or Plot?

ON JANUARY 13, 1943, President Franklin Roosevelt and Prime Minister Winston Churchill and their top aides convened at the stately old Hotel Anfa in Casablanca. After months of bitter fighting, German and Italian forces had virtually been swept from North Africa. Now the joint delegations would answer the key strategic question: Where would the next Anglo-American blow fall?

Hardly had the participants settled into their chairs than a heated debate erupted. General George Marshall, the low-key, silver-thatched U.S. Army chief of staff, spoke in favor of an assault across the English Channel against German-occupied northwest France. General Alan Brooke, the hawk-nosed and astute chief of the Imperial General Staff, proposed invading Sicily to force Adolf Hitler to reinforce his armies in the Mediterranean, which would require Hitler to pull away German divisions that were facing the hard-pressed Russians on the Eastern Front.

As the conference droned on, the American delegation found itself on the losing end of the verbal duel and, after four strenuous days, capitulated.

Before departing for home, President Roosevelt and Prime Minister Churchill agreed to meet with the press of the free world. There Roosevelt, in an off-the-cuff manner, let loose a thunderclap that would anguish and dismay other Allied leaders and would furnish a gleeful Hitler with a propaganda blockbuster.

With scores of journalists avidly taking notes, the American president casually observed: "Prime Minister Churchill and I have determined that we will accept nothing less than *unconditional surrender* of Germany, Italy, and Japan!"

Seated next to the president and drawing on a large, black cigar, Winston Churchill was stunned. That was the first time that the prime minister had heard the phrase "unconditional surrender" used with regard to the current war.

Churchill was deeply alarmed. With the Third Reich and its Wehrmacht still a powerful force to be reckoned with, he felt that the posture to be assumed by Allied leadership should be one of defiance. He was convinced that it was a blunder of the first magnitude to be dictating harsh terms to enemy nations at a time when victory or defeat still hung in the balance.

But the damage was done. Churchill could not, in the face of the free world's press, take issue with his war partner. He assured reporters that he concurred with the unconditional surrender ultimatum which he had only moments before heard for the first time. Within minutes, the news was flashed around the globe.

Later, a high official of the British government told Churchill: "Unless those terms are softened, the German army will fight with the ferocity of cornered rats." Already on public record, Churchill merely shrugged.

Lieutenant General George S. Patton, Jr., the profane, dynamic leader of American ground forces in the bitter fighting in North Africa, was nearly apoplectic, telling a close friend: "Our President is a great politician, but goddamn it, he's never read history. He and the people in our government can't understand the Germans. Look at this goddamn fool 'unconditional surrender' shit. If the Hun [German] ever needed anything to put a burr under his saddle, that's it. Now he'll fight like the goddamned devil. It will take much longer, cost us far more lives, and let the Russians take more territory!"

General Dwight Eisenhower, the Allied supreme commander, was flabbergasted, confiding to an aide: "If you are given the choice of mounting the scaffold or charging thirty bayonets, you might as well charge the bayonets!"

In Berlin, top Nazis rejoiced. The eloquent Dr. Paul Josef Goebbels, Hitler's cunning minister of propaganda, trumpeted to a gathering of Party leaders in Berlin: "Since the enemies of Germany are determined to enslave our nation, the war has become an urgent struggle for national preservation in which no sacrifice is too great!" Cheers echoed from the rafters.

In Junkers bombers over England and in Messerschmitt fighters above the fatherland, in U-boats beneath the cold, murky waters of the North Atlantic, in snow-covered foxholes in the frozen tundra of Russia, at dispersed outposts along the underbelly of Europe, those in the German military inwardly reaffirmed their vows to fight to the end—with courage, tenacity, and growing feelings of desperation.

Had Franklin Roosevelt, a cerebral politician long accustomed to speaking in the global spotlight, truly been so incredibly muddleheaded as to make the seemingly offhand "unconditional surrender" ultimatum? Or had this unrehearsed press conference been a carefully calculated scenario, cooked up by the president and a few key advisers in the White House to trap Winston Churchill into a situation wherein he could not disagree?

There were indeed top figures in the Roosevelt Administration who were promoting the theme that the war in Europe should not be concluded until the Third Reich had not only been crushed but dismantled. Chief among these alleged hard-liners were Secretary of the Treasury Henry Morgenthau, Jr.; Assistant Secretary of State Harry Dexter White; Bernard Baruch, who moonlighted as an adviser to Roosevelt; and Alger Hiss of the State Department.

Henry Morgenthau lived near the Roosevelt estate at Hyde Park, New York, and, in particular, had the ear of the president. Earlier, Morgenthau had drawn up a top-secret plan for dealing with a defeated Germany. It called for the destruction of German heavy industry and the flooding of mines, which would thereby deny the postwar nation the raw materials needed to produce consumer goods. In essence, Germany would be reduced to an agricultural entity. Its 90 million citizens would be kept in a gigantic ghetto with armed guards posted around the borders with orders to shoot any German who tried to get out. There was a long list of German officers and government officials to be summarily executed.

Conceivably, Morgenthau's plan had been created with the knowledge and approval of President Roosevelt. So against this background, had Franklin Roosevelt's stunning unconditional surrender proposal at Casablanca truly been an off-the-cuff remark, or had it been the result of a subtle scheme to assure that there would be no negotiated peace with Germany, no matter what the cost to young Americans who were doing the fighting?

Perhaps only Roosevelt, Morgenthau, and a few of the White House inner circle had the answer.[14]

Political Tangle
in the Balkans

ADOLF HITLER not only considered the Balkans to be the eastern frontier of the
Third Reich, he considered the region useful for furnishing his war machine
with valuable raw materials, especially oil. And Nazi elements in Bulgaria, Romania, and Hungary provided more than seven hundred thousand soldiers for
his armed forces.

Bulgaria, a mountainous country about 370 miles by 185 miles at its
widest point, lies on the Black Sea, bordering Greece on the south and Romania on the north. Bulgaria's role in the war had been a strange one. On December 12, 1941—five days after the United States was plunged into the global
conflict by the bombing of Pearl Harbor—Czar Boris III of Bulgaria declared
war on the United States and Great Britain. But for whatever his reason, he
had scrupulously avoided any hostile action against the Soviet Union, which
was fighting Nazi Germany.

In mid-1943, Hitler became alarmed when reports reached his battle
headquarters in East Prussia that Czar Boris was conniving to seek a separate
peace. Thus began one of the complex political tangles for which the Balkans
has been famous for centuries.

Fearful of losing the Balkans should Bulgaria "defect," the führer summoned Boris to Berchtesgaden, his mountaintop retreat in Bavaria. After a
stormy session, Boris agreed to remain with Germany.

Meanwhile, Josef Stalin, the Soviet dictator, had his eye not only on Bulgaria, but on the entire Balkan Peninsula, fertile ground for the expansion of
Communism. Moreover, oil and other raw materials from that region could
help feed Stalin's war machine.

At the same time, British and American agents had launched a clever deception campaign in the Balkans to coerce Hitler into believing that the Allies
intended to invade Bulgaria, thereby causing the führer to pour more troops
into the Balkans, keeping the forces out of western Europe.

On August 28, 1943, a few days after Boris returned to the Bulgarian capital of Sofia after his angry confrontation with Hitler, the czar collapsed in his
palace and died within an hour. In Berlin, Propaganda Minister Josef Goebbels
announced that the Bulgarian leader had succumbed to a rare poison, possibly
snake venom.

Clearly, Czar Boris had been murdered. But who had committed the
deed: the Germans, British, Americans, Soviets, or the Bulgarians themselves?
Whoever may have been responsible for Boris's demise—and many would pon-
der how a snake could have gotten into his palace—suspicion grew and unrest
and turmoil erupted in Bulgaria.

Czar Simon II was in line to assume power, but he was only a child. So
a regency council was formed, composed of Boris's brother Cyril, and two other

men. The council sent a secret delegation to Cairo to seek peace with the British and the Americans. No doubt fearful that Bulgaria was about to join the camp of the Western Allies, Josef Stalin further entangled the political situation in the Balkans by declaring war on Bulgaria.

In turn, on September 8 the Regency Council tried to counter Stalin's move by declaring war on its ally, Nazi Germany. Bulgaria then sent its 5th Army of ten divisions, which had been armed and equipped by Adolf Hitler, into an attack against the German army. While these two former allies were battling one another, the Bulgarian Regency Council was in Moscow, signing an armistice with the United States, Great Britain, and the Soviet Union.

Hardly had the ink dried on the "peace" agreement when Stalin broke the pact and sent his 3rd Ukranian Army plunging into Bulgaria. Communists took over the government, the Regency Council was arrested and executed, and a reign of terror erupted against "traitors," meaning known and suspected anti-Communists.

All of this intrigue, and the brutal takeover of Bulgaria by Josef Stalin, had been triggered by the death of Czar Boris III. It may never be known for certain who murdered him, but the finger of suspicion seems to point to Moscow. Or Berlin. Or London. Or Sofia.[15]

Ambush in the Sky

ON MARCH 22, 1944, Lieutenant Commander Harry C. Butcher, an aide and confidant of Allied Supreme Commander Dwight Eisenhower, penned in the daily diary he kept for his boss: "General [Carl] Spaatz [leader of U.S. bomber forces in Europe] is not too crazy about it but admits that strategic plans are supposed to draw the fire of the Luftwaffe over Germany."

Butcher was referring to Operation Pointblank, a massive Anglo-American bomber offensive that had two major objectives: the destruction of the German industrial base and baiting the dwindling Luftwaffe fighter squadrons to come up and fight so that the Allies would have air supremacy over northwest Europe on D-Day.

"If these aims—baiting the Luftwaffe and deceptions—are achieved, the sacrifices could mean the saving of thousands, perhaps tens of thousands, of lives on the beaches when the Allies land [in Normandy]," Wallace Carroll, head of the European branch of the Office of War Information (OWI), had told his bosses in New York City prior to Pointblank.

One evening, three weeks before Commander Butcher wrote his observations in Eisenhower's diary, Air Chief Marshal Arthur Harris, the fifty-two-year-old leader of the Royal Air Force (RAF) Bomber Command, listened while his meteorologist forecast that the weather over Germany that night might favor the German air defenses and not Bomber Command. Strong winds might splinter the bomber streams, there might be minimal cloud cover to conceal the aircraft, and the half moon might be brilliant. Despite this adverse forecast, Air Chief Marshal Harris announced that the target for that night (March 30–31) would be Nuremberg, deep in southeastern Germany.

RAF crew members who were to fly the mission were puzzled. The bomber stream would follow a route that would take it near what the British called Flak Alley—a thick concentration of Luftwaffe night-fighter bases around the Ruhr, the Reich's industrial heartland. What's more, there apparently was a deliberate effort to mislead the crews (or at least many of them) about weather conditions. Flight Sergeant Tony Fogarty of 115 Squadron would later remark: "We were assured that there would be ten-tenths cloud cover for most of the way."

Meanwhile in Germany at 5:30 P.M., General Wolfgang Martini, chief of Luftwaffe intelligence, had sent an urgent message to General Hans-Juergen Stumpff, head of the Air Defense Command: Between 700 and 800 RAF planes would attack the Reich that night. Actually, some 850 Wellingtons, Halifaxes, and Lancasters would be in the strike force. How had General Martini been so accurate in predicting the RAF strength? Had he had foreknowledge of the Nuremberg mission?

7:10 P.M.: General Stumpff, from his huge underground command post on the outskirts of Berlin, orders six air divisions to prepare for action and brings distant night-fighter squadrons to bases closer to the expected bomber-stream route.

10:01 P.M.: The stillness of the English countryside is shattered as the first RAF bombers lift off, rendezvous over southeast England, and set a course for the first leg of the long flight to Nuremberg. The bomber stream is sixty-five miles long and ten miles wide.

10:16 P.M.: Instead of the ten-tenths cloud cover they were promised, crews discover that the bombers are virtually naked in the brilliant rays of the moon. High winds begin to break up close flying formations.

11:07 P.M.: As the first bombers approach the German frontier, General Stumpff orders 1st and 2nd Fighter Divisions to rendezvous with the 3rd Division over Aachen and Frankfurt. Almost all the night fighters in western Europe are being concentrated along the exact route that the RAF bombers will fly.

11:23 P.M.: Two decoy raids, one by fifty Halifaxes across the North Sea toward Berlin and Hamburg, and the other by thirty-two Mosquitos against Aachen, Kassel, and Cologne, both missions designed to confuse German air defenses by simulating the approach of much larger forces, are ignored by General Stumpff. He orders his swarms of night fighters to concentrate on the main bomber stream flying toward southeast Germany.

11:37 P.M.: With incredible precision, Stumpff has calculated the time of the arrival over Germany of the RAF bombers and the flight time of his fighters. So Luftwaffe pilots are up in strength with full loads of fuel and ammunition, using a new type of radar—the SN-2—to direct them to their prey.

*Luftwaffe General Hans Stumpff
seemed to know details of the RAF
mission to Nuremberg. (U.S. Air Force)*

11:42 P.M.: Cries of *"Sieg Heil!"* ring out over the German night fighters' radio bands as they pounce, with cannons blazing, on the lumbering bomber stream illuminated by bright moonlight. It is a classic air ambush.

12:02 A.M.: Nuremberg air defenses are warned that the city might be the target—more than an hour before the RAF force is due to drop its bombs and at a time when the RAF can go in any direction to scores of other cities.

12:45 A.M.: A flaming funeral pyre of fifty-nine crashed Lancasters, Wellingtons, and Halifaxes stretches along the German countryside all the way to Fulda, where the leading British aircraft turn southeast for the seventy-two-mile run to Nuremberg. The change of direction is seemingly anticipated by Hans-Juergen Stumpff: He orders fighter squadrons into the final leg of flight to the RAF target.

1:10 A.M.: Most Nuremberg citizens are in their bomb shelters. Ordinarily, the Germans were able to furnish a warning only a few minutes before RAF night attacks. But the Fliegeralarm (air-raid warning) sounded thirty-two minutes before the bombers arrived.

1:12 A.M.: Thick clouds, absent throughout the British bombers' flight, now blanket Nuremberg. Hundreds of tons of bombs fall, and some damage is done to the industrial areas of the old city, but most of Nuremberg remains untouched.

1:28 A.M.: The long flight back to England begins, and the RAF bombers are attacked by Luftwaffe night fighters periodically until far out over the English Channel. Most of the surviving British bombers are riddled by machine-gun bullets, cannon shells, and flak.

5:00 A.M.: Climbing wearily out of their bombers at English airfields, the surviving airmen are bitter—and suspicious.

Flight Lieutenant Stephen Burrow would later recall: "It certainly appeared to me that Jerry [the Germans] was waiting for us, and there were rumors that the raid had been leaked."

The RAF Bomber Command had suffered its most grievous losses of the war: 745 crew members had been killed or wounded and 159 others had bailed out of damaged planes and were presumed to be German prisoners of war. Secret British intelligence documents were later said to disclose that 53 bombers had crash-landed in England, bringing the total airplane loss to 161.

Five Luftwaffe night fighters had been shot down and five others were damaged in the moonlit running shoot-out across German skies.

Had the Nuremberg mission been deliberately tipped off to the Germans? If so, who had perpetrated the leak? Fingers pointed to British cloak-and-dagger agencies whose job it was to mislead Adolf Hitler about the time and place of the looming invasion of France. There were unproven charges that Nazi spies, captured in England long before and "turned," had been directed by their British controllers prior to the bombers' takeoff to radio their former masters in Hamburg and Berlin information about the Nuremberg raid.

This ruse, it was alleged, was part of an intricate deception scheme code-named Bodyguard that was intended to convince the Germans that the Allied invasion would hit at the Pas de Calais, two hundred miles northeast of the true planned landing beaches in Normandy. Tipping off the Nuremberg mission, this conjecture held, would reinforce the turned agent's credibility and reliability with German intelligence, so when the agent fed the Wehrmacht *false* information on the site of the invasion, the Germans would trust and believe the spy. This meant that a certain number of men and even missions were considered expendable in order that D-Day might stand a better chance of success.

After the war, evidence surfaced that seemed to indicate that the Nuremberg raid had indeed been leaked as a component of the D-Day deception scheme. British airmen who had been shot down prior to the Nuremberg mission and who were being held as POWs at the time of the ill-fated venture stated that German intelligence officers had told them, more than four hours before the RAF bombers lifted off from England, that British aircraft were going to attack Nuremberg that night.

Perhaps the full story of the curious circumstances surrounding the Nuremberg mission will never be known. Yet there remain many who believe that nearly one thousand British airmen and scores of precious bombers had been sacrificed on the altar of Operation Neptune, the assault against Normandy.[16]

Was the Normandy
D-Day Necessary?

JUST PAST SIX O'CLOCK on the evening of June 4, 1944, the bell clanged on the large wooden door of the convent of the Sisters of St. Agonie at 127 rue de la Santé in Paris. Each time the bell sounded, Mother Superior Henriette Frede felt a surge of fear, expecting to be greeted by the Gestapo. For more than two years, the convent had been the headquarters of Jade Amicol, an underground network of French people created and directed by MI-6, Britain's secret service. Mother Henriette and her twelve nuns were couriers for Jade Amicol, risking their lives almost daily.

When the mother superior cautiously opened the door, she found herself face to face with a small, wiry, white-haired man in civilian clothes whom she recognized as German Admiral Wilhelm Canaris. Since 1933, he had been chief of Adolf Hitler's espionage agency, the Abwehr. But a few months earlier, after a power struggle in Berlin, Canaris had been relieved of his duties.

Although slightly flustered about finding herself suddenly in the presence of a German who had been dreaded throughout much of Europe, Mother Henriette quickly regained her composure. Before his arrival, she had been told by the Jade Amicol leader, the redoubtable Colonel Claude Ollivier (whose real last name was Arnould), that Canaris was coming that evening. She asked the visitor what he wanted.

"I have come to pray," he replied.

The mother superior invited Canaris inside and led him past the sacristy (above which were hidden a transmitter and a receiver for communicating with MI-6 in London) and into her own sitting room. There, Arnould was waiting. The two men shook hands solemnly. It was an incredible encounter: the chief of the underground in northern France and the German secret service leader whose function had been to wipe out the French resistance networks.

For four years, Canaris had been the moving spirit behind the Schwarze Kapelle, the anti-Nazi resistance movement in Germany, whose members included top military, government, civic, and religious leaders. All were convinced that Hitler was taking their beloved Germany down the road to total destruction, and they had been trying for months to get the support of the United States and England to "eliminate" Hitler and to end the war in the West. Even though the leaders in the Schwarze Kapelle included Field Marshal Erwin Rommel, a folk hero with the German people who was admired by his British and American adversaries, the Western Allies chose to ignore the secret organization's overtures.

Since early in 1944 when it had become clear to most of the world that the Western Allies were massing armies in England for an assault across the English Channel, Canaris had been providing Stewart Menzies, head of MI-6, with what was substantially the complete order of battle for the German Heer

Abwehr chief Wilhelm Canaris. (National Archives)

(army), together with the German generals' plan to smash the invasion. No military commander in history had ever had such priceless intelligence before going into battle as did General Dwight Eisenhower, supreme commander of Allied forces.

Canaris had sent his intelligence by trusted Abwehr couriers to the neutral capitals of Lisbon and Madrid, both hotbeds of espionage. The little admiral had a code name and this was used on all intelligence that came from him. In Lisbon and Madrid, his secret reports were slipped to British agents, then rushed on to London.

With the arrival of spring and the invasion nearly at hand, Canaris grew desperate. His pleas for the United States and Great Britain to publicly announce their support for the Schwarze Kapelle had resulted only in silence from London. He decided to make a final, desperate, personal appeal to save Germany from destruction. In so doing, he would throw caution to the winds.

Canaris made contact with an officer on the staff of General Karl-Heinrich von Stuelpnagel, the military governor of France whose headquarters was in Paris. Through the German officer, who also belonged to the Schwarze Kapelle, the admiral set up a rendezvous with Major Philippe Keun, Arnould's partner in the Jade Amicol.

Sometime in late May—about a week before the Allied invasion was to be launched—Keun slipped out of Paris and flew to London, presumably having been picked up by a British Lysander. These small aircraft landed on predesignated fields outside the French capital to bring in and take out spies. He had made the dangerous trip to receive final instructions on the role Jade Amicol was to play in the invasion, and he carried with him a personal letter from Canaris for MI-6 chief Stewart Menzies.

In his message, Canaris apparently pleaded once again for the Western Allies to work with the Schwarze Kapelle to head off the looming invasion. Had the little admiral only known his last-minute overture was doomed to failure. There could be only unconditional surrender by Germany.

It would have seemed logical for Menzies to ignore Canaris's letter. However, for whatever reason, the MI-6 chief wrote a personal reply. Philippe Keun brought it back to Paris and turned it over to Arnould at the convent of St. Agonie.

Arnould promptly telephoned his Schwarze Kapelle contact in General von Stuelpnagel's headquarters, and arrangements were made for Canaris to be at the convent that night, June 4. After the mother superior had escorted Canaris to her sitting room where Arnould was waiting, she departed. Arnould produced the letter from Menzies.

Canaris put on his eyeglasses, sat in an easy chair, and began reading the letter. The room was thick with silence. When he had finished reading, the admiral gave a gasp, then exclaimed: *"Finis Germaniae!"* (Germany is finished!)

Thirty-six hours later, Allied armies stormed ashore at five beaches in Normandy.

Because of the rebuff to the Schwarze Kapelle, there remains a haunting question: Had D-Day in Normandy been necessary? Charles V. P. von Luttichau, a prominent German-American historian, reflected the view of most Germans who had opposed the Nazi regime when he claimed, long after the war, that the invasion could have been avoided and tens of thousands of lives saved. He wrote:

> D-Day was one of the greatest political blunders of all time. If Great Britain and the United States had uttered a single word publicly of encouragement to the [German] conspirators, then Eisenhower and [General] Montgomery could have walked ashore, and Rommel would have been there to salute them. As it was, Great Britain and the United States were determined to destroy Germany.

Many years after the war, British Prime Minister Winston Churchill was among the first of the Western leaders to express regret that the Anglo-American alliance had ignored those who, in his words, represented the social, political, and even military conscience of Germany.[17]

Evidence of a High-Level Cover-Up

IN LATE NOVEMBER 1944, Obergruppenführer (SS General) Sepp Dietrich, a big, burly man with a rough voice, was just back from the Western Front and chatting amicably with guests at a convivial party in a Berlin hotel. Spending much time with Dietrich, a pal of Adolf Hitler's since the early days of the Nazi Party in the 1920s, was a beautiful Irish woman in her mid-thirties. She was the wife of a top Hungarian diplomat, who was nearly twice her age.

Because Hungary was an ally of Germany, Dietrich apparently felt free to discuss the war. He had no inkling, of course, that the diplomat's wife was an Allied spy. For many months, she had been notifying London about information she picked up at social affairs in Berlin.

Within hours, the Irish woman informed London that the Sixth SS Panzer Army, led by General Dietrich, was assembling secretly in the Ardennes forest of Belgium and Luxembourg. For whatever reason, an intelligence officer at SHAEF (Supreme Headquarters, Allied Expeditionary Force) apparently pigeonholed the alarming disclosure without as much as investigating its authenticity.

Thickly wooded, hilly, with a surfeit of deep gorges, and having few roads capable of supporting heavy tanks and vehicles, the seventy-five-mile-long Ardennes sector had become known as the Ghost Front. Due to the topographic limitations, General Omar Bradley, leader of the U.S. 12th Army Group, thinly manned this region with a combination of green divisions "just off the boat" and veteran outfits decimated and exhausted from brutal fighting in the Hurtgen Forest caldron, just north of the Ardennes.

For their part, the Germans used the Ghost Front for the same purpose. In early December 1944, American and German soldiers were within rifle distance of one another, but a sort of gentlemen's agreement had evolved: You don't shoot at us and we won't shoot at you. So although each side sent out occasional probing patrols, it was eerily quiet generally, except for the rustling of the tall, snow-covered fir trees.

Few, if any of those on both sides, were aware that German armies had invaded Belgium by pounding through this same region in 1870, again in 1914, and more recently, in 1940.

Despite the calmness along the Ghost Front, there were ominous signs that the Germans were cooking up something big in the area. Six weeks earlier, American troops had captured copies of a German order creating an English-speaking brigade under dashing Standartenführer (SS Colonel) Otto "Scarface" Skorzeny, who had gained worldwide fame the previous year for leading, atop a bleak mountain peak in Italy, the bold rescue of the Italian dictator Benito Mussolini from his captors.

On December 1, a captured German told about a panzer outfit that was assembling to the rear of Wehrmacht lines in the Ardennes, where no armored formations were thought to be. This unit was identified as the crack 2nd Panzer Division.

Another telltale sign that something of major significance was brewing behind German lines in the Ardennes: Buzz bombs (pilotless aircraft filled with explosives), which had been fired regularly for the past few months onto the key Allied supply centers at Liege and Antwerp, in Belgium, suddenly ceased. Moreover, all German communication radios had fallen silent.

On December 4, a German woman, for whatever reason, slipped through the lines in the Ardennes and told American intelligence officers about feverish activity behind German lines. This included movement of pontoons, small boats, and stream-crossing equipment. She also said she had seen large numbers of panzers and many pieces of artillery, all moving westward at night toward the Ghost Front.

Seven days later, a Feldgrau taken prisoner by a GI patrol said that members of German divisions manning the Ghost Front had been ordered to return immediately from furloughs, and that the Wehrmacht was planning to attack. Somewhere along the murky channels of Allied intelligence, this ominous report was erroneously translated to read that the POW said that the Germans were expecting the Americans to attack instead.

A courier from an SS outfit strayed into American lines by mistake and was taken into custody. On his person was a document from a divisional headquarters to a unit on the Ghost Front: "Previous message ordering your withdrawal was in error. Remain where you are and prepare for an attack which is planned."

That same night, along the Ardennes sector, a small German patrol was ambushed and captured. Taken from the patrol leader's coat was an order for a December 16 attack. The document had just been distributed to low-level German units. This alarming information was rushed up channels to the division headquarters, where it got lost in a maze of administrative tunnels.

The entire U.S. chain of command, from General Omar Bradley to GIs on outpost duty in the arctic Ardennes, were unaware that the Germans, in a masterpiece of logistics, had moved up to the Ghost Front by the night of December 15 about 650,000 troops, 1,906 artillery pieces, and nearly fifteen hundred panzers. It was the equivalent of silently transporting the entire population of San Francisco, together with their vehicles, for many miles, without anyone else in California being aware of it.

As the inky blackness of the bitterly cold early morning of December 16 started to dissolve into a gray overcast, the eerie stillness along the Ghost Front was abruptly shattered by the roar of hundreds of German artillery pieces and mortars. Forty minutes later, tens of thousands of German infantrymen, backed by swarms of panzers, plunged into the thinly manned and disoriented American lines and began racing deep into Belgium. Spearheading the onslaught was Sepp Dietrich's Sixth SS Panzer Army, whose presence the Hungarian diplomat's wife had pinpointed for the Allies two weeks earlier.

The Americans were taken by total surprise. Before the savage fighting concluded six weeks later with the Germans having been driven back behind the Siegfried Line, more than a half-million men on each side bled and suffered in what came to be known as the Battle of the Bulge.

Who was responsible for the colossal American failure to piece together the wealth of suspicious clues and arrive at a logical conclusion that might have prevented the Wehrmacht's great successes in the early days of the Ardennes death struggle? One reason for the colossal intelligence torpor was that Ultra had dried up since the Germans had ceased radio communications. Another was that the Germans had conducted a brilliant deception plan that had lulled the Americans to sleep. Perhaps SHAEF and other American headquarters staffs had developed a mindset that the Wehrmacht was no longer capable of conducting a major offensive.

However, there appeared to have been frantic efforts to cover up high-level remissness, even dereliction. It was not until twenty-five years after the war, when secret SHAEF papers were released, that British Brigadier Kenneth Strong, Dwight Eisenhower's chief of intelligence, learned that a covert investigation had been conducted under his nose into who or what had been responsible for the Allied intelligence breakdown.

At the same time, a quarter century after the conflict, General Strong was shocked to discover that both file copies of SHAEF intelligence summaries for the two-week period leading up to the Battle of the Bulge were "missing." One copy had been kept at SHAEF rear in London and the other in Eisenhower's headquarters in suburban Paris.

There is also evidence that surviving papers had been doctored. Hugh M. Cole, the U.S. Army's official historian, reported years later: "Sentences, phrases and punctuation marks from American intelligence documents of pre-Ardennes origin had been twisted and turned, noted in and out of context, interpreted and misinterpreted, in arduous efforts to fix blame and secure absolution."

The curious failure of the Allies to detect the huge German buildup that had been going on under their noses remains one of the war's most tantalizing mysteries.[18]

Part Two

Odd Coincidences

Reunited in an Operating Room

SHORTLY AFTER German dictator Adolf Hitler sent his jackbooted legions to seize the tiny nation of Austria in March 1938, Roman Turski quit his job as a flying instructor in Lyons, France, and headed back to his native Poland. Europe was on the brink of war, he was convinced, and Poland well could be Hitler's next target.

Turski lifted off from Lyons in his own airplane, but it developed engine trouble and he was forced to make an emergency landing for repairs in Nazi-held Vienna. While the work was being done, the Pole checked into a hotel to spend the night.

The next morning, Turski was leaving the front entrance of the hotel to buy some cigarettes before checking out when a man came running by, bumped into the Pole, and knocked him to the ground. Angry, Turski leaped up and grabbed the stranger by the lapels. White-faced with fear, the man tried to wrench himself free. He was perspiring and panting heavily.

"*Gestapo! Gestapo!*" he cried out.

Turski spoke little German, but understood that the petrified man was running from the dreaded Nazi secret police. Taking the stranger by the arm, the Pole rushed the man into the hotel lobby and up the stairs to his room, motioning for the frightened stranger to get under the bed. Turski draped the blankets and sheets over both sides of the bed, concealing the fugitive. Since Turski had slept in the bed the night before, it looked naturally rumpled. Then the Pole whipped off his coat and tie, and tried to look as though he had just arisen.

Moments later, two Gestapo men barged into the room; someone in the lobby apparently had told about the two men rushing up the stairs minutes earlier. The Germans shouted questions. Turski merely shrugged each time. After examining Turski's passport, the Gestapo men departed without searching the room.

Turski locked the door and let out a sigh of relief. The stranger wriggled out from beneath the bed, speaking a stream of German. Turski didn't understand any of it, but knew that the man was expressing his gratitude.

In a mixture of German and pidgin English, the Pole asked the other man why the Gestapo had been chasing him. Because he was a Jew, the man replied.

Then, through a combination of gestures and drawings, Turski made it known that he was flying to Warsaw. The stranger begged to be taken with him. Turski reluctantly agreed, knowing that his own freedom—and possibly his life—would be forfeited if he were caught trying to slip a Jew out of Austria.

Turski and the man were waved through customs at the Vienna airport after the Pole explained that his companion was along merely to see him off. Scrambling into the airplane, the two men lifted off, winged across Czechoslovakia, and with dusk approaching, landed in a large pasture near Cracow, just across the border in Poland. Since the fugitive might be arrested if Turski were to touch down at the Cracow airport, it was necessary to part company with the Austrian in this remote locale.

Using his map (on which the Pole had earlier printed his name in large block letters in the event it should become lost), Turski showed the man where they were. Then Turski gave most of his money to the man and wished him well. Wordlessly, with tears in his eyes, the man took his benefactor's hand, then slipped silently into the dark woods.

When the German Wehrmacht poured across the Polish frontier on September 1, 1939, Roman Turski fought the invaders as a fighter pilot. After Poland was conquered by the Teutonic Blitzkrieg in only six weeks, Turski escaped to England, joined the Free French Air Force, in 1940, and fought in the Battle of Britain.

While returning from a sweep over the English Channel, Turski was wounded by the guns of a German fighter plane. Bloody and dazed, he made it back close to his base, where he crash-landed his Spitfire. When he was pulled from the wreckage, the Pole was unconscious and suffering from a skull fracture.

Rushed to a hospital, Turski was examined by a team of surgeons, who debated whether an operation could save his life. However, surgery was performed, and when the Pole regained consciousness, he slowly became aware that a tall man wearing a white medical smock was peering down at him.

"Remember me?" the man asked in heavily accented English. Turski slightly shook his head in the negative.

"You saved my life in Vienna three years ago," the man said.

Despite his hazy mental condition, Turski did recall the episode concerning the Austrian Jew. The man in the smock explained that just before the German invasion of Poland, he had escaped to England. Turski asked how the man knew his name.

"You had it written on the map when you dropped me off in that meadow near Cracow."

Turski was thunderstruck as the white-smocked man continued. "Now I have had the chance to show you my gratitude for saving my life," the man continued. "You see, I am a brain surgeon—I was the one who operated on you this morning."[1]

Blue-Blood Nazi Spy

ROBERT TREECK, a suave, highly educated and wealthy German aristocrat, was an unlikely candidate to join Abwehr chief Wilhelm Canaris's espionage network. But in the late 1930s, with Adolf Hitler preparing for war, Treeck was one of the large number of Nazi spies infiltrated into Great Britain.

Treeck, a member of Germany's upper-crust society, had been sent to Britain to "cultivate"—that is, spy on—the British branch of The Blue International, a small, tightly knit political and business organization that wielded great power in Europe.

Adolf Hitler had the utmost contempt for the aristocracy, be it German or British, but agent Treeck's reports would be devoured avidly by the führer, for Hitler valued the views of England's upper classes who ruled a global empire.

But if Robert Treeck was going to impress Britain's wealthy fraternity, he would first have to display enormous affluence. So he rented a large estate at Luckington Manor, between Chippenham and Bath, in the lush green British countryside. He arrived with truckloads of expensive furniture, paintings, sculptures, jewelry, and wardrobe—as well as five trailers loaded with thoroughbred horses. Perhaps no Nazi spy had ever ensconced himself in such opulent splendor.

Also brought along or hired locally by Treeck were a butler and a chef, a horse groomer, a footman, two undercooks, three maids, three gardeners and a valet—plus a shapely mistress, Violetta Baroness de Schroeders.

Not surprisingly, forty-one-year-old Robert Treeck and the baroness became "socially acceptable" from the moment they arrived at Luckington Manor—just as the cunning Abwehr boss Wilhelm Canaris had envisioned. The dashing Treeck was promptly invited to join the Beaufort Hunt, a highly exclusive fox-hunting group that was influential in British government affairs. The Beaufort hunt master was the Duke of Beaufort, who was also the Master of the Horse at Buckingham Palace—the home of King George and the royal family.

Treeck soon learned that the neighboring estate, separated by a hedge, belonged to a man who worked in London during the week and who came to his country lodgings on Sundays. That neighbor was Stewart Graham Menzies, who had been born into a rich British ruling-class family that had provided courtiers for the throne for many generations.

Treeck also discovered a weird happenstance: the occupation of his neighbor. Stewart Menzies was acting chief of Britain's MI-6, whose function was to ferret out German spies such as Robert Treeck.[2]

Suspicious Arrow of Wheat

IN LATE JUNE 1940, England was an island under siege. She stood alone against the awesome threat of the Wehrmacht poised on the far side of the channel. Contingency plans had been drawn up to evacuate the royal family and the government to Canada, to which some eighteen hundred million pounds sterling worth of gold ingots had been secretly shipped by the cruiser HMS *Emerald*. Unprepared for total war, Britain was reeling in tumult and confusion.

Rumors of the most fantastic nature swept the British Isles. In the recent invasion of the Low Countries, German paratroopers had landed dressed as nuns—or so rumor had it. Now nuns were suspect, and ecclesiastics in Britain ventured out only for necessities. The BBC stoked the mania fires by reporting that German parachutists dropping into England wearing other than German uniforms were to be shot immediately.

Having heard tales of fifth columnists (enemy infiltrators) and spies paving the way for the Wehrmacht in Belgium, The Netherlands, and France, the people of Great Britain grew highly suspicious. Constabularies were flooded with reports of "odd-acting strangers" and of men who "looked German." "Queer" conversations overheard in pubs were promptly reported to police. Civilians grew panicky. They persisted in seeing all sorts of strange happenings: smoke signals, flashing lights, even unidentified men signaling in trees (who turned out to be telephone linemen).

Early one morning, British security agents rushed to a farm in East Anglia, where a number of large Royal Air Force bases were located, and intensely interrogated the bewildered tenant. Suspicions had been aroused that the forty-eight-year-old farmer was a Nazi spy, although he vehemently denied any wrongdoing.

What had gotten the Briton into trouble was that he had cut his field in a pattern that left standing an arrow-shaped wedge of wheat, about one hundred yards long. From the air, the arrow pointed directly toward an RAF base only about three miles away. Was this arrow designed to aid Luftwaffe bombers to find the target?

A week later, after intense investigation of the suspect's background, the security officers were convinced that the farmer was a loyal Briton and the episode had been a fluke. He had persuaded the security men that he had left the arrow of wheat standing because he "got bored of cutting the field the same way year after year" and had never dreamed that the arrow pointed to the RAF airfield.[3]

A Couple of Mixed-up Britons

IN JULY 1940, D. J. Page was a young British soldier stationed in England. Page was delighted when his long-awaited wedding photographs arrived, but he found that they had been opened by mistake by another young serviceman in Troop A. The recent bridegroom was in Troop H.

Accompanying the pictures was a very apologetic letter from the man who had inadvertently opened the wedding pictures envelope. But his action was not surprising, as it turned out, due to the incredible similarity between the two men's names and serial numbers. The name of the man who wrote the letter was Pape; the other's was Page. Pape's army serial number was 1509322; Page's was 1509321. Neither man had previously known the other.

A few months after the war, D. J. Page was working as a driver with London Transport. One day he noticed that the tax deduction on his paycheck was far too high, and he went to his superintendent to inquire about the matter. There Page learned that his salary had been mixed up with that of another London Transport driver, one recently transferred to the same garage, whose name was Pape—the very same man Page had encountered earlier. There was yet another coincidence: Page's license number was 29222; Pape's was 29223.[4]

A Postcard with a Unique View

IN 1942, Arthur Butterworth was in the British army, posted at a camp near Norwich, on the grounds of Taversham Hall. Butterworth ordered by mail a secondhand book from a London firm, and when the volume arrived two weeks later, he stood in the window of his hut and opened the package.

While removing the wrapping, a picture postcard fell out of the book, placed there, presumably, as a marker by the previous owner. Picking up the card, Butterworth saw that it was postmarked August 4, 1913—nearly three decades earlier. Then he turned it over to look at the picture and was flabbergasted. It showed precisely what he was seeing out his window—a view of Taversham Hall.

During World War II, British army camps, as a security measure, were not identified by name, but rather by a mailing code. So the bookseller, as a friendly gesture to a serviceman, could not have intentionally inserted the card in the book, for he had no way of knowing to which camp he was sending the package.[5]

Fifty Surgeons at the Right Place

A BRILLIANT SUN, rising majestically over Mount Tantalus, began drenching Honolulu, Hawaii, with its first warming rays. Even for the island of Oahu, this was an uncommonly glorious and peaceful Sunday morning. In Honolulu, the sound of pealing church bells summoned the faithful to mass. Except for its handful of aircraft carriers, the United States Pacific Fleet was roosting drowsily in Pearl Harbor. It was 7:00 A.M. on December 7, 1941 (U.S. time).

Over the mighty American naval base, the tranquility was suddenly shattered by the sounds of powerful airplane engines. Below, on scores of ships and boats, thousands of sleeping sailors partially opened their eyes, and roundly cursed the brass hats for disturbing their Sunday morning slumber with aircraft exercises.

Moments later, Japanese bombs began to rain down on the warships in Pearl Harbor and the Army Air Corps planes neatly lined up in rows at Hickam Field.

Within minutes, wounded soldiers were being rushed by a motley collection of civilian and military ambulances to Tripler Army Hospital, where the chief surgeon put in an emergency call for doctors in nearby Honolulu. Then occurred one of life's unbelievable coincidences. At that moment in Honolulu, about fifty civilian doctors were listening to a lecture on war surgery delivered by Dr. John Moorhead of New York. En masse, the surgeons leaped to their feet and rushed off for Tripler Army Hospital, where their skills saved numerous lives that otherwise might have been lost.[6]

A Timely Japanese Air-Raid Drill

IN LATE MARCH 1942, the Japanese government decreed a first, full-dress air-raid drill for the millions of people in Tokyo. It was stressed that this mass exercise was merely a precaution, that no American airplane would ever get near the Japanese homeland. Starting at 9:00 A.M. on April 18, the sprawling city would stage a three-hour alert, and all the military planes based on Honshu would form a protective umbrella above Tokyo throughout the drill.

A few days later, on April 2, while word of the air-raid exercise was making the rounds of Tokyo, the United States carrier *Hornet* put to sea out of San Francisco; aboard her were sixteen army B-25 bombers, Lieutenant Colonel James H. Doolittle, thirty-one other army pilots, and forty-eight air crewmen. Their mission was to bomb Tokyo on April 18. By chance the same day as Tokyo's first air alert had been chosen.

Jimmy Doolittle's pending raid was regarded as a pinprick in the overall war effort. But its primary purpose was more than a gesture of American derring-do. Rather, it was intended to lift the hearts and spirits of the home front, which, since the nation had gone to war five months earlier, had been flooded with gloomy news of one American setback after another around the world.

There was a second, unspoken purpose in what would be the boldest and most spectacular operation in American military history: A few bombs exploding on Tokyo would cause the Japanese warlords to "lose face" among countries all over the western Pacific.

At 8:18 P.M. (7:18 Tokyo time) on April 18, Colonel Doolittle made his run down the *Hornet's* short flight deck, took off into the forty-knot wind, cir-

Jimmy Doolittle's bomber lifts off from the carrier Hornet, *bound for Tokyo. (U.S. Air Force)*

cled the carrier until the other fifteen planes had joined him, then set a course for Tokyo, about eight hundred miles away. Almost at once, Murphy's Law took hold: "If anything can possibly go wrong, it will."

Most of the B-25s lost their way and came at Tokyo from all points of the compass, some attacking north up the bay, others approaching from the west. But the utterly bizarre pattern, contrived by faulty instruments, hard weather, and human error, miraculously turned into what seemed a stroke of genius. Because of these aerial meanderings, the shaken Japanese air defense commanders were wholly mystified and deceived about the source of the attack.

Since the Imperial Japanese high command had assured the armed forces that it would be impossible for American warplanes to even approach the homeland, Jimmy Doolittle's plane crossed over a Japanese cruiser that took no notice of him whatsoever. Doolittle's aircraft, and a few other B-25s that were more or less following him, reached the Honshu coast at 11:55 A.M. and made a beeline for Tokyo.

They flew over thousands of Japanese country folk who looked up and waved them on their way, convinced that the planes were their own aircraft. In Tokyo, the three-hour air-raid drill was just coming to an end. Barrage balloons were being hauled down. Traffic had begun to resume its normal flow. Pedestrians, however, continued to crowd the streets and sidewalks, gawking at the Japanese fighter-plane umbrella stunting directly overhead.

At 12:15 P.M., the first American bombs exploded on Tokyo. A Japanese antiaircraft battery, no doubt confused and thinking all this noise was merely a realistic component of the air-raid drill, fired a round uncertainly in Doolittle's direction, then broke off. No Japanese wanted to blast one of the emperor's warplanes out of the sky.

Above, the Japanese fighter planes, seeing the U.S. bombers, assumed that they were a part of the realistic air-raid alert. So they flew off to their bases. By a strange irony, Tokyo's first air-raid exercise, staged by a people who boasted that their country would never undergo the impact of an enemy bomb, had worked out as a heaven-sent gift to Jimmy Doolittle and his dauntless airmen.[7]

New York Uranium Merchant

IN JUNE 1942, an American army colonel, wearing civilian clothes, strolled briskly into the New York City office of Edgar Sengier, a Belgian mine operator. Assigned to the supersecret Manhattan Project, whose mission was to develop an atomic bomb, the colonel flashed his credentials and asked if Sengier could help the United States get some uranium ore from the Belgian Congo. All the colonel would reveal was that it was "crucial to the Allied cause."

Sengier, adventurous, tough and keen-witted, replied that, yes, he would be able to deliver a sizable quantity of uranium and inquired as to when the colonel would like to have the shipment.

"Right now," the officer declared. "But, of course, we'd settle for a few months from now."

"Well," remarked the Belgian, "I can produce it for you immediately. I have one thousand tons of the ore stored here in New York City."

Taken aback, the colonel thought Sengier was joking. But within an hour, the officer left with a bill of sale that had been drawn up rapidly on a scrap of yellow paper and signed by Sengier. The uranium vital to the success of the Manhattan Project had become the property of the United States government.

Perhaps the anonymous colonel never learned the full story of how one thousand tons of little-known uranium happened to be in New York City and ready for what amounted to an over-the-counter sale. Back when he was thirty-one years of age, Belgium-born Edgar Sengier moved to Africa to seek his fortune and settled in the Congo, which was rich in uranium and copper deposits. Production of those minerals was dominated by the Union Miniere, of which Sengier became president in 1939.

Sengier had been producing pitchblende since 1921. But in that era no one knew that the uranium contained in the ore had any value. However, by 1939—the year the war erupted in Europe—Sengier was approached by an anti-Nazi scientist who told him that German scientists were experimenting in atomic fission, and that it was possible that an atomic bomb might be developed out of uranium.

Edgar Sengier, who was staunchly anti-Nazi, feared a German invasion of the Congo, if for no other reason than to tap the needed uranium deposits. So on his own initiative, he arranged for the shipment of one thousand tons of rich pitchblende to the United States. The Belgian told no one of his action.

When the precious ore reached New York City in 1940, Sengier had it stored in steel drums in a warehouse. Then, he covertly informed appropriate officials of the United States government about the uranium cache, and his disclosure promptly got pigeonholed somewhere in the sprawling federal bureaucracy.

When the army colonel paid his visit to Sengier, he had known nothing about the uranium being in New York. He had played a million-to-one long shot that the Belgian might be able to provide him with clues about where a large amount of the precious mineral might be purchased in the shortest possible time.

The colonel's unexpected discovery played a key role in concluding the war without the loss of perhaps 1 million American and 5 million Japanese lives in an invasion of the Japanese homeland.[8]

The Spy Who Chose the Wrong House

IN THE FALL OF 1942, the SOE, the British cloak-and-dagger agency that Winston Churchill had ordered to "set Europe ablaze," was rapidly infiltrating France with scores of agents in order to have an extensive espionage network when the Anglo-American armies were ready to invade the Continent.

F section was a branch of the London-based SOE, and its function was to conceive and direct secret operations against German forces occupying France and French territories. Its chief was Colonel Maurice Buckmaster, who had been manager of the Ford Motor Company in Paris before Adolf Hitler's Wehrmacht invaded France in 1940.

Within a short period of time, F section agents had gathered together several important réseaux (espionage networks) in France, including "Priest," "Surveyor," "Orator," "Donkeyman," "Physician," "Bricklayer," and "Butler." Established were courier (secret mail), communications, actions, finance, intelligence, and medical branches.

One F section agent, Henri A. E. Dericourt, code-named Gilbert, was parachuted into France on the night of January 23–24, 1943, landing north of Orléans. A Frenchman by nationality, Dericourt had been a civilian pilot with Air France. He possessed great intelligence, nerve, and quick wit, and he was handsome and persuasive.

Henri Dericourt. (USIA)

Dericourt, as with other Allied agents, had been warned to keep an eye open for the presence of the notorious Hugo Bleicher, one of the Abwehr's most energetic, able, and successful spy catchers in France. Bleicher, it was whispered around Paris, could smell an Allied spy at fifty yards.

Dericourt made his way to Paris and moved by chance into a house at 58 rue Pergolèse, near the Avenue Foch. Greater Paris had an estimated 1.5 million houses and apartments, but the weird happenstance that espionage agent Henri Dericourt soon learned was that his next door neighbor was the redoubtable Hugo Bleicher, the Nazis' ace spy catcher.[9]

Two Deadly Foes Meet Again

FIGHTING WAS SAVAGE in the hilly region of northern Tunisia in the tip of the Cape Bon Peninsula. The men of Major General Omar Bradley's U.S. II Corps and elements of General Bernard Montgomery's British Eighth Army (the famed Desert Rats) were pushing to trap the remnants of the once vaunted Afrika Korps. The Germans were tenaciously contesting every yard of ground, even though their renowned commander, General Erwin Rommel, had been stricken with a serious illness and had been evacuated to the Third Reich. It was late April 1943.

During the struggle near places called Bald Hill and Mousetrap Valley by the GIs, a German panzer was charging toward an American machine-gun crew, whose bursts were ricocheting off the tank's thick hide. Suddenly, the tank ground to a halt: An American artillery shell had struck it at a vulnerable point—its treads.

Only one German tanker survived the blast. He crawled out of the damaged vehicle and was taken prisoner by the GI machine-gun crew that he had been trying to kill moments earlier. The Americans were in a foul mood, for the fighting had been a no-holds-barred donnybrook for weeks.

"Kill the bastard!" one GI snarled. His comrades voiced their approval.

"No," their sergeant replied firmly.

Moments later, a shell from a German .88-millimeter gun, the weapon the American ground soldiers feared most during the war, exploded in the machine-gun position.

When the American sergeant, who had been badly wounded, regained consciousness in a field hospital many hours later, he glanced toward the adjoining cot. Lying there was the Afrika Korps tanker whom he had saved from being killed by the other GIs. They had been the only survivors of the shell blast. Each had been evacuated separately, and by a curious circumstance, had been brought to the same field hospital and had been placed in adjoining cots.[10]

Look Out Below!

AT SEVERAL AIRFIELDS in the vicinity of Rome, 1,817 tough young German paratroopers were strapping on parachute harnesses as they prepared to board scores of black transport planes. It was 7:20 P.M. on July 13, 1943, the fourth day since Anglo-American armies had invaded Axis-held Sicily, the stepping-stone to Italy.

These members of the elite 1st Parachute Division, wearing their distinctive round steel helmets with cushioned lining designed to absorb heavy blows on landing, performed hurried last-minute inspections of their Schmeisser automatic pistols, MG-42 machine guns, and bolt-action rifles. Then they checked them yet again.

The Wehrmacht parachutists, perspiring heavily, waited nervously for the shouted order to get aboard the Junkers. Faces were grim. Jaws were set. Eyes narrowed to slits. There was little conversation.

The mission of the German parachute force was to drop behind the lines of Oberst (Colonel) Wilhelm Schmalz's Panzergruppe (armored group) which was dug in along the Simeto River on the east coast of Sicily, seeking to block the northward drive of General Bernard Montgomery's British Eighth Army toward the key port of Messina. There the Fallschirmjäger were to assemble and reinforce Schmalz's already strong defensive line at the southern edge of the Catania plain.

Just as the German transports were lifting off, some six hundred miles to the southwest in Tunisia, troop-carrier aircraft, crammed with grim-faced Red

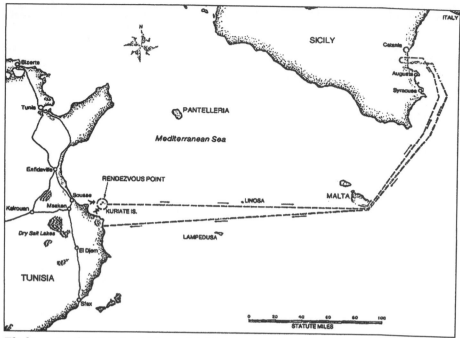

Flight route of British 1st Airborne Division.

Devils of Brigadier Gerald Lathbury's British Parachute Brigade, roared down runways and set a course toward the east coast of Sicily. Down below, the Mediterranean Sea was tranquil, even beautiful, in its clear blue shadings.

Had some omnipotent being been hovering over the central Mediterranean region at that moment, the being would have observed one of the strangest phenomena of the war—or any war. A force of German paratroopers, flying from Rome, and a brigade of British parachutists, taking off from Tunisia, unknown to each other, were winging through the dark skies bound for bailouts on the *identical* drop zone in Sicily, and at the *identical* time. Odds against such a coincidental happening are astronomical.

Darkness was drawing its veil over Sicily when elements of the German 1st Parachute Division, which had taken off from Rome two hours previously, jumped on a drop zone behind the lines of Wilhelm Schmalz's armored battle group. There was the customary confusion of a night drop, and the calm summer air was pierced by the shouts of commanders calling out orders. A rapid assembly was important as the Fallschirmjäger were to be in the front lines by dawn.

While trying to locate their units in the darkness, the German paratroopers heard the oncoming roar of a large number of airplanes and, peering upward, were startled to see scores of white parachutes billowing under the dark silhouettes of transports. Red Devil paratroopers were jumping almost upon the heads of the German parachutists who were in the process of assembling.

Confusion was augmented in German ranks by the unexpected appearance of additional parachutists floating to earth. The Germans on the ground did not know whether to open fire on the descending chutists because the newcomers might be Wehrmacht reinforcements.

As soon as the Red Devils touched ground, a violent series of chaotic firefights erupted. Neither adversary had been expecting to confront the other. Adding to the confusion were the virtually identical steel helmets worn by the German and British paratroopers, which made it impossible to tell friend from foe.

The hand-to-hand battle raged in the blackness. Geometric patterns of white and red tracers laced the sky, and the sharp explosions of hand grenades punctuated the fury. Here and there two shadowy figures grappled to the death in the darkness, their struggle ending with loud grunts as a trench knife found its mark in a neck or stomach.

One Red Devil was slipping cautiously across a field. Sten gun in hand and alert for any sign of an enemy, which might mean sudden death, he was glad to have a comrade walking alongside him in the blackness, particularly in the mass confusion. Curious as to his fellow parachutist's unit, the Briton was about to speak when the other asked, *"Hast du meinen Schmeisser gesehen?"* (Have you seen my automatic pistol?).

Startled to learn that he had been walking along with a German soldier, the Red Devil whipped his Sten gun around and squeezed off a burst at his "comrade."

By dawn, German and British paratroopers had untangled themselves, regrouped, and marched off on their respective missions. No doubt both sides speculated over how German and British commanders had decided to conduct airborne operations, and how both then had picked the same tiny patch of ground and the precise same time to bail out after each force had flown some 300 miles to the drop zone.[11]

Two GIs on Salerno Beachhead

EARLY MORNING DARKNESS was hovering over the towering limestone and marble Apennine mountain range of southern Italy as men of Major General Fred Walker's U.S. 36th Infantry Division were slugging it out with determined German defenders a short distance inland from the Gulf of Salerno. An hour earlier, Walker's assault troops had hit the beach during the first contested Allied invasion of Adolf Hitler's Fortress Europe. It was September 8, 1943.

An American sergeant, along with several comrades, had taken cover behind a low sand dune. A German machine gun only a short distance away sent bursts of tracers at the huddled GIs, clear targets in the light of flares.

"Stay here, I'll get the bastards!" the sergeant ordered.

Cradling his Garand rifle across his arms, the sergeant began arduously crawling through the sand toward the machine-gun nest. The Germans spotted him and concentrated their full attention in his direction. A tracer bullet glanced off his back pack, setting it on fire, but he managed to shed the pack and continued to slither toward his tormentors. A potato-masher grenade was tossed at him and exploded nearby, sending white-hot jagged chunks of steel into his body.

Blood began to form in a pool underneath the sergeant. Bullets continued to zip past just over his head. Summoning his inner spirit, the badly wounded and dazed GI inched forward until he was only fifteen yards from the spitting machine gun. Turning onto his side, he detached a grenade from a web belt and barely had the strength to pull the pin. With one final burst of determination, the sergeant tossed the grenade, heard an explosion, and saw an orange flame erupt at the German position. Piercing screams rang out above the din of the lethal melee swirling around.

The four German machine gunners crumpled into heaps—dead. His work done and bleeding profusely, the sergeant lapsed into unconsciousness.

A short distance away, another GI was working his way toward a German panzer that had been pouring rounds into his comrades. As the GI sought to gain a better position from which to fire at the iron monster, bullets ripped into both his legs. He lay on the ground helpless, and the enemy tank ground forward and ran over him.

GI medics later discovered an amazing coincidence. The sergeant who had been badly wounded while knocking out a death-dealing German machine-gun nest and the soldier a short distance away who had engaged in a lopsided duel with a panzer tank, each had the same name—Manuel S. Gonzales.[12]

Long Shot in the Dark

THE ALLIED BEACHHEAD at Salerno was black and eerie. Thousands of tense, nearly exhausted American and British soldiers were dreading the arrival of dawn, for that would bring a renewal of heavy German onslaughts. Only three days earlier, Allied troops under Lieutenant General Mark Clark, commander of the Fifth Army, had swarmed ashore. In response, the Germans had quickly surrounded the thin beachhead, launching powerful attacks, and they were on the verge of driving the invaders back into the Tyrrhenian Sea.

Now, Major William P. Yarborough, the thirty-one-year-old airborne adviser to General Clark, was standing in the middle of the DZ (drop zone) on the beachhead. It was 1:10 A.M. on September 14, 1943. Yarborough was anticipating the arrival of the first echelon of the 82nd Airborne, the twenty-one hundred paratroopers of Colonel James M. "Slim Jim" Gavin's 505th Parachute Infantry Regiment. Along with the Division's 504th Parachute Infantry

U.S. 82nd Airborne Division paratroopers bailing out over Salerno beachhead.
(Courtesy of Keith Rose)

Regiment, the "Five-O-Fives" were to jump behind American lines on the beachhead to add "numerical and psychological" reinforcement and to stave off Allied disaster.

Major Yarborough, who had planned the fire-alarm operation to bring in the 82nd Airborne paratroopers from southern Sicily, 350 miles from Salerno, had been told by General Clark to promptly locate and escort Colonel Gavin to Clark's headquarters for instructions. Time was crucial and Clark wanted to get the paratroopers into the front lines as rapidly as possible.

It was a tall order. Gavin might land anywhere on the DZ, which measured about eight hundred yards long and was a half mile wide. Or he might land outside the DZ, or even in the sea. Besides, Gavin's parachute coming down would look from the ground exactly like twenty-one hundred other white parachutes that would soon be blossoming in the dark sky. Yarborough reflected that it might take him two or three hours to locate Gavin—or he might not find him at all.

Minutes later, the first of 131 C-47s carrying the 505th Regiment roared overhead and hundreds of parachutes began descending. One trooper crashed to the ground almost on top of Bill Yarborough and began rolling up his chute.

Walking over to the tall, shadowy figure, Yarborough was astonished. It was Slim Jim Gavin himself.[13]

The Second Bill Purdy
Wins Out

FOR SEVEN YEARS prior to 1943, Private Bill Purdy of Ithaca, New York, had a steady girlfriend who lived in Buffalo. Then Bill was drafted. While Purdy was taking his basic training at Camp Croft, South Carolina, the young lady wrote to him several times each week, professing her undying love, and she often sent packages of cookies that she had baked especially for him.

Then, strangely, a second Bill Purdy was assigned to the same outfit. This second Purdy began to receive the first Bill Purdy's letters and cookies from the girl in Buffalo. Finally, Purdy "Number 2" wrote to her to explain the mix-up. Soon, their correspondence grew into a pen-pal relationship.

Months later, the first Bill Purdy visited Buffalo on furlough and learned that his longtime girlfriend had married the second Bill Purdy.

"I don't mind so much that he stole my girl," Purdy told newspeople. "What bothered me was that he swiped my cookies!"[14]

Pigeon Scores a News Scoop

IN LATE MAY 1944, invasion fever gripped the British Isles. Even Adolf Hitler and his Oberkommando der Wehrmacht knew that the mighty Allied force coiled in England was preparing to bolt across the English Channel and strike at Nazi-held northwest Europe. Only the precise date and locale were unknown to German intelligence.

Among those in England waiting nervously for the "Go!" signal were fifty-eight American war correspondents who were scheduled for what were called first-wave slots. These were the civilian men and women who would write, record, and photograph the Normandy invasion, one of mankind's mightiest endeavors.

Now these correspondents received a curious order: Wander up casually (no groups) to a block of flats in Edgerton Gardens, in London's Knightsbridge, and knock on the door of number 38. The man who always opened the door at number 38 in this cloak-and-dagger scenario knew all the American correspondents who came calling like thieves in the night and they all knew him— Major Barney Oldfield, press officer of the United States First Army, which would assault Normandy.

It was Oldfield's task to ride herd benignly over the correspondents while they were in England. Once they were on the Continent, Oldfield was to establish and protect their communications to the cableheads of London. He also was to transport, mess, and brief them, plus provide them with a guardian flock of military people who understood their wants and what they could write and pass through censorship.

Once inside number 38, each correspondent was asked for his or her current telephone number and address, and then was told that he or she would be contacted concerning which invasion unit the journalist was to join.

Major Oldfield, a qualified paratrooper who was once a newsman himself, had as his biggest headache (among hundreds) the job of making certain that the correspondents could get their stories back to London and the United States once the invasion struck. They would rely primarily on mobile radio transmitters, Teletype circuits, and a commercial radio installation, Press Wireless.

A speedboat courier system running between Normandy and England was established; motorcyclists were ready to roar to London from England's south coast with photographic and recorded materials. In addition, a landing strip would be opened on the Continent, so an air courier service could collect copy and other press materials and fly them directly to London.

Time was closing in on Major Oldfield and other planners, who were far from certain that everything possible had been done to assure that news stories and pictures would get out of the Normandy beachhead. And the awesome magnitude of the D-Day story resulted in sleepless nights for Oldfield and other press officers.

Only a few days before the June 6 D-Day (it had been postponed from June 4), an American correspondent, Robert Reuben, had come to Major Oldfield with a problem. Reuben was to jump into Normandy with the U.S. 101st "Screaming Eagles" Airborne Division six hours before the sea assault. Reuben was concerned that he would be isolated and unable to get his story back to England.

"How about taking a couple of pigeons with you?" Oldfield asked casually. Reuben thought the press officer was joking.

"*Pigeons?*" he almost shouted.

The major explained that the army in England had conducted experiments with pigeons, and had found that they were capable of flying forty-five miles per hour, and that they had been able to cover seven hundred miles back to their homing roosts in twenty-four hours. Reuben was hardly enthused. Pigeons, no matter how they were sized up, looked antiquated alongside the highly sophisticated electronic gear that would be set up in Normandy with the capacity for sending back to England perhaps 100 million words daily.

Shortly before midnight on June 5 — D-Day Minus 1 — Robert Reuben sat tensely in a planeload of 101st Airborne paratroopers as they winged through the blackness toward the drop zones in Normandy. Alone among all the correspondents, Reuben had decided to take up Barney Oldfield's suggestion to gamble on two carrier pigeons as part of his personal communications equipment. His feathered pals were resting comfortably in a cage at his feet.

At 9:31 A.M. on D-Day—about three hours after American, British, and French troops had hit the Normandy beaches—Colonel R. Ernest Dupuy, acting public relations officer for SHAEF, told scores of war correspondents in London: "This is it!"

Twelve hours after that electrifying pronouncement, an officer bolted into a tent near Portsmouth, SHAEF invasion headquarters on the southern coast of England.

"We finally have a story in from Normandy!" he blurted excitedly to Major Oldfield. "It came in at Dover!" "Dover?" one officer exclaimed. "Why Dover?"

"Well, it came by pigeon—and it's signed by Robert Reuben."

Suddenly, Oldfield was struck by a strange coincidence. Back in the 1840s, nearly a century earlier, Paul Julius Baron von Reuter, a German, laid the foundation for what would become a global news gathering agency—Reuters. He established a system of coaches, courier horseback riders, wigwag signals, telegraph, and other means to rush to Germany information about the up and down days on the London Stock Exchange before the Frankfurt exchange opened the next day.

However, there had been a gap in Reuter's patchwork system: the distance between the telegraphic terminus at Aachen, Germany, and the end of the French-Belgian telegraphic circuit at Verviers, Belgium. So Baron Reuter decided to use pigeons to span that gap and to outpace the fastest horseback riders of his competitors.

Now, some ninety-three years later, Robert Reuben also had used pigeons to beat *his* news competitors. Curiously, Reuben was a correspondent for Reuters.[15]

Parachute in a Million

AT AN AIRFIELD in the midlands of England, scores of powerful airplane engines howled. The entire region seemed to be shaking. Crowded around the planes were hundreds of paratroopers of Major General Maxwell Taylor's crack U.S. 101st Airborne Division—tough, dedicated, but never before in battle. All were tense. Some men felt like vomiting the stew they had eaten for supper.

Now, the troopers, burdened with about eighty pounds of gear, waddled toward the C-47 doors. Nobody sang. Nobody cheered. It was 9:30 P.M. (British double summer time) on June 5, 1944.

Crammed shoulder to shoulder in bucket seats, bleak-faced troopers craned their necks to get a look at the pilot. Standard procedure. If he was an "old" man of twenty-five, everyone felt better; he'd probably been through Flak Alley before. If the pilot was a fuzzy-faced youth of twenty, troopers grumbled, "Good God, we're being chauffeured by a choirboy!"

At several airfields, one by one C-47s began speeding down runways, and by 11:30 P.M., all of the 101st Airborne's 6,638 parachutists were winging toward Normandy where they would leap onto and behind German positions.

On board one craft carrying troopers of Lieutenant Colonel Robert G. Cole's battalion was Private Robert C. Hillman of Manchester, Connecticut. Hillman held his hand on his parachute.

A paratrooper's life hangs on his parachute. If it is faulty, he will plunge to his death in a "streamer" (a chute that fails to open). So all on board were painstakingly inspecting their lifesaving packs of silk. Hillman noticed that his pack had been inspected at the Pioneer Parachute Company, which was located in his hometown in Connecticut—and he was a personal acquaintance of the inspector whose initials he recognized.

"I know my chute is okay," Hillman told Wright Brown, above the roar of the two engines. Brown was covering the airborne assault for the NBC radio network.

"How can you be so sure?" the correspondent queried.

"Because my mother works for the Pioneer Parachute Company as an inspector, and her initials are on my chute!"

Perhaps as many as a million parachutes, manufactured by scores of American firms, had been distributed to the armed forces all over the globe. By an astonishing circumstance, Private Hillman had been assigned a chute inspected by his own mother.[16]

A Map Found in Normandy

Brigadier General James Gavin, the thirty-seven-year-old assistant commander of the 82nd "All American" Airborne Division, had been handed a tough nut to crack—forcing a crossing over the Merderet River eight miles west of Utah Beach in Normandy. Gavin's men were to spearhead the full-scale attack by Major General J. Lawton Collins's U.S. VII Corps westward across the Cotentin Peninsula. The VII Corps was to reach the sea and trap large numbers of Germans around the key port of Cherbourg to the north. It was June 9, 1944—D-Day Plus 3.

Dug in and fiercely defending the far bank of the Merderet was the first-rate 91st Luftlande (Air Landing) Division. Between the Feldgrau and the American paratroopers was a flooded area several miles long and some five hundred yards across. Stretching over this inundated region was the La Fière causeway (a built-up road). Gavin's attack plan was simple—and perilous. Because of the flood, the All Americans would have to charge along the narrow, exposed causeway. On the far bank, the Germans could be counted on to cluster their heaviest firepower along the sole avenue of approach.

At 10:45 A.M., after a fifteen-minute artillery barrage on the far bank, Gavin's boys, lead by Captain John B. Sauls of the 325th Glider Infantry, charged onto the causeway and were met by blistering machine-gun fire and exploding mortar shells. There was no place to take cover: The glidermen were naked in the gunsights of the enemy. Men went down like flies showered with a lethal chemical, and soon, bodies, dead and wounded, were sprawled along the elevated road.

Next, a company of paratroopers, led by Captain R. D. Rae, leaped to their feet and raced onto the causeway, yelling at the top of their voices. Miraculously perhaps, numerous All Americans survived the hailstorm of fire and reached the far bank.

Huffing and puffing like all of those in the arduous five hundred-yard dash, Jim Gavin reached the west bank on the heels of the first troopers to make the crossing. While gunfire crackled stridently on all sides, he began walking along a dirt road that was cluttered with litter, abandoned and destroyed vehicles and mortars, and other flotsam of violent conflict.

Shortly, the young general came upon a German mortar crew sprawled in a ditch where they had fallen after being gunned down by an American armored car that had come that way just ahead of Gavin. A Wehrmacht lieutenant in the ditch, dead but still limp, was lying face down, clutching a map of the La Fière region. Gavin took the map from him, hoping it would reveal German troop dispositions. It did not.

Disappointed, Gavin turned over the map. There, to his astonishment, was a map of the midlands of England. Clearly marked in red circles were the airports from which the 82nd Airborne had taken off shortly before midnight on the eve of D-Day. Had German spies ferreted out top-secret information? On reflection, the general decided that the map had been prepared for Operation Sea Lion, Hitler's planned invasion of England four years earlier. It was not the 82nd Airborne's departure fields that had been marked on the map, but, by a startling coincidence, Wehrmacht objectives for Sea Lion.[17]

The MacArthurs
Have a Houseguest

DURING THE TWENTY-NINE MONTHS that followed the driving out of the United States from the Philippines in the spring of 1942, the flame of armed resistance against the Japanese had burned brightly. Despite the vigilance of the Kempei Tai, the dreaded Japanese secret police, Manila was a hotbed of Filipino spies who were organized and directed from far-off Australia by Major General Courtney Whitney, Sr., of General Douglas MacArthur's staff.

Since March 1942, when he climbed into a PT boat, broke through a Japanese air and naval blockade of Corregidor, a tiny rock island perched in the mouth of Manila Bay, and escaped to Australia, MacArthur had been focusing on going back to the Philippines at the head of a powerful force. "I shall return!" had become a rallying cry among Filipino guerrillas and spies alike.

General Douglas MacArthur. (MacArthur Memorial)

In August 1944, Courtney Whitney received a message from a spy who was masquerading as a bellhop in the Manila Hotel, where Douglas Mac-Arthur, his wife Jean, and young son Arthur had lived. The MacArthurs had left their household furniture behind and had evacuated the city rapidly when Japanese troops poured in on Christmas Eve 1941. Whitney took the message to his boss, then stood by as MacArthur scanned its contents while puffing on a corncob pipe. In a curious coincidence, Field Marshal Hisaichi Terauchi, supreme commander of Japanese forces in the South Pacific and MacArthur's opposite number, had not only moved into the Manila Hotel, but was occupying the suite that had belonged to the MacArthur family.

Handing the cable back to Whitney, MacArthur remarked dryly: "Well, he should like it. It has a pair of vases given by the [Japanese] emperor to my father [General Arthur MacArthur] in 1905."[18]

Sad Discovery in a Cemetery

WHEN THE U.S. 101st "Screaming Eagles" Airborne Division was bivouacked near Utah Beach in Normandy, waiting for the boats to take it back to England in early July 1944, a teenage trooper by the name of Fritz Nyland received shocking news. The company commander of his brother William's outfit in the

508th Parachute Infantry told Fritz that his brother had been killed in action during the vicious fighting in Normandy.

Fritz Nyland, fighting back tears, came to see Captain Francis L. Sampson, a regimental chaplain known affectionately to the Screaming Eagles as Father Sam. Clearly troubled, Fritz told the parachute padre of William's death and said that he was buried in a cemetery at Sainte-Mère Église, six miles inland from Utah Beach.

Father Sam and Fritz climbed into a jeep and drove the twenty miles to the cemetery. But when he checked the cemetery roster, the chaplain could not find the brother's name. Could there have been a mistake about his reported death?

"There's no William Nyland listed here," Father Sam said encouragingly, "although there is a Roland Nyland listed."

It was another jolt for Fritz: "Father . . . that's my brother, too. He was a lieutenant in the 90th Infantry Division."

Fritz had come seeking one brother's grave and had found another dead brother's resting place instead. After saying a few prayers at Roland's grave, the two troopers went to another cemetery just a few blocks away. There they found the grave for which they had been looking. In addition, only two weeks earlier, a third brother had been killed in the Pacific. Mother Nyland had seen four sons go off to war; now she had only one.[19]

Rommel and Montgomery

SIX WEEKS AFTER the Western Allies stormed ashore in Normandy on June 6, 1944, Field Marshal Erwin Johannes Eugen Rommel climbed into his staff car—a six-wheeler Mercedes—after visiting at the headquarters of *Obergruppenführer* (General) Sepp Dietrich, commander of the 1st SS Panzer Korps and long a crony of Adolf Hitler. The Mercedes headed back to Rommel's headquarters at the Château de La Roche Guyon, nestled in a bend of the River Seine north of Paris.

Rommel was known as *Der Junge Marschall* (the Boy Marshal) and his popularity in the fatherland rivaled that of the führer himself. Energetic, devout, and courageous, Rommel had been awarded Germany's highest decoration for bravery, as a company commander in World War I. Twenty-two years later, in the North African desert in the early 1940s, Rommel's star had risen as a result of his numerous victories over British General Bernard Montgomery. At the age of forty-nine he became the youngest field marshal in German history.

Above the brutality of war, the two generals even became admirers of one another. Montgomery had a portrait of his Teutonic rival on his trailer-headquarters wall. Rommel often referred to the Briton as "my friend Montgomery." Their names and destinies became indelibly intertwined.

These stills are from moving pictures taken during strafing run by U.S. Air Corps pilot Lieutenant Harold O. Miller. Was this Field Marshal Erwin Rommel's car? (U.S. Air Force)

In Normandy, Rommel and Montgomery were again foes: the German as commander of Army Group B and Montgomery as leader of Allied ground forces during the invasion.

Now, on July 17, 1944, at four o'clock in the afternoon, Rommel's Mercedes was speeding along what was known as the Livarot Road after his visit to General Dietrich's headquarters. Beside the field marshal was his longtime aide, Captain Helmut Lang, and in the front seat was Corporal Walther Holke, whose job it was to keep an eagle eye open for marauding fighter bombers.

Suddenly, Holke called out that two Allied planes were banking and heading toward the staff car. Staff Sergeant Daniel, who had been Rommel's driver since North African days, put on a burst of speed. At the edge of a village just ahead, the Typhoons swooped in and a burst of machine-gun fire caught the Mercedes in the rear. Rommel was hit in the left cheek and left temple. Sergeant Daniel, the driver, was killed instantly, and the car went out of control, hit a tree stump, careened across the road, and halted in a ditch.

Rommel was thrown from the car by the impact, and lay in the road while a Typhoon zoomed in to rake the macadam with bullets. Captain Lang and Corporal Holke dashed into the road and carried the unconscious and bloody field marshal to cover in the roadside ditch.

Even in this isolated episode, Erwin Rommel could not escape from the image of his longtime nemesis-friend, the British general. Near to where Rommel lay was a sign that told the name of the village—*Montgommery*.[20]

Lost Dog Tag

A SKY TRAIN of 396 C-47 transport planes, stretching out for more than one hundred miles, was nearing the French Riviera in the predawn darkness of August 15, 1944. On board were 5,607 infantry, engineer, and artillery

Missing for 45 years:
Eugene Brissey's dog tag.
(Courtesy General Richard Seitz)

paratroopers who were spearheading Operation Dragoon, the Allied invasion of southern France. The remaining 3,400 men of the 1st Airborne Task Force would bail out and land in gliders later on D-Day.

As each flight neared its designated drop zone, green lights flashed on in cabins, and out the paratroopers plummeted into the black unknown. One of those troopers was Trooper Eugene L. Brissey of Loveland, Ohio, a member of Colonel Rupert D. Graves's 517th Parachute Regimental Combat Team. Brissey crashed hard into thick shrubbery; his dog tag and its chain were ripped off.

Scrambling to his feet, Brissey shucked his parachute, then stalked off through the foggy darkness in search of his company. The least of his thoughts was the lost dog tag, although it did flash through his mind that if he were killed, he might be buried with the word *Unknown* marked on his wooden cross. However, Brissey survived the war.

Thirty-seven years later, Colette Saeys, who lived inland from the French Riviera, was raking her yard when she noticed that a small metal object had been collected with the leaves and brush. Picking it up, she saw the name Eugene L. Brissey stamped on it. Mrs. Saeys put the dog tag in an envelope and stored it in a drawer.

Eight years after she found the dog tag, Mrs. Saeys and her husband were visited by two Americans, a man and his wife, from Albuquerque, New Mexico. At that time, the French woman returned the tag to the man who had lost it in her yard forty-five years earlier during the heat of battle—Eugene L. Brissey.[21]

A "Dead" Soldier Reappears

A HOWLING SNOW STORM was pounding the thick pine forests of the Ardennes in Belgium, as grim, half-frozen men of the U.S. 509th Parachute Infantry Battalion were forming up to assault the German-held town of Born. Captain Carlos C. "Doc" Alden, the battalion surgeon, who had been tending the wounded at an aid station, hurried forward through the deep snow to join in the attack. It was January 7, 1945.

Captain Carlos C. Alden. (Carl Alden painting)

Doc Alden was a legend among many American paratroopers. Earlier, during the fighting in North Africa and in Italy, the Buffalo native had been awarded the Distinguished Service Cross and numerous other decorations for gallantry. Three times while behind enemy lines, he had been captured; three times he had escaped.

During his early combat in North Africa, the thirty-three-year-old Alden had worn the traditional red cross on his helmet. But after he had been shot at and had a number of his medics gunned down, the surgeon began going into battle armed to the teeth. He carried a tommy gun or a BAR (Browning automatic rifle), and had a .45-caliber pistol on his hip and a .38-caliber pistol in a shoulder holster. Alden also carried a trench knife and a few grenades. And, he was an expert in the use of all these weapons.

With a straight face, Doc Alden explained to curious outsiders, who knew that a medic carrying weapons was prohibited by the Geneva Convention, that, when treating wounded soldiers in the field, he used his arsenal to ward off wild animals.

Now, in frontline position outside Born, Alden was told that a fellow paratrooper was wounded seriously and was lying in a shell hole 250 feet ahead, in sight of the Germans defending the town.

"Cover me," Alden said. "I'll go have a look."

Crawling and slithering alternately, the surgeon reached his comrade. Semiconscious, the trooper looked as though a huge meat cleaver had struck him on the chin, then had sliced off his face to the right ear. His head was a blob of blood, almost unrecognizable as a human body part. Alden dragged the man's heavy weight out of the hole, then slung the injured trooper over a shoulder and trudged back to his own lines.

The surgeon felt the man's pulse, listened to his heartbeat, and examined his face, which was mutilated hideously. A parachutist whispered to Alden, "What chance has he got, Doc?"

"Slim and none. I doubt if he'll make it alive back to the aid station."

Minutes later, the 509th Parachute Infantry Battalion, its ranks severely depleted after heavy fighting in the Ardennes, attacked Born. After a ferocious clash with SS troops, the town was captured.

Five years after the war, Carlos Alden was attending a reunion in Chicago when he was approached by a tall, rather handsome man.

"I bet you don't remember me, Doc," the stranger said.

Alden studied the man's smooth facial features, then admitted that he could not place him.

"Well," the man replied, "you rescued me from that hole outside Born during the Battle of the Bulge!"

Unbeknown to Alden, Army doctors had performed a miracle in snatching the man from the jaws of death after he had been evacuated and then, in numerous operations over many months, plastic surgeons had worked their magic in rebuilding his face. Doc Alden stared as though he had seen a ghost, then muttered, "Good God!"[22]

Kamikaze Hits the *Calloway*

ON JANUARY 3, 1945, Admiral Jesse Oldendorf's bombardment and fire-support ships set sail from the central Philippines for Lingayen Gulf off northern Luzon Island. Oldendorf's heavies were the spearhead of General Douglas MacArthur's U.S. Sixth Army that would storm ashore on Luzon along the gulf, and drive southward to capture Manila.

Included in Oldendorf's flotilla of 164 vessels were the "ghost ships," battlewagons that had been sunk at Pearl Harbor and raised from the mud to fight again.

Twenty-four hours later, while en route to Lingayen Gulf, the naval spearhead ran into a hornet's nest. Japanese kamikaze pilots by the score swooped down and plunged their aircraft into American escort carriers, destroyers, and cruisers. The suicide airmen took a deadly toll as Oldendorf's naval force ran a gauntlet of fire all the way to Lingayen Gulf.

At 7:55 A.M. on January 6, a kamikaze hit the bridge of the attack transport *Calloway*, which was manned largely by U.S. Coast Guardsmen and loaded with 1,188 army assault troops. Splinters from the Japanese Zeke (as the kamikazes were called) and from the transport's bridge sprayed everywhere, and flaming gasoline was splashed over the main deck.

Twenty-nine Coast Guardsmen were killed and twenty-two were wounded. In a curious twist of fate, not a single army man received as much as a scratch.[23]

A Sister's Startling Discovery

IN JANUARY 1945, a young lady named Theresa Fisco was hard at work performing her job as a typist for the United States Army at a large city in the eastern United States. Her function was to type the commendations of American fighting men who had been awarded medals.

Each day since her brother, Sergeant Richard D. Fisco, had gone overseas with the 509th Parachute Infantry Battalion two years earlier, Theresa had prayed to the Holy Mother for his safe return. In common with countless other women on the home front, she was worried at this time especially, because she knew a pitched battle was raging in Belgium and she presumed that her brother was involved in it.

On this day, Miss Fisco completed typing the wording on one decoration and routinely picked up another official army form from her desk. A startled look came over her face. It was a million to one chance occurrence. She noticed excitedly that this award of a Silver Star for gallantry was easily the most important one that had ever reached her desk—it was that of Sergeant Richard D. Fisco of the 509th Parachute Infantry Battalion, her brother.[24]

Inseparable Twins

EARLY ON THE MORNING of February 16, 1945, hundreds of C-47 transport planes carrying the U.S. 503rd Parachute Infantry Regimental Combat team were heading toward Corregidor, a tiny rock island nestled in the mouth of Manila Bay in the Philippines. The DZ (drop zone) was the parade ground on Top Side, a 550-foot-high elevation that dominated Corregidor.

At 8:32 A.M. the GIs began bailing out of the aircraft. A death struggle for what General Douglas MacArthur called the "Holy Grail of Corregidor" had begun. Early in the war, powerful Japanese forces had overrun the island and imprisoned the U.S. survivors under incredibly brutal conditions.

Down below the transport planes, six thousand Japanese were burrowed in caves and man-made holes. Within a few minutes, the smoky blue sky over The Rock (as it was known) was awash with billowing white parachutes. Most of the troopers jumped at five hundred feet, and a twenty-four-mile-per-hour wind heightened the danger that they would be blown far off target and would plunge to their death in Manila Bay.

A PT-boat crew rescuing American paratroopers who fell into the sea during the attack on Corregidor. (Courtesy Alyce Mary Guthrie)

Throughout the parachute drop American PT boats, swift, heavily armed craft designed mainly for hit-and-run attacks against enemy ships often fifty times their size, cruised back and forth some 150 yards offshore. The PT boats' mission: to fish paratroopers out of the water. These craft had to move in a hurry; a paratrooper, loaded with between fifty and ninety pounds of gear and ensnarled in his chute harness would be dragged under in seconds to a watery grave.

Now, a PT boat was racing toward two paratroopers who had plunged into the bay within forty yards of each other. The first to be pulled out of the water was Private First Class Ammizon B. Impson, Jr., of the 462nd Parachute Field Artillery Battalion.

The drenched trooper had an identical twin, Private First Class Jack N. Impson, who was also a member of the same artillery battalion and who was jumping in the same mission. Ammizon and Jack had been inseparable during their nineteen years of life. They had joined the army together and had volunteered together for the paratroops.

As Ammizon Impson lay gasping for breath, his thoughts were on his twin. Had Jack Impson hit the DZ? Had he made a safe landing? Moments later, the PT-boat crew began hauling the second paratrooper from the bay. In a curious twist of fate, it was Jack Impson.[25]

A Nazi Bigwig Slept Here

FOR THE WAR CORRESPONDENTS attached to Lieutenant General William H. Simpson's U.S. Ninth Army, the accommodations into which they were moving exceeded in creature comforts anything in their fondest dreams. Their temporary home on March 12, 1945, was Schloss Rheydt, an ancient castle dating from about 1275 A.D.

Located near the German city of München-Gladbach, Schloss Rheydt was overpoweringly German in its architecture, and it was moated all around, with a single drawbridge entry. The dining hall had been built on the grand scale, with a high ceiling, and the hall was outfitted with a series of long tables at which stood high-backed chairs. The fireplace at the entrance end of the dining hall was ten feet across and as high as the average man. In it were burned seven-foot logs. Meals, prepared by hired civilians, were tasty.

Clearly, the absentee Teutonic master of Schloss Rheydt was a man of great power and wealth within the Third Reich. Large color portraits of Hermann Goering and other top Nazi nabobs adorned the walls. In one large room hung personally inscribed photographs of German celebrity actors and actresses.

On the first night in Schloss Rheydt, Wes Gallagher and Henry Griffin of the Associated Press, Gordon Gammack of the *Des Moines Register-Tribune*, and Vic Jones of the *Boston Globe* were ensconced in the castle's largest and most pretentious bedroom, which had been occupied by the owner when he was in residence.

It was an ironic situation. Schloss Rheydt was the country estate of Nazi Propaganda Minister Josef Goebbels. By a curious coincidence, four American correspondents, who embodied the free press concept, were now sleeping in the bedroom of Goebbels, who, for fourteen years, had put a clamp on so much of Europe's print and who had stifled free-enterprise journalism within greater Germany.[26]

A German General's Homecoming

ON THE AFTERNOON of May 1, 1945, Major General James M. Gavin, the leader of the U.S. 82nd Airborne Division, jeeped into the village of Ludwigslust in northwest Germany. The streets were jammed with Feldgrau, who had thrown their arms away. Crippled and healthy, wounded and robust, old and young, they were fleeing the oncoming Russians westward through American

Lieutenant General Kurt von Tippelskirch (right) leaves his former home after surrendering the German 21st Army Group. (Courtesy Mrs. James M. Gavin)

lines. Once the scourge of Europe, the Wehrmacht had disintegrated into a rabble.

Gavin's spirited troopers were continuing to push eastward beyond Ludwigslust, and more Germans, their faces stricken with fear over their fate should they fall into the hands of the Soviets, were pouring through the town. The general, clad in a jumpsuit faded by three years of war and with his trademark M-1 rifle slung over one shoulder, was standing on a downtown street intersection when a GI came up and said that a German general was looking for an American general.

"Send him over," Gavin ordered.

Within a half-hour, the enemy general, wearing the Iron Cross at his throat, strolled up to Gavin, rather haughtily, the American reflected. The German refused to believe that Gavin held two-star rank: He was too young and didn't look like a general. Besides, he was carrying a rifle just like any other GI.

Gavin quickly set the other general straight. Then the German said that he represented Lieutenant General Kurt von Tippelskirch, leader of the German 21st Army Group, who wanted to discuss surrender terms. Happy to oblige, Gavin replied, "suggesting" that von Tippelskirch be at Gavin's command post at 8:00 P.M. Both men agreed to the arrangement.

Gavin's headquarters had been set up by his staff in a resplendent palace, the opulence of which none of the 82nd Airborne men had seen during the war. Leading up to the palace was a huge, well-manicured courtyard. Inside, the high-ceilinged rooms had silk wall coverings. Expensive, lovely chandeliers scintillated as the evening light reflected off the mirrors and highly polished parquet floors.

With the customary bevy of aides, General von Tippelskirch arrived at the stroke of eight. Minutes later, he agreed to surrender the 21st Army Group to the 82nd Airborne, provided that Gavin tell the Russians to cease their attacks against his unit. Gavin pointed out that he had no control over the Russians, and that von Tippelskirch could either capitulate unconditionally or the 82nd Airborne would continue to attack eastward until it linked up with the oncoming Soviets.

Von Tippelskirch finally agreed to those terms and signed a document that had been hurriedly typed. Then he asked if he could remain in the palace overnight. Gavin gave his approval, but was curious: Why did von Tippelskirch make that request? In a strange quirk of fate, this ornate palace, in which the German had just undergone the humiliation of surrendering his entire army group to a single American division, had been the home of von Tippelskirch, a wealthy banker by profession, and he wanted to spend one final night in it before going into captivity.[27]

Nabbing a Nazi Nabob

EARLY IN MAY 1945, with the Western Allies approaching Berlin from the west and the Russians closing in on the German capital from the east, Radio Berlin announced Adolf Hitler's "heroic death." He had shot himself through the head in a bunker. The once vaunted Wehrmacht (armed forces) was battered and in total disarray. Germans were surrendering by companies, battalions, and even divisions.

Rumors were rampant that numerous Nazi big shots were holed up in and around Berchtesgaden, the Alpine village in Bavaria in southeastern Germany indelibly linked with Adolf Hitler and Nazism. On a towering peak overlooking Berchtesgaden was the Adlerhorst (Eagle's Nest), which had once been the führer's secluded retreat.

On the night of May 3, Colonel Robert F. Sink's 506th Parachute Infantry Regiment of the U.S. 101st Airborne Division received orders to rush sixty miles and capture Berchtesgaden. Near there, the paratroopers took charge of a top Nazi, Field Marshal Albrecht Kesselring, the Oberfehlshaber West (commander in chief, west), who was comfortably ensconced in the *Brunswick*, his private nine-car train parked on a siding.

Then the paratroopers hauled in another large Nazi fish. Acting on a tip from a German priest, a few GIs rushed to a shoemaker's house in Schleching, where they dragged a sleeping figure from his bed on the third floor. The German protested violently. But a short time later, a local Bergermeister (mayor)

Self-styled Nazi "Jew-baiter" Julius Streicher was captured by a Jewish GI. (National Archives)

identified him as Dr. Robert Ley, a longtime Hitler crony and leader of the Nazi Labor Front.

A week after Ley was collared, Major Henry Plitt of the 101st Airborne received an anonymous telephone tip. Plitt quickly gathered a few of his men and headed for a farmhouse outside the Bavarian village of Waldring, where Julius Streicher was thought to be holed up.

Streicher was one of the most violent and crude "Jew-baiters" (as he called himself) in the Nazi Party, and he had been a close associate of Hitler since the early days of 1923. That year he had founded *Der Stürmer*, a newspaper with a semiofficial status that specialized in scurrilous and pornographic sensationalism, mainly directed against Jews.

When Major Plitt and his troopers arrived at the farmhouse, they found a bearded man who gave his name as Sailor. He was leisurely creating a painting on a canvas.

"Sailor, hell!" Plitt exploded. "You're Julius Streicher, you bastard!"

"No, no," the German protested. "I am a painter. I have never had any interest in politics."

Under intense interrogation, the man finally broke down and admitted he was Streicher. Capturing Streicher was of special satisfaction to Henry Plitt, a highly decorated Jewish officer.[28]

Part Three

Curious Happenings

United States Tunes In
to Hitler

IN THE LATE SUMMER of 1939, Europe was gripped with war fever. In the Third Reich, Admiral Wilhelm Canaris, the shrewd, white-haired chief of the Abwehr, placed his sixteen thousand agents around the world on a war alert. On the grounds of a tree-shaded estate outside Wohldorf, a few miles north of the Baltic port of Hamburg, Abwehr radio men scurried to their shortwave sets in the Europa Saal, a hall in a concrete dugout containing twenty listening posts, each in a separate soundproof booth. Each shortwave set was tuned to a different frequency, monitoring the flood of incoming messages that was pouring in from secret agents at scattered points around Europe.

Nearly all of the spies were calling in on Afu radios, or Klamotten (junk), as the hand-carried suitcase transceivers were known in Abwehr jargon. Unknown to the Wohldorf radiomen, Adolf Hitler had decreed that war would break out on September 1, 1939, with an invasion of the fatherland's eastern neighbor, Poland.

All through the month of August, while five German armies in excess of 1.5 million men were being deployed along the Polish frontier, Wohldorf was broadcasting a conveyor-belt stream of peremptory orders, issuing emergency rules, or seeming to chitchat with shadowy figures identified only by strange call signs or by quaint nicknames such as "Snow," "Mutt," or "Peacock." But it was far from idle talk. Each one of these spies with a strange call sign or name was being issued specific orders that were to be implemented as soon as war erupted.

It was the first time in history that wireless was being used so profusely for the transmission of secret intelligence. The air was saturated with the strange sounds, filling those in British agencies who were eavesdropping on the broadcasts with a sense of foreboding.

It was not only British intelligence that was tuned in to Adolf Hitler's war preparations. In New York City, radio station WOR recorded the German wireless traffic, much of it gibberish, and rebroadcast it to hundreds of thousands of Americans, who, curiously, were then able to listen to the eerie sounds of impending war.[1]

An Anti-Nazi Paces Hitler's War

ADOLF HITLER envisaged conquering neighboring Poland by massing troops along the Polish frontier and then making a lightninglike, unimpeded advance into the heart of the weak nation before Poland even had the opportunity to mobilize its forces. Admiral Wilhelm Canaris's Abwehr was given a critical part to play in the execution of the Blitzkrieg (lightning war), including the destruction of bridges and roads that the Polish army would want to use.

In late April 1939, four months before the invasion, Canaris received special instructions from Colonel General Wilhelm Keitel, chief of staff of the German high command. The Abwehr was to put together sixteen Kampfgruppen (combat teams, or K-teams) to pave the way for the armies' charge into Poland. In an order for the teams' employment, the German high command authorized Admiral Canaris to engage them in specific offensive operations up to twelve hours prior to the launching of hostilities—against a nation with which the Germans would still be at peace.

Just past noon on August 24, Lieutenant Colonel Adolf Heusinger, an operations officer in the German high command, informed Canaris that the führer had set 4:15 A.M. on August 26 as the time for the invasion of Poland. Eight hours later, Heusinger called back to tell the Abwehr chief to send the Kampfgruppen into action beginning at 8:00 P.M. on the following day.

On the evening of August 25, Canaris received an urgent telephone call from Heusinger: The führer was postponing the jump-off for political reasons. Hitler ordered the Abwehr boss to "do everything possible to halt your combat teams."

The hour was late—8:05 P.M. But by superhuman effort, Canaris and his aides managed to halt the K-teams—all except one. That team, led by young Lieutenant Albrecht Herzner, had the mission of securing Jablunkov Pass, through which a key railroad line ran.

It was a weird situation. Lieutenant Herzner was secretly a violent anti-Nazi with a passion for eliminating the Hitler regime. Only a few weeks earlier, he had been meeting clandestinely with a group of German officers dedicated to that task. All were convinced that the führer was recklessly taking the fatherland down the road to total destruction, beginning with the invasion of Poland.

By a curious roll of the dice, Albrecht Herzner had been chosen to lead a K-team and now he, the anti-Nazi who had been plotting the assassination of Hitler, would pave the way for the führer's war, which he fervently opposed.

Unaware of any change in plans, Lieutenant Herzner's "lost" K-team opened fire at the railroad pass at one minute after midnight on August 26, drove off a group of Polish defenders, seized the nearby railroad station, and waited for the panzer division for which it had carved out a path to arrive. The hours passed. Dawn came. No sign of the expected division. What had gone wrong? Had Herzner's group inadvertently seized the wrong railroad pass and station? Baffled by the mystifying circumstances, Lieutenant Herzner asked a captured Polish major: "What's going on? Aren't Germany and Poland at war?"

"Not that I'm aware of," the Pole replied with a shrug.

Herzner found that the telephone in the railroad station still worked, so he called the base of the panzer division which was supposed to have arrived hours earlier. The lieutenant was told by a frantic intelligence officer to drop everything—prisoners, enemy equipment, booty—and to rush back behind the German border as rapidly as possible.

It was too late. Herzner, the anti-Nazi plotter, with conspicuous gallantry, had already fought and won his war. His K-team had fired the first shots in World War II, six days, four hours and forty-four minutes before its "official" outbreak at 4:45 A.M. on September 1, 1939.[2]

Dame Fate Foils a Kidnapping

ADOLF HITLER had grown furious—and frustrated. In the spring of 1940, his mighty, booted legions had overrun Belgium, The Netherlands, Luxembourg, and France, and had driven 337,131 waterlogged British Tommies—minus their guns, tanks, and artillery—from the Continent at Dunkirk, France. Great Britain had suffered a shocking military disaster and was virtually defenseless, an island at bay.

In Berlin, Hitler ranted to confidants that "[Winston] Churchill and his clique," and King George VI to a lesser degree, were obstacles to his granting England magnanimous peace terms. The führer held the notion that there was a large "peace movement" in Britain. So if Churchill and the king could be disposed of, peace would return to Europe—with Adolf Hitler reigning as lord and master.

While planning for Operation Sea Lion, the Wehrmacht invasion of the British Isles, was progressing, Hitler concocted a scheme for dispatching the pair of "obstacles to peace" Churchill and King George. The wildeyed machination centered on the Duke and Duchess of Windsor.

To "be with the woman I love" was the reason the duke had given when, in 1937 as King Edward VIII, he had abdicated the British throne to marry a commoner. The duke and the duchess had been in Paris when France surrendered. The couple had then moved to Madrid, where they were living still.

According to Hitler's plan, the duke and duchess would be kidnapped, and in some undetermined manner the Nazis would return the duke to the British throne, presumably whether he wanted to wear the crown or not. When King Edward VIII was ruling once again, the comic-opera script went, he would bounce Churchill from office (or have him arrested), boot out his brother, King George, and, presto, Sea Lion would be unnecessary.

The task of snatching the Duke of Windsor was given to an SS officer, twenty-nine-year-old Walther Schellenberg, whose character was a blend of a keen and innovative mind with the instincts and morals of a gangster. Wearing civilian clothing, Schellenberg and a few handpicked SS men flew to Madrid, posing as German business representatives.

Then, on July 30, 1940, Eberhard von Stohrer, the Nazi ambassador in Madrid, fired off an urgent message to Berlin: A German spy had learned that the duke had been appointed governor of the Bahamas, and that he and the duchess were going to sail for the island on August 1, departing from Lisbon, Portugal, on the American liner *Excalibur*. Word was flashed to Walther Schellenberg, who rushed from Madrid to Lisbon to head off the duke and duchess.

Apparently, it was proposed that the duke be abducted in Lisbon before he boarded the *Excalibur*, and then he would be flown to Berlin. Since the world would not know that the former British king had been kidnapped (and no doubt drugged in the process), it would appear that the duke had gone to Berlin voluntarily in a dramatic effort to seek peace and to denounce the "warmonger" Churchill and the duke's own brother, King George.

Before the Nazi conspirators could snatch the duke, he and the duchess unexpectedly drove to the Lisbon dock three hours before sailing time. Presumably, Edward was unaware that he was a kidnapping target. Only at the last minute did Walther Schellenberg hear that the duke had left early to board the *Excalibur*.

Luck was with the German conspirators. Rumors had spread at the dock that a bomb had been planted on the ocean liner, so the captain delayed sailing for an hour while the vessel was searched. Meanwhile, Schellenberg and three of his men leaped into an automobile and began racing hell-bent for the dock, determined to grab the duke before he could get up the gangplank.

Then, Dame Fate intervened. At a Lisbon street intersection, a truck pulled in front of the Schellenberg automobile, and a jarring collision resulted. The Nazis' car was badly damaged and was inoperable. As Schellenberg desperately tried to obtain another vehicle, the Duke and Duchess of Windsor sailed on the *Excalibur*—unaware that they had been saved by a timely fluke.[3]

Dead Spy Put to Work

In July 1940, Hitler's powerful legions were poised in northwest France, ready to leap the English Channel and conquer Great Britain, whose armies had suffered a major disaster at Dunkirk a few weeks earlier.

Now, the British army was in disarray; the Royal Air Force, while of high quality, was far outnumbered by the Luftwaffe, and the Royal Navy, although still one of the world's largest and most capable fleets, was seriously overextended in its operations to keep open vital supply routes between the United States and England.

In order to mask Britain's woeful military weakness, a stable of Nazi agents, captured in England by counterintelligence and security agents within weeks after war had erupted, would be utilized. These double agents had been given a choice: to be summarily hanged or to radio back messages contrived by the British to their former spy masters in Hamburg and Berlin. To a man, they chose to become double agents.

Late in August, Scotland Yard detectives were summoned to a deserted air-raid shelter in Cambridge to investigate a possible murder. Although hundreds of Britons had been killed in a Luftwaffe blitz in full swing at that time, murder was still a serious matter in England.

Papers were found on the dead man indicating that his name was Jan Villen Ter Braak. His suitcase contained an Afu radio set, the precise kind the Abwehr issued to its agents before parachuting them into remote parts of England. It was quickly determined that the mystery man had committed suicide—and that Jan Villen Ter Braak was a fictitious name and his papers were also fraudulent, created by Abwehr technicians in Hamburg.

The true identity of Ter Braak would never be known. But in death, he performed a valuable service to the nation he had come to spy on. British deception agents, using the secret code and instructions found on his body, used Ter Braak's radio to periodically flash "high-grade intelligence" to the dead Dutchman's controllers in the Third Reich, phony information that indicated that the British armed forces had rapidly been rearmed with tanks and guns from America.[4]

A Cooperative German Commandant

AFTER ADOLF HITLER'S powerful war juggernaut smashed the once vaunted French army in an amazing six weeks in the spring of 1940, captured French officers were herded into Colditz Castle, a massive, ancient structure surrounded by a thick wall and perched on a height in Saxony, a region in east-central Germany. The castle had been designated Oflag IVC, an abbreviation of Offizierlager, meaning officers' place of detention.

Colditz was a Sonderlager, a special camp to hold captured enemy officers who, for various reasons, merited a more careful watch than was kept on other prisoners of war. Among those who were incarcerated in the castle were those who were regarded as likely candidates to escape.

In mid-1941, Lieutenant Pierre Mairesse Lebrun, a tall, ruggedly handsome French cavalryman, was among the three thousand officers, mainly British, Dutch, and French, being held in Colditz. When Lebrun and his group arrived, they were told by the Kommandant of the camp: "You cannot escape from here; *Sie beissen hier auf Granit.*" (Here you will bite into granite.)

Lieutenant Lebrun felt challenged to "bite into the granite" and escape, as had several POWs. Most had been caught, returned to Colditz, and given terms of solitary confinement in cells. During a recreation period in the castle's courtyard on June 9, Lebrun, aided by several diversions that attracted the attention of the guards, climbed into the rafters of an open-sided pavilion.

After the other prisoners had been returned to their quarters, as pre-arranged, a bugle blown by a POW from a castle window signaled an "all clear." Having changed into a gray suit made from pajamas sent by his family a few months earlier, Lebrun scrambled over the wall and walked to a station six miles away to catch a train for Leipzig.

At the ticket office, he offered a one-hundred-mark note that had been smuggled into Colditz. The clerk immediately recognized that the note was invalid; it dated back to pre-Nazi days. Police were called and Lebrun was hustled back to Colditz to serve twenty-one days of solitary confinement.

Undaunted, Lebrun began scheming to make another escape. Less than a month later, prisoners in the castle heard a volley of rifle shots ring out from the courtyard far below. Minutes later, Lieutenant Lebrun was back in a cell serving thirty days for his latest escape attempt.

Soon the Frenchman was ready to try again. While strolling around the courtyard with other prisoners during a two-hour exercise period, Lebrun paused nonchalantly next to the eight-foot-high wire fence. As prearranged, another POW clasped his hands; Lebrun put one foot in them and was boosted over the wire. Crouching, he began running a zigzag course for the castle wall fifty yards away. Guards began shooting. Bullets hissed past the Frenchman's head as he clawed his way up the wall and dropped down on the far side.

Clad in a T-shirt and the running shorts he wore during exercise period, Lebrun dashed for nearby woods and crossed a stream twice, hoping in that way to throw tracking dogs off his scent. Being dressed in shorts, he did not want to be seen by civilians, so he hid in a cornfield for three days and nights.

Then Lebrun began walking southward during the hours of darkness. He slipped into the town of Zwickau and stole a bicycle. By then he was fifty miles from Colditz, and he looked like an average German on tour, a common sight, so he pedaled on the bicycle during the daytime. Along the way, he waved at German army field policemen, whose job was to capture escaped prisoners. He bought food snacks with thirty Reichsmarks that had been smuggled into Colditz by fellow officers.

Nearly exhausted, Lebrun eventually reached Switzerland—four hundred miles from Colditz—and freedom.

Back at the castle, meanwhile, the Germans had carefully inspected the belongings Lebrun had left in his small quarters. On a label tied to a suitcase containing the few things he treasured, a terse note stated: "Herr Kommandant. If I succeed, I would be grateful if you would arrange for my personal possessions to be sent to the following address [in Switzerland]."

Amazingly, the Kommandant complied with the request. A few weeks later, Lebrun received a box containing his suitcase, inside of which were the belongings from his stay at Colditz. Perhaps it was the first time in history that a prison-camp commander had forwarded the possessions of an inmate who had made a successful escape.[5]

A Pilot's On-the-Job Training

SEATED AT HIS DESK in Tokyo, Japanese Premier Hideki Tojo sifted through reports from commanders of the rampaging Imperial Army, which was performing one conquest after another in a breath-taking sweep through the South Pacific that paled Adolf Hitler's Blitzkriegs in Europe. The latest victory had taken place earlier that day when Tojo's armed forces overran the Indonesian island of Java. It was March 10, 1942—just more than three months after Pearl Harbor.

In the rush to flee Java, Allied forces had inadvertently left behind eighteen Americans, who were huddled near a deserted and bomb-scarred airfield. The only one in uniform was Master Sergeant Harry Hayes, a ground crew chief. Scattered about the tarmac were three badly damaged B-17 Flying Fortresses.

Hayes declared the obvious: "We've got to get out of here—fast!" With that, he left the field and returned in an hour with sixty Dutchmen, who went to work stripping two of the four-engine Flying Fortresses and transferring the usable parts to the third B-17, the least crippled of the bunch. In four days, the big plane had been repaired—in a fashion. It looked to Sergeant Hayes and the others like a puzzle assembled by a committee, but, hopefully, it would fly.

Next came the moment of truth. Hayes called the seventeen Americans together and said, "I want you to know that you are putting your lives in my hands. I have never flown a plane before." However, he was fully knowledgeable about the instruments and had often watched pilots go through procedures prior to takeoffs.

No one else spoke a word. Then the sergeant continued: "I can't promise you that she'll get off the ground, or that I can get her off. So if anyone thinks he or she will be safer here, he is quite free to remain."

No one wanted to stay behind. Grimly, all eighteen Americans climbed aboard the Flying Fortress. Sergeant Hayes sat behind the controls and, one by one, the engines coughed, groaned, and burst into life.

Unheard above the Fortress engines' roar, seven Japanese Zero fighter planes had zoomed down and they began to pour a fusillade of bullets toward and into the B-17. Its terrified passengers cringed on the plane's floor. Then, the enemy planes, apparently out of ammunition, streaked for home. Incredibly, none of the Americans had been hit and only minor damage had been done to the plane.

Hayes's hand moved the throttle and the great ship started rolling down the runway, gathering speed. He kept yet another haunting specter to himself: Even an unloaded B-17 required a three-thousand-foot runway to lift off; his plane was filled with people—and the runway was only twenty-eight hundred feet long.

Hayes pulled the controls back and the plane lifted, her engines wheezing and the entire craft wobbling. Seconds later, the Fortress was in the air and over the Sea of Timor. All hands breathed collective sighs of relief. However, if Zeros were to catch the lumbering, coughing plane in the sky, all on board would be doomed.

Without maps, without instruments, and with a man at the controls who had never before flown an airplane, the Flying Fortress headed for Australia, about twelve hundred miles southeast of the Java airfield. A seemingly endless amount of time later, someone shouted, "Land ahead!" The northern coast of Australia came into view.

There was wild cheering. But Hayes knew the toughest job of all remained—setting the B-17 down. He spotted a clearing near the beach and began lowering the plane's nose. Striking the ground with a crunching noise, the Fortress skidded for several hundred feet; then it ground to a halt.

Not a single person on board was hurt. They all scrambled from the plane. The man who previously had never flown a plane had made it. Looking back at the sky, Harry Hayes remarked casually, "You know, I'd like to be a *real* pilot someday!"[6]

Ghost Pilot of Kienow

AN HOUR BEFORE darkness settled over eastern China, a steady rain was pelting the tiny airfield near Kienow, where eight Warhawk P-40 fighter planes of the China Air Task Force were based. For a week, the Americans, whose outfit was formerly known as the famed Flying Tigers, had been grounded and they were itching for action. It was April 1942.

Suddenly, the silence was shattered in the operations cave as telephones began to jangle raucously. A Chinese officer attached to the outfit said that distant outposts had reported that a lone, unidentified airplane was coming toward Kienow, flying low. The Americans were puzzled. The Japanese never sent out single aircraft, nor did they fly so far inland in bad weather. However, it might be a trick to catch the P-40s on the ground and destroy some of them.

Taking no chances, Flight Leader John Hampshire ordered six P-40s to remain in place. He told one pilot to go with him and to stay on his wing; then the two men raced to their separate aircraft and lifted off. From the radio cave, Hampshire was given word that the unknown plane was by then only thirty miles to the east.

A Chinese soldier stands guard over P-40 Warhawks flown by American pilots.
(U.S. Air Force)

About ten miles from the Kienow airfield, the two pilots spotted the mystery plane zipping along at only two hundred feet above the ground. Hampshire and his wingman prepared to attack this unidentified aircraft that was coming from the direction of enemy territory. Both men fired bursts, then Hampshire shouted into his radio: "That's an American insignia—it's a P-40!"

The plane had been literally shot to pieces before Hampshire and his fellow pilot had even intercepted it. The fuselage was a sieve; the cockpit had been nearly blasted away. They could make out the pilot behind the shattered glass of the windshield. His face was a mask of blood. But the P-40 was holding a steady course.

Only later would the pilots at Kienow airport learn that the pilot in the mystery plane was "Corn" Sherill, who had been dubbed with that nickname because he was fond of corn liquor back in his home state of South Carolina. After the fall of the Philippines to powerful Japanese forces in the spring of 1942, Corn Sherill and eleven mechanics cannibalized a few decrepit airplanes on the southern Philippine island of Mindanao, which had not yet been occupied by the Japanese. They decided to load a plane with an auxiliary fuel tank and the few bombs they had and Corn would fly one last mission "where it will do the most good."

And a bold mission it would be: against a Japanese naval base on the island of Formosa, far west of Mindanao. After dropping his lethal cargo and strafing, Corn, if he nursed his dwindling fuel, might make it to the airfield of

Kienow, 250 miles farther to the west. At Kienow, the China Air Task Force had no way of knowing of Corn Sherill's last-gasp raid.

Five hours after lifting off from a grass field on Mindanao, Corn was over Formosa. Down below on an airfield, a large number of fighters and bombers, each bearing the rising sun insignia of the Japanese empire, were lined up in neat rows. The American zoomed in and fired burst after burst against the juicy targets. Soon, planes were burning and exploding. Corn's bomb load then made a direct hit on the Japanese offices. By now, ack-acks were firing madly and Corn's P-40 was riddled with shrapnel.

Within minutes, Japanese Zeros, buzzing around him like angry bees, poured scores of rounds into Corn's already battered plane. (The Japanese would later confirm the carnage that this lone pilot had wreaked.)

Then the P-40 zipped up into the clouds and set a course for Kienow. Badly wounded, Corn was flying by the seat of his pants—he had no working instruments. (The Chinese air-defense warning net would later reveal his course.) Somewhere between Formosa and Kienow, Corn Sherill died. In some manner, perhaps by bracing his stick between his knees, the P-40 continued on course—flown by a dead man, a phantom pilot.

Within minutes after Flight Leader John Hampshire and his wingman intercepted the mystery P-40 and began escorting it to Kienow, one plane on either side, Corn Sherill's mission suddenly ended. His plane plunged to the ground and exploded.[7]

Make-Do Bombardier Scores Big

KARL MAY was a young private in the U.S. Army Air Corps stationed in China, where his bomber group was based to launch attacks against Japanese forces. May, a gung ho type, was an armorer and was striving diligently to become a member of a combat crew. It was May 1942.

May kept pestering his commanding officer until the ground-crewman was allowed to go on two combat missions. Then, he made ready for the third one, a raid on the Japanese base at Hankow on the Yangtze River. When May climbed into his Mitchell B-25, he discovered that there were two defects: The interphones were out of commission and there were no racks for fragmentation bombs.

With typical GI ingenuity, these defects were remedied. May would squat by the photo hole with a stack of fragmentation bombs and when the turret gunner nudged him in the rear end, he was to drop the explosives, one by one, out the window. It was a primitive arrangement. But at this stage of the war, everything was primitive in China.

While winging up the Yangtze toward the target at Hankow, an observer from Washington grew chilly, saw that the photo hole was open and decided to ask the private hunched along side it to close the window. May had his back turned, so the observer went about getting his attention by means of a gentle nudge with his toe in May's buttocks.

Eager beaver that he was, Karl May began frantically dropping the fragmentation bombs out through the open window. After May had set loose three of the explosives, the B-25 commander managed to stop him. May was chagrined to find that the two-engine aircraft was still far from Hankow, that he had not been given the signal by the designated rear-end thumper, and that he had just wasted hundreds of dollars of Uncle Sam's money.

When the flight reached Hankow, Private May dropped scores of fragmentation bombs properly, but on the way back to the base his heart was heavy over his earlier, embarrassing goof. What's more, he knew that his buddies in the squadron would never let him live it down.

Twenty-four hours later, an intelligence report arrived from the Chinese army. Two bombs dropped on a Japanese barge on the Yangtze had scored direct hits, sinking the craft and drowning scores of Japanese soldiers. These were two of the three fragmentation bombs that Karl May had mistakenly pitched out far short of Hankow.[8]

A Journalist Beats the Odds

ABOVE THE ROAR of powerful engines and the rush of angry wind through the open doors of the C-47 transport plane came the shout: "Stand up!" Among those struggling to their feet while burdened with heavy equipment was the *Chicago Tribune's* John H. Thompson, who would be the first American correspondent to jump with paratroopers in a combat operation.

"Hook up!" Metal fasteners on parachute static lines were snapped to overhead anchor cables that ran the length of the cabin.

Silent and tense, the thirty-four-year-old Thompson, whose bushy beard had earned him the nickname "Beaver," and the GIs waited to bail out into the unknown over the enemy-held Youks les Bains airfield in eastern Algeria. Winging through the sky with Thompson's plane were twenty-one other C-47s carrying men of the U.S. 509th Parachute Infantry Battalion. It was November 18, 1942.

Beaver Thompson, an unflappable type, was the only novice in the entire parachute force. The others had jumped earlier to spearhead Operation Torch, the Allied invasion of North Africa and the first major U.S. offensive of the war. In addition, the 509ers had been training for jumping into combat for many months, and most had a few score training bailouts to their credit.

Three days earlier, on hearing that Thompson would be jumping with them onto Youks les Bains airfield, the GIs predicted personal disaster for the correspondent. Perhaps he would land on his head and be killed. At best, Beaver could hope to escape with only two broken legs, for a parachutist crunched into the hard, unyielding ground with the equivalent impact of a

Chicago Tribune *reporter John H. "Beaver" Thompson.*
(Courtesy Jim Phillips)

man leaping off the top of a railroad freight car that is traveling thirty-five miles per hour.

"Poor Beaver," the troopers moaned. "He *was* a nice guy!"

In preparation for the Youks les Bains jump, correspondent Thompson's "training" had taken place two days earlier. It consisted of twenty minutes of instruction by an officer who began with, "Now this crazy-looking thing is what's known as a parachute . . ."

Now in the C-47 armada approaching the airfield target, "Go!" rang out, and men barreled though the doors in piggyback fashion. Soon, the bright, blue sky was awash with white canopies interspersed with the red, yellow, and blue ones that were carrying equipment and ammunition bundles. A combination of the relatively low jumping height (about four hundred feet) and the rarefied air (a mile above sea level) resulted in jolting collisions with the ground.

Around the field, hardly a single trooper failed to receive at least cuts, scrapes, bruises, or a turned ankle. Many others writhed in agony. Captain John Berry broke his leg in several places, and the battalion surgeon, Captain Carlos Alden, cracked three bones in his foot. A few jumpers suffered compound leg fractures, and splintered, bloody bones protruded through their flesh.

Despite this deluge of injuries, the key airfield was captured in less than an hour. Beaver Thompson, the parachute novice whose demise had been roundly predicted, was about the only one who jumped at Youks les Bains to land unscathed.[9]

Nazis Aid U.S. A-Bomb Creation

IN 1937, five years after Adolf Hitler seized power, a team of German scientists, headed by world-renowned physicists Otto Hahn and Fritz Strassman, was reputed to be far ahead of anyone else in the world in theoretical research into nuclear energy. A year later, Hahn and Strassman split the atom when they bombarded uranium with neutrons. They called this process fission. Unknowingly, they were on a course toward developing the most powerful weapon that humankind has known.

Although Hitler and his generals were drawing up plans to go to war in 1939, the führer clearly did not grasp the significance of nuclear energy as an ultimate weapon. So he raised no objection to Hahn and Strassman publishing their findings in scientific publications distributed around the world.

In the United States, Albert Einstein, who had fled from Germany in 1933 when the Nazis confiscated his property and ousted him as director of the prestigious Kaiser Wilhelm Institut because he was Jewish, was haunted by the specter of an A-bomb in Adolf Hitler's hands. So on August 2, 1939, he wrote to President Franklin Roosevelt, explained the nature of the danger, and urged the government to become involved in what would become a race with Germany to develop an atomic bomb.

An alarmed Roosevelt set up the Uranium Project to study the possibility of unleashing atomic energy, and in early 1940, American scientists received their first funding for research.

Meanwhile, powerful German armies conquered their neighboring country, Poland, in only six weeks. After the invasion, Nazi bigwigs who had become aware of the military potential of nuclear energy, put a ban on the export of uranium, a key ingredient in the development of the A-bomb, and they tried to import the element from the Belgian Congo, the principal source of uranium.

In mid-1940, after Hitler's legions invaded and rapidly overran Norway, German leaders were even more enthused about the prospect for creating an ultimate weapon, although atomic research was still in its infancy. Norway's Hydro-Electric Company's large electrolysis plant at Vemork, which the Nazis took over, produced Europe's only supply of deuterium oxide, known as heavy water, a prime ingredient for the creation of an atomic bomb.

Most of the German nuclear research was conducted at the Kaiser Wilhelm Institut in Berlin and in a facility in Leipzig, where the first German atomic reactor was built in early 1942. Although the reactor was primitive and designed to conduct experiments that would result in the development of a workable apparatus in which nuclear fission could take place, Adolf Hitler was demanding "The Bomb"—*immediately*.

In June 1942, the German nuclear program received a major setback: The Leipzig uranium reactor exploded. However, Hitler apparently felt certain that his scientists were on the brink of a revolutionary breakthrough. When Field Marshal Erwin Rommel flew from North Africa to Berlin later that year to demand more supplies, fuel, weapons, and troops to spare his famed Afrika Korps from being destroyed by British and American armies, Hitler made a startling remark. He alluded to a "new secret weapon" which had such explosive power that the blast would "throw a man off his horse at a distance of two miles." Rommel was puzzled, but did not pursue the topic, perhaps believing that the führer was on one of his periodic flights of fancy.

Meanwhile, Niels Bohr, a prominent Danish physicist who was a sort of confessor to the international scientific community, received a visitor from Germany. Professor Werner Heisenberg, a principal figure in the German program to develop the atomic bomb, had come to ask his friend Bohr a perplexing question. Was it morally correct for a physicist to engage in the development of an ultimate weapon, even in wartime?

Bohr replied with a question: Did Heisenberg mean that the Germans believed such a weapon was feasible? Sadly, the German said that such was the case. The conversation left Bohr deeply shocked. He warned the underground secret intelligence service in German-occupied Denmark and said he was convinced that the Nazis were on the threshold of developing an atomic bomb. The underground contacted MI-6, the British secret service agency in London, with the frightening news.

Prime Minister Winston Churchill and his key advisers were greatly alarmed over the disclosure. MI-6 sought out Professor Lief Tronstad, a chemist who had helped build the heavy water plant at Vemork. Tronstad had escaped from Norway and had become the Norwegian government-in-exile's secret service chief in London.

Under Tronstad was an agent named Einar Skinnerland, a native of the Vemork region. On March 29, 1942, Skinnerland parachuted onto the rugged, desolate plateau in southern Norway where the plant was located. He soon made contact with Jomar Brun, the facility's chief engineer, who reported that the Germans were increasing the plant's production of heavy water.

In the United States, meanwhile, Enrico Fermi, a thirty-nine-year-old physicist who had fled from Benito Mussolini's fascist Italy in 1938, and other scientists had been experimenting with nuclear fission at the University of Chicago. On December 2, 1942, Fermi and his team scored an unexpectedly early success in producing the first controlled atomic chain reaction. It had

Albert Einstein. (Princeton University)   *Enrico Fermi. (Chicago University)*

taken place in an improvised laboratory under the spectator stands at Stagg Field, an abandoned football stadium at the University of Chicago.

This astonishing achievement led to the construction of huge plants for the production of plutonium and uranium—and to the birth of the supersecret Manhattan Project, code name for the development of the A-bomb.

Never had security been so tight as it was around the Manhattan Project. Stagg Field was known as the Chicago Metallurgical Laboratory; the gaseous diffusion plant at Oak Ridge, Tennessee, was K-25; a facility at Los Alamos, New Mexico, was Site X; and the scientist in charge of the atom-splitting operation at Stagg Field had the title Coordinator of Rapid Rupture.

Despite the tight security, American leaders were jolted early in 1943, when the FBI uncovered a chilling message sent from Abwehr headquarters in Hamburg to a contact in the United States:

THERE IS REASON TO BELIEVE THAT THE SCIENTIFIC WORKS FOR THE UTILIZATION OF ATOMIC ENERGY ARE BEING DRIVEN FORWARD INTO A CERTAIN DIRECTION IN THE UNITED STATES. CONTINUOUS INFORMATION ABOUT THE TESTS MADE ON THIS SUBJECT ARE REQUIRED.

In the Third Reich, Colonel Josef "Bippo" Schmidt, chief of Luftwaffe intelligence, wrote the high command: "Work in the field of nuclear physics is already so far advanced [in the United States] that, if the war is prolonged, it could become of considerable significance."

In early February 1944, after the U.S. Eighth Air Force heavily bombed the plant producing heavy water at Vemork, Norway, Reichmarschall Hermann Goering, who was responsible for Hitler's atomic program, ordered the facility and its heavy water to be evacuated to Germany.

Within days, MI-6 agents in Norway learned about Goering's plan. Six hundred and thirteen kilograms of heavy water and fourteen tons of fluid in thirty-nine large drums were to be put aboard a ferry train at Rjukan, near Vemork. The train would travel a short distance to Lake Tinnsjo, where it would edge onto the railroad tracks on the ferry *Hydro*, which would cross the body of water. On the far side, the train would roll off the ferry onto land rails, then continue the trek to Germany.

Two days before the ferry train from Rjukan was to arrive, Knut Haukelid, a Norwegian and an MI-6 agent, boarded the *Hydro* for a routine crossing of Lake Tinnsjo. He knew that the lake was particularly deep—thirteen hundred feet near the middle—and concluded that if the ferry was to be sunk there, the cargo could never be retrieved.

The next night, February 19, Haukelid and two of his men snuck aboard the docked *Hydro*, which, incredibly, had been left unguarded. The agents set time bombs to explode forty-five minutes after the vessel shoved off with the train aboard.

At ten o'clock in the morning, the ferry train, with its precious cargo of heavy water aboard, headed for the far shore of Lake Tinnsjo. Forty-five minutes later, an enormous roar echoed for miles—and Adolf Hitler's hope for an atom bomb that would bring him rapid world domination plunged to the bottom of the lake.

In August 1945, the United States dropped an atomic bomb on Hiroshima, Japan, bringing an end to the butchery in the Pacific and preventing perhaps 1 million American casualties and some 5 million Japanese casualties that would have occurred if U.S. forces had had to invade and conquer Japan.

Unwittingly, Adolf Hitler and Nazi Germany had played a major role in the eventual development of the ultimate weapon by the United States. Had Albert Einstein not been forced to flee Germany, he would not have been in the United States to warn President Roosevelt about the danger of Germany's nuclear research. Otherwise, Uncle Sam might have slept on for months—or years—perhaps until Hitler had A-bombs in his arsenal.

Had the führer ordered the nuclear studies of Otto Hahn and Fritz Strassman kept secret back in 1938, Enrico Fermi, who had been run out of Italy by Hitler's crony, Benito Mussolini, might not have created the first controlled atomic chain reaction in 1942.

And had Fermi not made his scientific breakthrough, President Roosevelt may not have ordered the creation of the Manhattan Project.[10]

Piggyback Ride on a U-Boat

LIEUTENANT CHARLES H. HUTCHINS, commander of the destroyer USS *Borie*, stood on the ship's bridge and gave the order to switch on the searchlight. Moments later, the brilliant beam split the blackness of the Atlantic Ocean and

USS Borie *found itself on top of a surfaced German submarine such as this one.* *(U.S. Navy)*

zeroed in on a dull gray target—a surfaced German U-boat. A duel to the death began. It was mid-June 1942.

The searchlight also gave the Germans a nice target at which to shoot. Crewmen scrambled out of the submarine's conning tower and manned the deck machine guns. Streams of tracer bullets pinged off the *Borie*. In turn, the destroyer's gunners poured fire into the U-boat, sweeping the German sailors off the deck.

Then the submarine, still on the surface, began to flee, and the *Borie* gave chase. When the destroyer finally caught up with the submarine, Lieutenant Hutchins called out over the intercom: "All stations stand by for ram!"

Men on the *Borie* braced for the expected jolting crunch—but there was no crunch. Instead, just as the destroyer was about to crash into the submarine, a huge wave lifted the *Borie's* bow high out of the water and put it down gently on the deck of the U-boat, just forward of the conning tower.

Thus the two vessels, both scarcely damaged, came to rest, bow over bow, in an "X" configuration. It was one of the weirdest naval episodes of the war— an American destroyer riding piggyback on a surfaced enemy submarine.

Skipper Hutchins was momentarily in a quandary. Nothing he had learned at the U.S. Naval Academy had prepared him for such a unique situation. Depth charges could not be lowered onto the U-boat, for they would blow up the *Borie* as well. *Borie's* machine guns could not be brought to bear, because the German sailors were inside the submarine.

About fifteen minutes after the vessels had became entangled, they worked themselves free of one another. Battling for its life, the U-boat scampered away, bobbing and weaving like a championship boxer. The *Borie* followed in hot pursuit, firing her four-inch guns at the submarine's conning tower and scoring several hits.

After an hour and ten minutes, the German craft began taking on water, and soon afterward it sank to the bottom of the Atlantic with the doomed crew still inside.[11]

A Spy for Both Sides

JUST BEFORE TWO O'CLOCK on the morning of December 10, 1942, a German bomber winged over fields glistening with frost in Hertfordshire. Encumbered by an Afu radio set, Nazi agent Fritz parachuted onto English soil near Ely. His mission would be one of the most daring of the war: to blow up the sprawling de Havilland aircraft works at Hatfield, a short distance north of London.

During the next few days, Fritz radioed his Abwehr controller in Paris and said that he had gone to Hatfield several times and had crept around at night to case the target. The spy also reported that he had located a quarry near Hatfield, and that its owner was willing to sell him all the explosives needed.

On January 27, 1943, Fritz radioed Captain Stephan von Grunen, chief of the Abwehr station in Paris: "Will attempt sabotage this evening at six o'clock."

Just before dawn, von Grunen received another signal from Fritz: "Mission accomplished. Powerhouse blown up."

Von Grunen, an experienced secret service officer, was skeptical. How could one man create such enormous damage to what must have been a closely guarded airplane plant? He arranged for two reconnaissance planes to confirm Fritz's triumphant report. Von Grunen was elated by the aerial photographs. They revealed that the damage was even more extensive than Fritz had indicated.

Von Grunen recommended Fritz for a German decoration for valor. But it seemed that Fritz might not get back to Paris to be honored. His daily radio contacts indicated that British counterintelligence agents were hot on his trail. On February 16, he signaled: "Am closing transmission. Too dangerous to work."

What Von Grunen did not know was that the British, through Ultra, a top-secret device that intercepted and decoded German wireless messages, had been keeping track of the movement of German agents long before they arrived in England. No sooner had Fritz shucked his parachute on his de Havilland mission than he was pounced on by waiting British security agents. He was given a choice: be hanged as a German spy or become a double agent for the British XX-Committee (Double-Cross Committee), whose function was to "turn" German spies and employ them to the panel's own designs. The phony messages that Fritz had been sending to Captain von Grunen in Paris after landing in England had been created for him by the XX-Committee.

Fritz's real name was Eddie Chapman. Before the war, he had made a living in England as a skilled safe-blower. Later, he joined the crack Coldstream Guards, but deserted in 1939.

In early 1940, Scotland Yard had been hot on Chapman's heels for a variety of crimes, so he fled to the Channel Islands off the coast of France. There he was thrown in jail for another criminal offense and was released by the Germans after they occupied the islands a few months later. In gratitude—or so Chapman said—he had volunteered to spy for the Germans, and his offer had been accepted by the Abwehr.

After extensive training at the Abwehr's espionage school in a chateau near Nantes, France, Chapman (code-named Fritz) was assigned the task of sabotaging the de Havilland works.

After Chapman's capture, the British knew that the Abwehr would try to verify his claimed success in blowing up the de Havilland powerhouse. So a violent explosion was rigged outside the aircraft plant, one that could be heard for miles around—by the ears of any lurking German agent. Then Major Jasper Maskelyne, who in civilian life was an accomplished magician and illusionist, and his crew created fake bomb damage at the de Havilland plant for the benefit of German aerial photographers. The entire roof of the powerhouse was covered with a relief canvas and painted on it, in color, was the damage that was supposed to have occurred.

Meanwhile, the magician's workshop hurriedly built papier-mâché dummies that resembled pieces of the "sabotaged" generator. Those pieces, along with dummy chunks of brick, cracked cement blocks, splintered furniture, and other props, were scattered about the premises. Royal Air Force photos of the scene stumped British interpreters, who were not told whether the damage was real or fake.

To add to the realism, the British press headlined stories about the "destruction" of much of the de Havilland plant, and, at the urging of the XX-Committee, blasted the ineptitude of the home security forces. British newspapers were flown routinely to neutral Lisbon, Portugal, almost every day, and eventually the publications reached the Abwehr in Paris and Berlin.

Eddie Chapman assured XX-Committee agents that his loyalty always had been with Great Britain, and that he had agreed to the de Havilland mission as a means to get back to England. Eagerly, he accepted an offer to become a double agent and to work for the British. He was to radio back reports on German army movements in France. Arrangements were made for Chapman (aptly code-named Zigzag by the British) to "escape" from England. In January 1943, he sailed for Lisbon aboard the steamer *City of Lancaster*, posing as a steward.

Ten days later, Chapman arrived at Abwehr headquarters in Paris, where he was hailed as a hero. That night at a champagne celebration for him at fashionable Maxim's, Fritz regaled admiring German officers with tales of outwitting the British secret service. Later, he collected the fifteen thousand pounds sterling (about seventy-five thousand U.S. dollars) he had been promised by the Abwehr to sabotage the de Havilland plant.

More than a year later, in late June 1944, after Allied troops were ashore in strength in Normandy, Chapman agreed to another espionage assignment for the Abwehr, which, apparently, had decided that his previous interception by British security agents had been a fluke. Out of the night sky, Chapman parachuted near Cambridge, England. He was loaded down with two radios, cameras, six thousand pounds sterling—and a contract with the Abwehr for one hundred thousand pounds sterling (about five hundred thousand U.S. dollars) to report where the German buzz bombs were falling.

Again a British reception committee was waiting to greet Fritz (or Zigzag). Again he was given two choices. He chose to become a *double* double agent for the British and was put to work radioing false information to the Abwehr. However, when security agents tailing him heard Zigzag loudly telling his story in a crowded pub, his case was "terminated" and he was locked up without fanfare for the remainder of the war.

Eddie Chapman did not surface again until several months after Victory in Europe Day. At that time, reports reached London that a man with a high-pitched voice, stylishly dressed and displaying two gold teeth, was making the rounds of high society in Belgrade, Yugoslavia. He had a yacht, a Rolls-Royce, and a large health farm.

"This has to be Eddie Chapman," declared J. C. Masterman, the former wartime chief of the XX-Committee.

When a British reporter caught up with Chapman in Belgrade, the spy was asked: "Tell me, Eddie, just whose side were you *really* on?"

Chapman/Zigzag/Fritz grinned and responded with a wink.[12]

A Lifesaving Candy Bar

BEFORE THE INVASION of Italy at Salerno in September 1943, Allied hopes were high. For the GIs, it looked like a victory march northward up the long, narrow, green country full of beautiful women and oceans of wine. The Italian government had capitulated a day earlier, so it appeared that everything was coming up roses for the invaders.

But within hours, first-rate Wehrmacht formations were rushed to the Salerno landing locale, and in the weeks that followed, one of the most ferocious slugfests of the war erupted in the rugged Apennine Mountains. It would become known as The Forgotten War.

Just below one mountain peak, the Germans had blasted a cave into solid rock and were using it as a perfect OP (observation post) for artillery officers to bring down accurate, murderous fire on GIs in the valley below. That cave had to be taken out—and a three-man patrol of U.S. combat engineers was assigned the seemingly suicidal task.

Staff Sergeant Charles Corella of Ajo, Arizona, and two comrades, concluded that it would take five hundred pounds of TNT exploded above the upper ledge of the German OP to collapse the excavation and render it unusable. This required the tiny patrol to make eleven trips, creeping and crawling, up the rocky slope, with their faces on the ground as if they were kids again, rolling peanuts across a room.

All the while, the three GIs sweated out the arrival of German artillery or mortar shells. It seemed as though the enemy had to spot them as they slithered time and again above and onto the upper ledge. In the OP, the enemy artillery observers remained blissfully unaware that a project intended to smother them under tons of rock and dirt was in the making.

Finally, the five hundred pounds of explosives were in place. Three fuses were attached and the three Americans scrambled to a rocky crevice some fifty yards away. Then they turned the handle of the electric fuses and a mighty roar shook the mountain. A fog of smoke and dust concealed what had once been the opening of the OP excavation.

The GI engineers began racing down the mountainside toward their positions and, it seemed to the trio, that every machine gun, mortar, rifle, and artillery piece in the Wehrmacht was focused on them. Miraculously, none of the three men received a scratch. However, Sergeant Charles Corella discovered that the Gods of War had smiled on him. A jagged piece of shrapnel had pierced his pocket, deflected off a spoon, and lodged in a candy bar in another pocket.

Corella held up the German fragment and said with a straight face: "Those dirty Kraut bastards! They ruined my candy bar!"

Moments later, in private, he was on his knees thanking God for the miracle that had spared him.[13]

A Bolt Out of the Blue

IN MID-SEPTEMBER 1943, German soldiers in Italy were in an especially foul mood. The war had been going badly on all fronts, and now their longtime allies, the Italians, had just signed an armistice with the Anglo-Americans. To the Germans, all Italians were now traitors.

So mountainous was the region of Italy along the German front that the artillery of both sides had as visible targets only the tiny villages that were tucked in the slopes. The village buildings with their thick masonry walls served as strongholds for each side. Into one of these villages, a tiny place of twenty houses, wandered a group of German soldiers. The Nazis broke into the houses, filled themselves with vino, and used wine barrels for target practice, laughing uproariously when the liquid gushed onto the ground. The native people were petrified.

Eventually, American artillery shells began exploding in the vicinity and, one or two at a time, the Germans began scampering out of the village. All except for one particularly drunk German, who collared all the Italian civilians he could find and lined them up against a high wall. Snarling and cursing, he was about to squeeze the trigger of his Schmeisser and mow down the quaking hostages.

Just then, like a bolt out of the blue, an American shell exploded on the roof of a building behind him. Slate and other rubble cascaded down from the roof, struck the German and killed him instantly. Already on their knees, the intended Italian victims looked skyward and thanked God for delivering such a timely blow.[14]

Lady Luck Saves a Sailor

ON JANUARY 25, 1944, the intelligence officer at the advanced U.S. PT-boat base at remote and desolate Papua, New Guinea, informed Squadron 8 that a Japanese submarine had been spotted just south of Gasmata, New Britain. The submarine was in shallow waters and it looked ripe for a kill. Two PTs were assigned to stalk and sink the enemy underwater vessel.

One craft, PT 110, had just arrived at the base before it was assigned the mission. Twenty-three-year-old Yeoman 1st Class Joseph M. Kline, Jr., knew the skipper, who invited him to accompany the crew on the patrol. Kline eagerly accepted. He gathered his gear and headed for the dock to board the PT 110.

Nearby several of his comrades were swimming and one called out, "Hey, Joe, where do you think you're going?"

"Just where in the hell does it look like I'm going?"

"Who took your watch (being on duty in the radio shack on the base)?"

"What watch? Do I have watch tonight?"

"You sure as hell do!"

Yeoman Kline told the PT 110 skipper that he would check out the duty roster and if he were on watch, he would have no problem in swapping the duty with a friend. Rushing to the radio shack, he glanced at the watch bill and saw that he was to be on duty between midnight and 4:00 A.M.

Kline dashed to his quarters and asked one comrade after the other if he would take the yeoman's watch. All had one excuse or another and turned him down. Kline was infuriated.

Returning to the pier, he informed the PT 110 skipper that he had to stand the midwatch, and he wished the crew well in their first mission. Then he stood by and watched the PT boat, a speedy, eighty-foot craft with a powerful sting in her tail, head out into the open waters of the Solomon Sea for the one-hundred-mile trek to Gasmata and the encounter with the Japanese submarine.

In the communications shack, around 3:00 A.M., Joe Kline heard shouts of "May Day! May Day!" (the traditional distress signal) over his radio. PT 110 was in big trouble. PT 114, the companion boat on the patrol, reported that there had been an explosion and PT 110 had been "blown clear out of the

PT-boat squadron's radio shack in the South Pacific. (Courtesy Alyce Mary Guthrie)

water and destroyed." A frantic search for survivors was launched. None were found.

After going off duty, Joe Kline thanked all of his friends for not taking his watch. Through a curious roll of the dice by Dame Fate, the squadron yeoman had escaped death.[15]

A German Pilot
Joins His Victims

It was midafternoon on February 7, 1944, and twenty-year-old Corporal Charles H. Doyle, a member of the U.S. 509th Parachute Infantry Battalion, was reclining on his cot as a patient at the tented 95th Evacuation Hospital on the Anzio beachhead in Italy. Doyle had mixed feelings about his lot. In the tent, he was warm and dry, was fed hot food, and had a reasonably comfortable place to sleep. But, like other combat men who were patients in the medical facility along the shoreline, Doyle had a creeping suspicion that it might be "safer" in frontline foxholes—at least during periods of static warfare. For Anzio beachhead had no rear echelon. Anybody could meet sudden death anywhere at any time—a quartermaster clerk, a female nurse, or an upfront GI or British Tommy.

As Charlie Doyle lay on his cot, he could hear shells screaming to earth around the hospital, blasts that rocked the terrain. And there were regular visits from the Luftwaffe. While the hospital tents were clearly marked with huge red crosses on fields of white, the beachhead was so jammed with troops, supply dumps, command posts, and installations that errant German artillery shells and bombs from the air struck the hospital on occasion.

Now, Doyle's sensitive ears perked up as he heard a familiar roar in the sky. He could not see the sky from under the canvas, but a Luftwaffe fighter and a British Spitfire were engaged in a dogfight over Anzio. To gain altitude, the German pilot dropped his bombs, and they landed directly on the surgery area of the 95th Evacuation Hospital. Twenty-three persons were killed, including three female nurses, a female member of the Red Cross, and a number of Medical Corpsmen and patients. Sixty-eight were wounded, including Colonel George Sauer, who commanded the facility.

Moments later, the German plane was riddled by Spitfire bullets, and the wounded pilot parachuted onto the beachhead, where GIs took him prisoner. In a curious twist of fate, he was taken for treatment to the same hospital that his bombs had accidentally struck—the 95th Evac. Although the surgical facilities were no longer as good as they had been, the American doctors and nurses treated the Luftwaffe pilot with the same professional skill given to the GI patients, and he survived.[16]

Bombing Patriots Out of Prison

HUGO BLEICHER was one of the most clever and effective German counterintelligence agents in France. His job was to root out Allied spies. In early 1944, while powerful American and British armies were in England preparing for a cross-channel assault against Fortress Europe, Adolf Hitler became worried about the rising tempo of espionage and disorder in France, a likely target for der Grossinvasion.

Consequently, the führer ordered his secret service agencies to launch Operation Donar, named after the god of thunder, to destroy all the forces of resistance, sabotage, and espionage in France. Hugo Bleicher was in the forefront of this massive effort. French patriot after French patriot—men and women—were collared in the dragnet. Most were tortured to extract information, then were executed by firing squads.

In London, a representative of the French government-in-exile approached British Air Vice Marshal H. E. P. Wigglesworth with an extraordinary request. Would the Royal Air Force send low-flying bombers to blast a prison at Amiens, a city of seventy-five thousand people eighty miles north of Paris. The emissary explained that the German agent, Hugo Bleicher, and his men had rounded up some fifty members of the French resistance—many of them important leaders of underground networks—and they were going to be executed soon.

After the Frenchman had departed, Wigglesworth barked to an aide, "Who the hell do they think they are? Have you ever heard of anyone making holes in walls with bombs to let people escape?"

"How do you know it can't be done?" queried Solly Zuckerman, a British intellectual who had long been involved in picking out bombing targets for the Royal Air Force.

Wiggles, as he was known to friends, looked at the other in amazement. "Do you mean it can really be done?"

When Zuckerman replied that he did think so, the air marshal called for an assistant to bring in the diagrams that the Frenchman had left. They were laid out on a table and thoroughly studied. The thickness of the stone walls as shown on the plans was recorded.

"Now I'm sure it can be done," Zuckerman declared. "Provided that really skilled pilots are willing to risk their lives, and that the overall gain to the underground operations in France is worth the danger."

On February 18, 1944, RAF Squadron Leader Charles Pickard was leading nineteen Mosquito fighter-bombers as they approached the Amiens prison at virtually treetop level. Moments later, the speedy aircraft, one after the other, skidded their bombs into the sturdy prison, blasting wide holes. The French patriots waiting for execution lost no time: Nearly all of them bolted through the smoking openings and escaped.

The bold attack had gone according to plan—except that Squadron Leader Pickard was killed.

The operation made history, however. For the first time, a jail break had been implemented by airplanes.[17]

Sleeping His Way into Battle

ENGLAND WAS GRIPPED by "invasion fever." Clearly, the long-anticipated Allied assault across the English Channel was only days—perhaps hours—in the offing. It was June 5, 1944.

All that day, Private Charles Schmelze of Pittsburgh, Pennsylvania, had been servicing a large glider at an airfield in the midlands of England. The motorless craft was designed to carry soldiers of the U.S. 101st Airborne Division into battle.

Britain was on double daylight time, so when Schmelze, thoroughly pooped, climbed into the glider to rest after supper, dusk had not yet arrived. After picking out a comfortable spot, Schmelze promptly fell asleep.

A few hours later, the glider, towed by a plane piloted by Lieutenant E. G. Borgmeyer of St. Louis, Missouri, crash-landed in Normandy amid heavy fighting. Presumably, the glidermen who rode with Schmelze thought that the service technician was authorized to be aboard. Private Schmelze had slept his way into the thick of the greatest military operation in history.[18]

Freakish Farewell to Arms

CLEVELAND-BORN ROGER GREENE, an Associated Press correspondent, crossed the English Channel in an LCIS (landing craft, infantry small), knowing that he would be the first reporter to hit the beaches on D-Day in Normandy. With him were one hundred green-bereted commandos. It was June 6, 1944.

When the landing craft crunched onto the ocean bottom just offshore, Greene and the others started swarming down the narrow spider-walk into the surf. German batteries had the range: Shells were splashing all along the waterfront and on both sides of the craft.

As the last fighting man left the craft, Greene, burdened by a sixty-five-pound rucksack, dashed across the open deck and started scrambling down the spider-walk. Halfway down, a sudden lurch of the LCIS sent the reporter pitching headlong into the sea . . . and saved his life. Seconds later, when he came sputtering to the surface, he saw that the spider-walk was but twisted wreckage, having been hit by a shell burst.

Edging past bodies floating face down, Greene waded fifty yards to shore and huddled in sardine formation with ten British Tommies behind a sandbank, while the Germans played a tattoo of artillery and mortar explosions around them. Lying prone when a shell hit in their midst, the reporter felt the blast. Nine out of ten of the British were killed or wounded. Greene escaped without a scratch.

In the following months, Roger Greene had one narrow escape after another. Each one threatened to short-circuit the goal that consumed him in the war: to be present when the Nazi armed forces surrendered.

One afternoon, Greene drove up to an especially hot spot that was under direct visual observation by German artillery spotters, and he raced through a ghostly shambles called "Hell's Corner" without hearing as much as a rifle shot or a mortar-round explosion. On his way back to the press camp, and safely out of the danger zone, Greene pulled into a casualty clearing station just as German shells plastered the site, wounding numerous men for the second time and killing others. The AP reporter was unscathed and still hoped to witness the Wehrmacht "throwing in the towel."

Another night, Roger Greene and his Cockney driver went forward to watch a tank-and-infantry team jump off in an attack. Suddenly, flares illuminated the dark sky and bombs dropped by circling Luftwaffe planes shook the ground violently. Many Tommies were killed and wounded. Greene's lucky star was still shining brightly.

AP correspondent Roger O. Greene.
(Yank)

On yet another occasion, the Princeton University graduate was flying in a tiny artillery observation plane, watching a fascinating duel between German shore batteries along the Belgian coast and Allied warships offshore. While Greene was cruising over one large vessel, it received a direct hit and an enormous thunderlike clap shook the midget airplane, spun it around, and twisted and hurled it hundreds of feet through the air. The ammunition ship below had been blown to bits. Miraculously, Greene's pilot righted the dizzily spinning light aircraft. Upon landing, Greene was convinced that the gods of war were on his side and that he was destined to see the Third Reich capitulate.

Roger Greene had been in the thick of the action from Normandy, all the way across France into Belgium and Holland, and to the Rhine in Germany. He wanted badly to go on to Berlin. But in March 1945, before witnessing the final curtain fall on the mighty drama in Europe, the AP correspondent left for London and a brief rest.

Within hours after his arrival in the British capital, Greene fell on a blacked-out staircase, suffering a head injury and breaking several ribs. It was his farewell to arms. In a hospital, he would only read about the Nazi surrender to the Allies in an old brick schoolhouse in Rheims, France, five weeks later.[19]

Belated Surrender on Guam

LIEUTENANT GENERAL TAKESHI TAKESHINA, commander of the eighteen-thousand-man Japanese garrison defending the Pacific island of Guam, pledged to fight to the last man after United States Marines stormed ashore there on July

21, 1944. Takeshina himself was killed by machine-gun fire a week after the invasion. When the ferocious fighting was officially concluded on August 11, 17,300 Japanese had been killed and only 485 prisoners had been taken. In addition, some armed Japanese survivors fled to the hills and holed up in caves.

Eventually, one of those who had lived an animal-like existence in remote regions of the twenty-eight-mile-long island, Sergeant Soichi Yokoi, emerged from hiding and gave himself up to a group of Guam fishermen — in late January 1972, twenty-eight years and a generation after Americans had landed on Guam.

Why had Sergeant Yokoi held out for so long, ignoring leaflets announcing his nation's surrender in September 1945? "We Japanese soldiers were told that death is preferred to the disgrace of getting captured alive," Yokoi explained.

More than two years after Yokoi had rejoined the civilized world, Lieutenant Hiroo Onoda of the Japanese Imperial Army decided that he had had enough. On March 10, 1974, Onoda, believing that the war was still raging in the Pacific, emerged from the jungles of the Philippines. Why had he waited three decades to take this action? "I had never received an order to surrender," the lieutenant declared.[20]

Fluke Wound in an Aid Station

TOMOYUKI YAMASHITA, one of Japan's most able generals and a folk hero on the home front, was defending the Philippines, which had been seized from a woefully unprepared and ill-equipped American and Filipino force in early 1942. Six feet, two inches tall and husky, his bullet-shaped head completely shaved, Yamashita had concluded that General Douglas MacArthur's powerful invasion army, sailing toward the Philippines, would strike at Luzon, the largest island in the chain. On Luzon were virtually all of the worthwhile military objectives in the islands. Typically, MacArthur struck where least expected. On October 20, 1944, his assault troops hit the beaches of eastern Leyte, a large, primitive island three hundred miles southeast of Luzon.

Spearheading MacArthur's westward drive to split Leyte in two was Major General Joseph Swing's U.S. 11th Airborne Division, which landed from the sea. Swing, in turn, handed Colonel Orin "Hardrock" Haugen's 511th Parachute Infantry Regiment the toughest nut to crack: hacking through the towering, jungle-infested Mahong Mountains for some forty miles to reach the west coast of Leyte.

Haugen's huffing and wheezing troopers, burdened by heavy packs and equipment, struggled over narrow, slippery trails to the tiny village of Manarawat, high in the Mahong Mountains. Manarawat sat on a plateau surrounded on three sides by sheer cliffs, and it was accessible only by means of a steep slope from the rear. A small clearing was hacked out of the jungle and word was radioed to 11th Airborne Division headquarters far in the rear to send L-5s (light observation planes) to drop badly needed food.

Meanwhile, Japanese mortars pounded the plateau. A corporal was hit in the buttocks by numerous shell fragments and was carried to a makeshift open-air aid station in Manarawat. A battalion surgeon administered an anesthetic and began stitching up the gash while the trooper lay with his arms outstretched.

Minutes later, three L-5s swooped in and dropped food. One parachute container, bearing a large box of chocolate, landed on the unconscious corporal's outstretched right arm, breaking it neatly near the elbow. Without missing a beat, the surgeon finished sewing up the man's buttocks wound and then splinted his arm.

Later, when the corporal awoke in a haze, the surgeon was gone. Two stretcher bearers came in and hauled the paratrooper away, all the while thinking that the man had "gone psycho." He kept demanding to know: "Why am I wearing an arm brace for a piece of iron in my ass?"[21]

A German Courier Gets Lost

ON THE MORNING of January 3, 1945, Field Marshal Hasso von Manteuffel, leader of the German Fifth Panzer Army, held no illusions: Adolf Hitler's gamble in the Ardennes Forest of Belgium had collapsed eighteen days after it had been launched with high hopes. But the führer, in his anger over the stubborn stand of the U.S. 101st "Screaming Eagles" Airborne Division at Bastogne, now ordered the diminutive Baron von Manteuffel to capture the town, no matter what the cost in blood of German boys.

Bastogne's most serious crisis loomed. The Wehrmacht was getting around to doing what it had not done during the two weeks the Screaming Eagles had been surrounded—launching simultaneous assaults in strength at separate points around the town's perimeter.

At dawn, four German divisions struck Bastogne from the north, and all day Major General Maxwell Taylor's fighting men beat off vicious attacks. That night, with the 101st Airborne Division's fate still in doubt, Corporal William Davis of the 502nd Parachute Infantry Regiment was hunkered down in a slit trench at a machine-gun outpost when a dark figure tapped him on the shoulder from behind.

"Wo ist die Kompanie Hauptquartier?" (Where is the company headquarters?) the newcomer asked, his teeth chattering from the subzero cold.

Davis quickly bagged the enemy soldier and escorted him to the 101st Airborne command post. The German proved to be an intelligence gold mine. A member of the 9th SS Panzer Division, he had been sent to deliver attack orders to a company command post, but had gotten lost in the darkness and thick forest.

The SS man "volunteered" the information that an all-out assault against Bastogne would hit at 4:00 A.M. One hour before that time, several American artillery barrages plastered a woods north of Longchamps, where the German force was assembling, and the attack from that direction never came.

Had it not been for the astounding coincidence of the lost enemy courier asking an American paratrooper for directions, the powerful German attack force might well have smashed on in to Bastogne.[22]

An Old German in a Garden

ALONG A FRONT of more than four hundred miles, powerful Allied armies were pushing toward the broad and majestic Rhine River, for centuries the barrier to invasion of Germany from the west. So in early March 1945, Adolf Hitler issued strict orders that the scores of bridges crossing the Rhine were to be blown on the approach of American, British, or French spearheads.

General Dwight Eisenhower, Allied supreme commander, and his planners had held out no hope that a Rhine bridge would be found intact. But on March 6, Brigadier General William M. Hoge, leader of Combat Command B of the U.S. 9th Armored Division, stood on a cliff overlooking the Rhine near the town of Remagen, and couldn't believe his eyes. Stretched out intact below him was the Ludendorff Bridge.

Bill Hoge had no way of knowing that the one-thousand-foot span would have been blown, as scores of others had been along the Rhine, had not faulty dynamite charges failed to ignite. All he knew was that the Ludendorff Bridge, if quickly captured, could save countless American lives and hasten the end of the war in Europe.

A radio call was put in to Lieutenant John Grimball of Columbia, South Carolina, leader of a platoon of Pershing tanks that were a short distance from the Rhine.

"Grimball, get the hell to the bridge!" was the stern—and excited—order.

Lieutenant Grimball swiftly cranked up his tank platoon and raced toward the bridge. Along Grimball's route, an old German was casually working in his garden on the outskirts of Remagen. One of the American soldiers suspected that he might be a member of the Volksturm (people's army), a motley force of elderly men that Adolf Hitler had mobilized to defend the borders of Germany. Perhaps he had been ordered to stay behind and use his age as protection.

In any event, the trigger-happy GI squeezed off three quick rifle shots at the man in the garden as the armored column rolled past, hell-bent for the Ludendorff Bridge. The elderly German sprawled in the dirt but was uninjured.

A short time later, the Americans charged up to the bridge, and Lieutenant Karl Timmermann of West Point, Nebraska, knowing that the span

Konrad Adenauer, who was spared from wild GI shots. (National Archives)

could blow at any moment, raced across the Ludendorff at the head of his infantry platoon.

Only years later would Lieutenant John Grimball learn the identity of the old man who had hit the ground to avoid being killed by the three rifle shots. The target had been seventy-year-old Konrad Adenauer, who, four years after the incident, would serve as Chancellor of the West German Republic and become a staunch ally of the United States in NATO (North Atlantic Treaty Organization).[23]

Snoozing on Iwo Jima

IWO JIMA HAD BEEN the costliest battle in human lives in the history of the United States Marines. When the savagery ended in mid-March 1945, some five thousand leathernecks had been killed. There were but a handful of Japanese prisoners. Virtually all of the twenty-two thousand defenders had chosen to die for their emperor. It was the most expensive piece of real estate the United States had ever purchased—550 lives and 2,500 wounded marines for every square mile of the bleak Pacific islet 750 miles from Tokyo.

By early April, seven thousand Seabees (navy construction battalions) were working ten-hour shifts, seven days a week, to move 3 million square yards of earth, leveling the central plateau of Iwo Jima into a giant airfield for B-29 Superfortresses. Referring to the older ages of the navy construction men, the standard joke of the marines, whose average age was about eighteen, had long been: "Never hit a Seabee—he might be your grandfather."

More than one thousand Seabees had come ashore by the afternoon of D-Day, and their casualties had been heavy. Chief Carpenter's Mate A. W. Barker, a former Arkansas deputy sheriff, had led a forty-man section in the second wave. Before it was dark, half of them were dead or wounded.

Grateful B-29 air crews named their planes for the marine units that had fought on Iwo Jima. Some twenty-four hundred Superfortresses would make emergency landings there before the war ended. More than twenty-five thousand airmen's lives were saved, and hundreds of priceless B-29s were spared to bomb Japan again.

Long after the Iwo clash was over and the island had taken on the trappings of a secure rear echelon base, Japanese survivors slipped out of their caves at night to kill the "Yankee devils." One of these diehards was Sergeant Toshihiko Ohno. One black night, Ohno, loaded down with hand grenades, reached a large group of tents undetected. Silently, he surveyed the tents, and picked out the largest as his target. No doubt it was a command post, and by choosing it as his target, he could kill the most American officers with his supply of grenades.

Stealthily lifting the flap of the tent, Ohno found that it was not a command post, but a mess hall. Its only occupant was a lone soldier, possibly the mess sergeant, who was sound asleep on a cot and snoring loudly. Perhaps the GI had been fortified with torpedo cocktails, a mixture of medicinal alcohol and pineapple juice.

Fearing detection if he remained too long, Ohno pulled the pin and tossed a grenade under the snoozing soldier's cot. It failed to explode. The second one only hissed and did not go off. Frustrated, the Japanese pitched his third and last grenade—a dud. Weeks of dampness in his cave had ruined the grenades.

Before he could steal back out of the tented area, Sergeant Ohno was spotted by a GI who was heeding the call of nature. A cry brought other Americans on the run and they pounced on the Japanese survivor and locked him in the stockade until he could be shipped back to Japan after the war ended.

As for the soundly snoozing mess sergeant, he probably never learned that Providence and a wet cave had spared his life.[24]

A Sub Sinks Itself

AS THE SUN BEGAN TO RISE over the western Pacific on October 25, 1944, the U.S. submarine *Tang* was hunting Japanese shipping vessels in the Formosa Strait, a stormy body of water one hundred miles wide that separates Formosa (later known as Taiwan) from mainland China. Skippered by Commander Richard H. O'Kane, the *Tang* had sunk three tankers and two transports in a bold surface attack two nights earlier. Then the submarine made contact with another Japanese convoy, stalked it through the night, and launched a torpedo

Commander Richard H. O'Kane, skipper of the submarine Tang. *(U.S. Navy)*

salvo that badly damaged a warship and blew up a seven-thousand-ton merchant vessel.

That bonanza brought the number of ships sunk by the *Tang* during her eight-month tour of duty in the Pacific to twenty-four—a figure that could not be matched by any other U.S. submarine or surface vessel.

Now the *Tang* was left with only one torpedo, causing O'Kane's executive officer, Lieutenant William Leibold, to quip that they should keep it as a souvenir. O'Kane laughed, but said that he was going to use this last "fish" to sink the warship the submarine had crippled the night before.

A short time later, the *Tang* caught up with the limping warship, which had been left to fend for itself while the remainder of the convoy continued onward. Because the enemy vessel was clearly out of action, the *Tang* surfaced and fired its last torpedo. As soon as O'Kane could see the target sinking, he planned to head for Pearl Harbor, Hawaii, and a brief respite for the crew.

Suddenly, a voice on the bridge called out: "Look!"

O'Kane and others on the bridge spotted the telltale phosphorescent trail of a torpedo: It was heading directly toward the *Tang*, but was still a considerable distance away. The skipper was puzzled: There were no other Japanese warships to be seen and sonar sweeps disclosed the presence of no enemy submarines.

O'Kane immediately ordered evasive action, confident the submarine could dodge the oncoming fish. Then he was shocked: The torpedo was scurrying around the *Tang* in a wide circle—and the circle was getting smaller all the time. The submarine was trapped, not knowing which way to bolt to escape the torpedo.

Down below in the submarine's compartments, the men were unaware of what was happening. Then came an enormous explosion: The torpedo struck the *Tang* near the stern, killing or trapping all of those in the three closest compartments.

Up above, O'Kane, just before the torpedo struck, had shouted to close the conning-tower hatch; then the mighty blast hurled him and eight others into the water. No one had been wearing a life jacket. Within seconds, there were only four survivors in the sea: O'Kane, William Leibold, and two others.

Tons of water poured into the submarine, and she sank fast, finally nestling on the bottom of Formosa Strait. O'Kane's split-second order to close the conning-tower hatch had saved many lives, as thirty members of the crew eventually made it to the surface by using an escape apparatus known as Momsen Lungs.

There had been eighty-eight officers and men aboard the *Tang*: only fifteen, including O'Kane and Leibold, survived to be picked up by Japanese warships that had rushed to the scene. For these men, the ordeal was far from over. They were hurled into a prison camp on Formosa and subjected to months of brutal treatment.

When the Japanese empire surrendered in August 1945, the camp that held the *Tang*'s men was occupied by U.S. forces. Only Commander O'Kane, Lieutenant Leibold, and seven others were still alive.

Only after the *Tang*'s survivors were freed did the Pentagon learn what had happened to the submarine. In a grotesque twist of fate, the *Tang* had sunk herself. Her last torpedo had left the tube routinely, but its steering mechanism had gone awry. The fish circled the mother craft until it finally crashed into her.[25]

An Urgent Signal Saves a Ship

LIEUTENANT COMMANDER ADELBERT SCHNEE, one of the bold, dashing German U-boat skippers who had inflicted colossal carnage on British and American ships for more than four years, was prowling the North Atlantic in a revolutionary kind of submarine known as the Type XXI. This was the first; 119 others just like it were nearing completion at shipyards in Germany and in Nazi-occupied Norway. It was the spring of 1945.

Grand Admiral Karl Doenitz, Befehlshaber der Unterseeboote (commander in chief of submarines), had recently assured Adolf Hitler that these new craft might yet turn the war around in the Third Reich's favor by severing the Western Allies supply lifeline between the United States and the European continent.

The Type XXI was a giant boat, swift and able to remain underwater indefinitely. Its rubber skin deflected radar, making it "invisible," and it had an advanced search receiver that warned the crew when an enemy ship was nearby. Armed with new torpedoes called Lut, six of which could be fired at one time from 160 feet below the surface, the Type XXI submarine was an ominous threat. The Lut set their own course and in a series of wide, sweeping turns, homed in on the target and were impossible to track.

Now, in the North Atlantic on the afternoon of May 4, 1945, Commander Schnee, unaware that the führer had committed suicide in a Berlin bunker five days earlier after naming Admiral Doenitz to be his successor, was gazing into the periscope of his submerged U-2511. He was exhilarated: Between the crosshairs was an unsuspecting British cruiser. There was no doubt that his technologically advanced Lut torpedo could home in on the enemy warship and sink it.

Firing preparations were quickly made. Schnee looked through the periscope again for a final aiming adjustment. Just then, a bearded junior officer rushed up to the skipper: Admiral Doenitz had just signaled that the war was over; all U-boats were to cease hostile action and return to their bases in the Third Reich. Onward sailed the British cruiser, unaware that she and hundreds of her crew had been saved from a watery grave by a fortuitous fluke of timing.[26]

Was There a Plot to Kidnap Hitler's Corpse?

REICHSFÜHRER HEINRICH HIMMLER, owl-faced and inscrutable, was probably the most feared man in Nazi Germany. By a diligent and unrelenting pursuit of personal power, the onetime chicken farmer had made himself, by the final year of the war, the leader of the SS, the elite, black-uniformed army within an army; chief of the Gestapo (the dreaded secret police); commander of the Replacement (Home) Army; and Minister of the Interior.

With this enormous concentration of judicial, police, and military power in his hands, Heinrich Himmler was the instigator of gigantic cruelties (as he would freely admit to the Allies after the war), and his diabolical mind conjured up bizarre machinations to achieve his goals.

Himmler, who professed undying loyalty to Adolf Hitler, was not above treachery when it suited his purpose. In early 1944, when the handwriting was on the wall for the führer's one-thousand-year Third Reich, Himmler began conspiring to save his skin and to seize power from his benefactor, Adolf Hitler. Himmler's conduit for making peace overtures to the Anglo-Americans, behind the führer's back, was a shadowy figure named Dr. Felix Kersten, who alternately billed himself as a masseur and a physician.

*Führer Adolf Hitler (left) and Reichsführer Heinrich Himmler in better days.
(National Archives)*

Kersten, who was a Swede, lived in Stockholm and traveled to Berlin once a month to give the forty-four-year-old Himmler a back rub, a rather long journey for such a mundane function. The Reichsführer, an odd duck in many respects, once told an aide that Dr. Kersten was "my only friend, my Buddha."

While getting his back rubbed, Himmler disclosed to his Buddha all of the führer's plans. Himmler no doubt was aware that Kersten was in contact with agents of the American Office of Strategic Services (OSS) in Stockholm. As intended, Kersten passed along to the OSS everything he had learned from Himmler in Berlin. The idea was to win over the OSS as friends of the Reichsführer.

Meanwhile, Himmler had another pipeline into the Allied camp. He had dispatched his trusted subordinate, thirty-two-year-old SS General Walther Schellenberg, to Stockholm for clandestine talks. Schellenberg's contact in the Swedish capital, a hotbed of international intrigue, was Abram S. Hewitt, a wealthy New York lawyer, a graduate of Oxford and Harvard, and now an OSS operative.

Schellenberg was masquerading as a German businessman. A lawyer by profession, his character blended intellect with the instincts and morals of an Al Capone gangster—the precise traits Reichsführer Himmler wanted in his SS leaders.

Heinrich Himmler's "peace plan," as presented to Abram Hewitt, was simple. His good friend Adolf Hitler would be bumped off, and a new German government would be formed with Himmler as the president. Then, England and the United States would grant Germany reasonable peace terms, after which the three nations would gang up and fight the Russians.

In the weeks that followed, Himmler's emissaries continued to hold covert negotiations with the Americans. Then, in April 1945, with Allied armies closing in on Berlin from three directions, the Reichsführer holed up on the Baltic coast, two hundred miles north of the German capital. Hitler, he knew, was in the Führerbunker at the Reich Chancellery. Now Himmler concocted a bizarre scheme to pull his own chestnuts out of the fire with the Allies.

Around 9:00 A.M. on April 28, with Soviet troops only a few blocks down the street, a wireless operator in the führerbunker picked up a Swedish radio report in German. It had originated in San Francisco, seven thousand miles away, where statesmen of the free world were giving birth to the United Nations. Heinrich Himmler, the radio report declared, had put out peace feelers to the Americans and British.

When handed the bulletin, Adolf Hitler threw a classic tantrum, screamed, hollered, paced about, and castigated Himmler for his treason. He ordered the Reichsführer to be reduced in rank to SS private. (Such an order was actually cut.)

Minutes later, General Wilhelm Bergdorf, long the führer's personal adjutant, rushed into Hitler's office, shouting that Himmler had compounded his treachery. Himmler, Bergdorf spluttered, had promised to have the führer's dead carcass kidnapped and flown to England as a means of impressing General Eisenhower of Himmler's serious intent to set up a new government in Germany. It was not clear if Hitler was supposed to be murdered by an unknown Himmler accomplice in the bunker, or whether it was anticipated that the führer would commit suicide to evade the clutches of the Russians.

Apparently, as part of the ghoulish scenario, the murderer or another Himmler confederate was to do the corpse snatching and then rush the führer's remains to the historic Brandenberg Gate. Near there, two weeks earlier, General Hans Baur, Hitler's personal pilot, had supervised the rapid construction of an emergency air strip, and a few planes were standing by. The script called for Hitler's corpse to be loaded on one of those planes and flown to England.

Had Heinrich Himmler truly concocted such a weird scheme? Later, a Hitler aide in the Berlin bunker swore that a document spelling out the details of the body snatching did indeed exist. Certainly Himmler, who had been responsible for the murders of hundreds of thousands of persons in Germany and elsewhere in Europe, would have had no qualms over having Hitler killed and whisked off to the enemy camp.

Only Reichsführer Himmler and a few of his close associates would know the true answer to the reputed carcass kidnapping. But Himmler committed suicide after being captured by the Americans a few weeks later. Also taking the secret to his grave was General Wilhelm Bergdorf, who had claimed that the Himmler body-snatching plot had indeed existed.[27]

Living Unknown Serviceman

WHEN VICTORY IN JAPAN DAY was proclaimed by President Harry Truman in September 1945, the world was at peace again for the first time in nearly a decade. Hundreds of millions of people rejoiced. But in a hospital in Boston, a man who identified himself as Charles A. Jameson was not among the celebrants. He had taken part in achieving that victory, and had paid a heavy price, but no one knew his true identity—no military unit had the name in its listing.

Jameson and a group of other wounded Americans had been brought across the Atlantic on the navy transport USS *LeJeune*, and had been removed from the ship at Boston on February 8, 1945. Since medical records made in theaters of operations were necessarily sketchy (due to medical staffs pursuing their primary task of keeping wounded men alive), a tag tied to him read merely: "Charles A. Jameson, 49; religion, Catholic; citizenship, American. Cutty Sark." That was it.

The patient was in a coma. Examination revealed that his back was riddled with infected shrapnel wounds. There was also an ugly head wound which, doctors feared, might affect the patient's memory should he regain consciousness.

It was three years before the infected wounds finally healed. Meanwhile, the patient had regained consciousness, but when asked to identify himself, he repeated one line: "Charles A. Jameson, 49, Catholic, American, the Cutty Sark."

Military authorities tried vigorously to identify the patient. The Red Cross searched diligently through its records and found no listing for a Charles A. Jameson. Neither did the United States Navy, the Merchant Marine, nor the Coast Guard.

Through scribbling on pads, Jameson was able to name every major steamship company in the world. From photos, he recognized and could describe in minute detail the Royal Navy's gunnery school at Gosport, England. So the British Maritime Registry and the admiralty were asked to conduct a search of their records for Charles A. Jameson. Nothing was found.

It was thought Jameson might have been a crewman on a merchant ship *Cutty Sark.* That vessel turned out to have sailed a century earlier.

Jameson communicated mainly by writing on a pad. One day, he wrote that he believed that he had been on the merchant ship *Hinemoa* as first mate. "We were carrying nitrates from Chile to England when we were sunk by a German cruiser in the Atlantic," Jameson scribbled.

Naval authorities found that the *Hinemoa* had indeed been sunk by a German warship, but in the English Channel, not in the Atlantic. Investigators interviewed surviving crewmen of the *Hinemoa* and showed them Jameson's photo. No one could remember anyone by that name, nor did anyone recognize his picture. Had Jameson been the first mate, that certainly would not have been the case.

Later, it was learned that the patient had been deaf for four years, apparently since the time he had suffered his horrendous wounds.

The true identity of the man known as Charles A. Jameson remains a mystery. No relative or friend ever visited him in the hospital where he was a patient for nearly twelve years, even though his photo had been published in countless newspapers.

Charles A. Jameson was truly the American "Living Unknown Serviceman."[28]

Part Four

Uncanny Riddles

Did Britain Try to Bribe Hitler?

Europe was teetering on the brink of war. In embassies around the world, diplomats were conjecturing not if the conflict was going to erupt, but when it would do so. In this tension-packed global climate, Franz Wohltat, a top official in Adolf Hitler's financial administration, attended a conference in London on whaling between July 18 and 21, 1939.

During this period, he was approached by Horace Wilson, head of the British Civil Service, who, Wohltat would later claim, led him to believe that the British government was prepared to offer the führer what amounted to a bribe. What's more, Wohltat would state, the offer had the approval of British Prime Minister Neville Chamberlain.

Wohltat claimed that Horace Wilson suggested that Great Britain would make available to the Third Reich a loan of up to 1 billion pounds sterling (roughly 5 billion U.S. dollars) to cover the cost of German disarmament if Hitler would relent on his hostile attitude toward Poland.

This proposal, if indeed it was ever offered, was outside Franz Wohltat's authority. Wohltat claimed that he said he would have to obtain a reply from an undisclosed person in Berlin—no doubt Adolf Hitler. There the matter rested and Horace Wilson heard no more about it.

If Great Britain had indeed offered a bribe, the führer would have brushed it off. At that time, hundreds of thousands of German troops were already massing along the Reich's eastern frontier, and a date had been set to invade Poland late in August—only a month away. (This date was later advanced to September 1.)

Had lanky, sixty-nine-year-old Neville Chamberlain acquiesced to the proposed blackmail of a ruthless dictator who had been rattling his saber for months and who had stridently threatened to avenge the wrongs of the World War I treaty with the Allies that had virtually reduced Germany to a feudal state? There was prior evidence that the prime minister might have done just that, although no such transaction was ever committed to writing.

During the previous year, while the führer gobbled up the Rhineland, and at that present time, as Hitler was threatening to take over Austria and Czechoslovakia, Chamberlain had remained the leader of the forces of appeasement. As the crisis deepened, the prime minister, with hat in hand, flew to Hitler's Bavarian retreat at Berchtesgaden to seek a peaceful solution to the problem.

We, the German Führer and Chancellor and the
British Prime Minister, have had a further
meeting today and are agreed in recognising that
the question of Anglo-German relations is of the
first importance for the two countries and for
Europe.

We regard the agreement signed last night
and the Anglo-German Naval Agreement as symbolic
of the desire of our two peoples never to go to
war with one another again.

We are resolved that the method of
consultation shall be the method adopted to deal
with any other questions that may concern our two
countries, and we are determined to continue our
efforts to remove possible sources of difference
and thus to contribute to assure the peace of
Europe.

[signatures]

September 30, 1938

Hitler-Chamberlain
"peace" agreement.

Chamberlain wished to avoid war at any cost: The cost was handing over Czechoslovakia to the German dictator. On September 30, 1938, Chamberlain and Hitler signed a document pledging that Great Britain and Germany would "never go to war with one another again."

A day later, Neville Chamberlain flew back to London, climbed from his transport plane, waved the piece of paper which he and Hitler had signed, grinned broadly, and proclaimed that the document meant "peace in our time."

So as desperate as was Neville Chamberlain for "peace in our time," it is conceivable that he would have given his approval to a British scheme to bribe Adolf Hitler from going to war for 1 billion pounds sterling.[1]

Did the Allies Aid the Pearl Harbor Plan?

JAPAN HAD BEEN geared for war since 1931, when her armies invaded Manchuria. At home, the warlords controlled the nation. Emperor Hirohito, who had great power as a spiritual leader, was a timid, indecisive man who did nothing to curb the admirals' and generals' ambitions to conquer the western Pacific and to establish what they called "The Greater East Asia Co-Prosperity Sphere."

Since 1927, the Imperial General Staff had known that war with the United States was "inevitable" in order to achieve Japan's goals. It was eleven years later, however, when specific plans were being drawn up to inflict a massive blow that would demolish the U.S. Pacific Fleet in one fell swoop.

Architect of that plan, which envisioned a sneak attack at the American naval base at Pearl Harbor, Hawaii, was Admiral Isoroko Yamamoto, chief of the Imperial Fleet. Yamamoto had attended a prestigious American university and had spent two years in Washington, D.C., as a military attaché—and director of a widespread Japanese spy ring in the capital city.

As preparations continued in Tokyo for striking Pearl Harbor, it appeared that Admiral Yamamoto, a tall, husky, bullet-headed man who spoke English fluently, had unlikely allies—the Americans and the British.

A key figure providing U.S. help to Yamamoto in creating the Pearl Harbor strike plan was Klaus Mehnert, a young German intellectual and Nazi fanatic, who taught anthropology at the University of Hawaii in Honolulu. A highly regarded professor on campus, Mehnert was also a clever and productive spy, one deeply imbued with the ideals of Nazism.

In 1938, Professor Mehnert learned of the vulnerability of Pearl Harbor when U.S. Navy Captain (later chief of naval operations) Ernest J. King launched a successful mock air strike from the carrier *Saratoga* to conclude major war games called Fleet Problem XIX. Lifting off two hundred miles from their target, King's pilots sneaked through Pearl Harbor's defenses undetected and "bombed" the naval base, anchored warships, and nearby airfields.

Mehnert, under the guise of conducting field research, eavesdropped on the naval exercise, and sent to his masters in Berlin an exhaustive report in which he (accurately) detailed woefully weak spots in the Hawaiian Islands' defenses. An astute student of naval tactics, the professor suggested that a daring and skillfully executed air attack by a foreign power (that is, Japan) could easily infiltrate those defenses and strike a telling blow against the United States fleet.

Since Germany and Japan were locked in an espionage alliance negotiated three years earlier, Mehnert's report was eventually shuttled on to Tokyo. (After World War II, some top United States Navy Intelligence officers concluded that Klaus Mehnert's hand was visible in Japan's grand strategic design for conquest in the Pacific.)

In mid-1940, Isoroko Yamamoto reported that his operational plan for the sneak assault against the United States Pacific Fleet anchorage was nearly completed. Then, an event occurred halfway around the world that may have inspired the Japanese admiral to include its strategy in his own plan.

On November 11, 1940, a British air reconnaissance carried out from the Mediterranean island of Malta disclosed that six battleships were neatly congregated in the Italian naval base at Taranto in southern Italy. So, twenty-one Swordfish aircraft, eleven of them fitted with torpedoes and ten with bombs, lifted off from the Royal Navy aircraft carrier *Illustrious,* some two hundred miles off Taranto.

Caught by total surprise, the Italians did not even activate the harbor's smoke screens. Although the flak was thick, the Swordfish launched their torpedoes and six scored hits. It had been a disaster for the Supermarina (the Italian fleet). All six battleships were either abandoned or put out of action for many months.

So a curious riddle has endured. Had the Americans, through Captain Ernest King's mock air assault, and the British, through the Taranto torpedo strike, furnished Admiral Yamamoto with inspiration and strategy for the surprise bomb-and-torpedo attack against Pearl Harbor in December 1941?[2]

Was Frau Goebbels Defecting?

DR. PAUL JOSEF GOEBBELS and his beautiful and vivacious wife, Magda, were outwardly loving and caring toward one another. They were also the model Nazi couple, for between them they had produced five handsome Aryan children: Heidi, Helmut, Helga, Hilde, and Hedde. Privately, Joe and Magda detested each other, but their marriage remained intact for years because of their obligations to the Third Reich and Adolf Hitler.

Herr Doktor Goebbels, the Nazi propaganda minister, was an educated man with literary pretensions who had joined the Nazi Party in 1924 at the age of twenty-six. Later, with Hitler in power, he controlled all aspects of communications in greater Germany—newspapers, magazines, publishing, theater, radio, and movies. Goebbels was completely cynical and a compulsive liar; at various times, he attributed his limp to a World War I wound. However, it was much more likely to have been caused by him having had infantile paralysis as a youngster.

Goebbels had a reputation in Berlin as a great lover, one who was always on the prowl, and in 1941, he had a torrid romance with the beautiful Czech movie star Lida Baarova. Not to be outdone, Magda Goebbels found time from caring for her large brood to engage in a lurid liaison with young, tall, handsome Karl Hanke, an SS lieutenant colonel who was one of her husband's aides.

Adolf Hitler and his Nazi Party could not tolerate a public scandal involving members of what had been billed as the "First Family of the Third Reich." But one night at a gala celebration, Magda broke down in tears and confessed to the führer that her life was intolerable and that she was going to divorce Herr Doktor.

The führer took direct action, ordering Goebbels to jilt Lida Baarova and to fire his aide and wife's lover, Karl Hanke. Hanke, good Nazi that he was, helped untangle what threatened to become a highly political time bomb by volunteering to go to the front and fight.

Goebbels and Magda got back together. In Berlin society circles, it became known as The Great Reconciliation. Actually, Joe and Magda now hated one another even more intensely. Goebbels was still madly in love with Baarova (who Hitler had ordered to remain in Prague) and Magda was heart-broken over the absence of Karl Hanke.

Then the smoldering situation burst into flame. In the spring of 1941, Magda put her children into the family car, climbed in and drove southward, bent on fleeing Germany. But Goebbels soon learned of her departure and flashed word around the Third Reich. Magda was halted and arrested just short of the border with neutral Switzerland. Still in custody, she was flown back to Berlin.

What had been Magda Goebbels's true motive for her hectic flight south-ward? Had she planned to defect from the Third Reich? If that had been the case, the episode would have provided a propaganda bonanza for the Allies. Switzerland had more Allied spies per square yard than any other country in the world. Had Magda planned on contacting the Americans or the British through espionage agents in Berne, Geneva, or Lucerne? If so, as the wife of one of the four top Hitler functionaries, she could have provided information that would have vastly aided the Allied war effort.

Four years later, Magda Goebbels and Herr Doktor committed suicide in the closing hours of the war in Europe. So her motive in trying to flee Germany and enter Switzerland remains open to conjecture.[3]

Could $212 Have Prevented a U.S. Disaster?

COULD THE AMERICAN DEBACLE at Pearl Harbor, Hawaii, on December 7, 1941, been avoided had a tightfisted federal government been willing to cough up 212 dollars to cover freight costs more than a decade earlier? There is considerable evidence that this could have been the case.

In 1926, an article in a German publication aroused the interest of the U.S. Army Signal Corps. It described a revolutionary "secret writing machine" (later to be known as Enigma). It was capable of producing 22 billion different code combinations, and it would take forty-two thousand years for one person, working continuously day and night and trying a different cipher key every minute, to exhaust all combination possibilities.

So Major General Marlborough Churchill, the chief of intelligence of the United States Army, was asked to investigate the potential of this bold and exciting new machine. Inquiries were made in Berlin, where the Kryha Coding Machine Company was based, and an expert was rushed to New York to demonstrate the machine to American cryptanalytical experts.

One of these authorities was thirty-four-year-old Major William F. Friedman, chief cryptanalyst of the Signal Corps and regarded as one of the world's best in his field. Evidently, Friedman, who had been born in Russia and had come to the United States with his family a year later, was deeply interested by the demonstration. For on January 15, 1927, the Signal Corps ordered one each of two models of the machine.

It was an era in which the United States Army was an impoverished agency. Only a decade earlier, World War I—billed by politicians as "the war to end all wars"—had made an army obsolete. Or so concluded most members of Congress and the majority of American citizens. So before the United States Treasury Department would approve the modest expenditure for the two secret writing machines, the Signal Corps was asked for their precise cost, freight charges, and import duties.

Prices were quoted. The Treasury balked. Too much money. Finally, the contract was signed and the two machines were shipped from Berlin. Then, the transaction hit a snag. The Kryha Company had not paid the freight and import charges as it had agreed to do, and the Signal Corps had no funds for that purpose. The bill came to 212 dollars.

The two secret-writing machines languished in a New York warehouse for many months. Then, on April 5, 1928, the Signal Corps rustled up enough money to pay the charges, and the machines were released from storage. Then, Bill Friedman began the task of penetrating the machine's secrets. It was a slow, painstaking and agonizing process. Moreover, Friedman's staff consisted of only three young and inexperienced cryptanalysts and two clerks.

Friedman's efforts were constantly impeded by official Washington, which referred to the army's crucial cryptanalytic service as the Black Chamber. In 1929, a horrified Secretary of State Henry L. Stimson withdrew his agency's support for the project.

"Gentlemen don't read other gentlemen's mail," Stimson had sniffed.

In the meantime, the "gentlemen" in Tokyo were not so squeamish about such clandestine activities. They were the Japanese warlords who, in 1927, had created a document called the Tanaka Memorial—a blueprint for conquest of a vast region of the western Pacific and for eventual war with the United States.

Friedman learned that the Japanese had purchased an advanced model of Kryha's secret-writing machine, so in 1934, he began focusing on the Japanese cryptosystems, based on his own penetration of the earlier model of the same machine, which he had acquired in 1928. However, it was not until early 1942—a few months after Pearl Harbor—that United States cryptanalysts began reading the Enigma traffic of the Japanese navy and the Japanese Foreign Office. These intercepts were code-named Magic.

In the light of the timing of this cryptanalytic breakthrough, Pearl Harbor conceivably might have been avoided. If Bill Friedman and his tiny staff had not been forced to cool their heels for almost a year back in 1928 while efforts were made to pry 212 dollars from the Treasury in order to get the Kryha machines out of hock, would American cryptanalysts have used the extra year to unbutton the Japanese code *before* the devastating sneak attack on December 7, 1941? No one will ever know.[4]

Reinhard Heydrich's Secret

TALL, HAWK-NOSED Reinhard Heydrich was chief of the SD, the intelligence branch of Adolf Hitler's elite military force, the SS, during the early years of the war. Brilliant and with the instincts of a barracuda, the highly ambitious Heydrich had long been a bitter rival of Admiral Wilhelm Canaris, the Abwehr chief, who had sixteen thousand agents sprinkled around the world.

It was Heydrich's secret goal to discredit the fifty-seven-year-old Canaris in the eyes of the führer, in which case the Abwehr would be absorbed into the SD. Heydrich, of course, would become chief of the one German intelligence agency, and as such, he would be the Reich's second most powerful figure, behind Adolf Hitler himself.

As cunning and ruthless as he was, Reinhard Heydrich, the son of an opera singer and an actress, had more than met his match in the cagy Canaris, who had spent a lifetime in the shadowy world of espionage and political infighting. Heydrich could only bide his time and wait for an opportunity to destroy Canaris.

SS General Reinhard Heydrich.
(National Archives)

Meanwhile, Heydrich's star continued to rise in the Nazi hierarchy. When the Wehrmacht invaded Russia in 1941, the thirty-seven-year-old Heydrich was put in charge of the Einsatzgruppen (extermination squads), which murdered Jews in the occupied eastern territories by the hundreds of thousands. It was Heydrich who drafted the protocol for the "Final Solution of the Jewish Problem," which led to the systematic slaughter of European Jews in the extermination camps of the east.

Reinhard Heydrich stood out in the Nazi leadership, not only for his cunning, but for his inhumanity. It was said that he sent tens of thousands of Jews to their deaths without as much as blinking an eye.

In one of the unsolved mysteries of the war, Reinhard Heydrich achieved his place near the top of the Nazi totem pole despite the fact that Adolf Hitler had in his possession incontrovertible proof that the man who sent so many Jews to be slaughtered was himself half-Jewish. That evidence had been provided to the führer by Heydrich's arch foe, Wilhelm Canaris, who had discovered Heydrich's background in the Ahnenliste, the ancestry list compiled by the Abwehr of everyone in the Nazi Party.

Since Hitler had proof that Heydrich had 50 percent Jewish blood, why had he permitted the man known as Heinrich the Butcher to remain in power? That question may never be fully answered.[5]

A Crucial Page Disappears

IN LATE SEPTEMBER 1942, German intelligence was beginning to get wind of Operation Torch, an impending invasion of French Northwest Africa. It would be the first major operation for the United States since the Argonne Forest offensive in World War I.

Lieutenant General George S. Patton, Jr., a bold tactician, would command the Western Task Force, one of the three—and largest—in the complicated invasion. It would sail directly from Hampton Roads, Virginia, for more than three thousand miles, then storm ashore at Casablanca.

Torch had been hastily mounted as the result of Soviet Premier Josef Stalin's demand that the Grand Alliance (the United States and England) open a Second Front in 1942 in order to keep Russia from being knocked out of the war. The date for the operation would be November 8, 1942.

Prior to sailing from the United States, General Patton confided to his diary: "[This is] as desperate a venture as has ever been undertaken by any force in the world's history."

As the day grew closer and Nazi agents and the highly efficient German wireless intercept service, the B-Dienst (for Beobachtungsdienst), labored feverishly to unlock the secret of Allied intentions, an alarming security flap occurred right in 20 Grosvenor Square, London, the headquarters of Allied Supreme Commander Dwight Eisenhower. Central figure in the turmoil was Lieutenant Commander Harry Butcher, Eisenhower's aide and confidant.

Butcher, a congenial officer who was a New York radio-network executive in peacetime, kept a detailed daily diary for the supreme commander. One morning, page 117 came up missing. It had simply vanished. On the page were numerous top-secret details of Operation Torch, including the directive from the Combined Chiefs of Staff outlining objectives of the invasion.

A frantic search by all ranks, from Eisenhower on down, failed to turn up the missing page 117. Army security officers launched intense interrogations of countless individuals in the headquarters. No one was above suspicion. Had the missing sheet gotten into German hands, a bloodbath could be awaiting the American and British invaders. General Eisenhower discussed with his staff the possible recommendation that Torch be cancelled.

Investigators failed to ever locate the vanishing page, nor did they ever gain a clue as to how it had gotten out of Commander Butcher's diary, which was held closely under lock and key. Was it an "inside job?" No one will ever know for sure.[6]

A Nazi Report Vanishes

IN THE FALL OF 1942, Adolf Hitler was starving for concrete intelligence that would disclose where the Western Allies intended to strike. The führer knew that a vast naval force was assembling in Great Britain for some expedition— but what was the target? Southern France? Sicily? Italy? Norway? Denmark? Northwest Africa? Of all the possible objectives, Northwest Africa seemed to be the most unlikely to Hitler and his high command.

Strangely, elements of German intelligence were incredibly well informed about Anglo-American plans for the looming major offensive—but word never reached the führer. Captain Herbert Wichmann, the Abwehr station chief in Hamburg, had obtained a detailed, accurate, and timely report from an A 1 source. There was no doubt about it. Northwest Africa was the Allied target!

Captain Wichmann, a navy officer, was a low-key, dedicated and clever operative. He possessed a vital trait for success as a spymaster: an intense passion for anonymity. Because of his skills, Wichmann had been assigned to Hamburg since 1938, for that teeming Baltic seaport station conducted the main espionage operations against the United States and Great Britain.

After Wichmann received the report identifying Northwest Africa as the Allied objective, he rushed the electrifying document to the German high command in Berlin as a priority delivery and under the highest-grade security. The spymaster was elated. Here was an intelligence bonanza seldom equaled in the annals of warfare. Now the Wehrmacht could inflict a catastrophic blow, one from which the American and British might never recover. With such high priority and security, it seemed logical that the document would reach the desk of Field Marshal Wilhelm Keitel, the stiff, humorless chief of staff who had been Adolf Hitler's closest military confidant since 1939.

Ten days later, in Hamburg, Captain Wichmann no doubt was astonished to learn that the Americans and British had not only invaded Northwest Africa virtually unmolested by the Germans, but that they had achieved total surprise. He would learn that the crucial intelligence document had mysteriously vanished. No one seemed to know what had become of it.[7]

The Luftwaffe Spares Doolittle

THE FOUR-ENGINE Flying Fortress, with Brigadier General James H. "Jimmy" Doolittle aboard, lifted off from a British airfield and set a course for Gibraltar, the huge rock at the western entrance to the vast Mediterranean Sea. Gibraltar would be the Allied headquarters for Operation Torch, the invasion of North Africa, and Doolittle would command American air forces. It was November 6, 1942. Zero hour for Torch was less than forty-eight hours away.

Jimmy Doolittle, a diminutive, forty-five-year-old flying veteran, had electrified the United States the previous spring. Then a lieutenant colonel, he had led a bold raid on Tokyo in which squadrons of two-engine B-25s had been launched from the aircraft carrier *Hornet*. Doolittle became a national hero and had been awarded the Congressional Medal of Honor for his role in the mission.

Now, arrowing southward toward Gibraltar over the Bay of Biscay, Doolittle heard a shout: "Bandits at nine o'clock!"

Moments later, bullets began ripping through the lumbering Flying Fortress, as four Luftwaffe fighters bored in for the kill. One of the enemy slugs tore into the arm of the copilot; others hissed past the head of General Doolittle.

A terrific racket erupted inside the heavy bomber as the youthful GI gunners, most in combat for the first time, returned the fire. "I got one! I got one!" a boyish-faced waist gunner yelled excitedly. No one saw an enemy plane go down.

As suddenly as they appeared, the German fighters, after making only a single pass against the lone, unescorted Flying Fortress, banked sharply and headed back toward France. Unflappable, Jimmy Doolittle ignored his brush with death and returned his attention to maps of Morocco and Algeria.

It had been a curious episode. Had the Luftwaffe pilots known that the famous hero of the free world was aboard the bomber? The German B-Dienst was experienced and capable. Perhaps American radio communications, whose security was often lax at that stage of the war, had tipped off the Germans that Jimmy Doolittle was on the plane. It would have been a major propaganda bonanza for the Third Reich if it could have announced that the "invincible" Luftwaffe had destroyed the American celebrity's plane.

General James H. Doolittle. (U.S. Air Force)

Whatever may have been the case, the German fighter squadron's actions had been most strange. When they had had a slow-moving Flying Fortress caught like a duck sitting on a huge pond, why had the pilots made but one pass, then scamped away?

Doolittle's narrow escape would remain a stitch in the mystery tapestry of the war.[8]

The Weasel Goes on the Lam

IT WAS A STANDARD JOKE in the United States Army just before and during the war: There was an entire battalion of generals who did nothing but crisscross the nation in airplanes, seeking likely locales for building camps to train millions of men. When one of these generals spotted a godforsaken, remote, desolate parcel of treeless terrain, he immediately staked it out as an ideal place for a military post.

One such place was Fort Harrison, outside of Helena (wartime population thirteen thousand), in the western part of Montana. There, in late 1942 and early 1943, the First Special Service Force, a mixture of twenty-three hundred tough and resourceful American and Canadian soldiers, learned to parachute, ski, and climb seemingly endless mountains.

This was an elite outfit of handpicked men led by a West Pointer, thirty-five-year-old Colonel Robert T. Frederick, a wiry, soft-spoken, mustachioed officer who was destined to become a battlefield legend in the U.S. Army. There had been good reason for the Forcemen, as the members of the outfit were called, to be assembled and trained in that secluded region: They were to conduct a secret mission of crucial importance to the outcome of the war.

As far back as April 1940, the international scientists' grapevine—notoriously indiscreet and often uncontrollable—had indicated that the Kaiser Wilhelm Institut in Germany was conducting extensive experiments aimed at splitting the atom. Then, in 1942, just as the United States was secretly setting up the Manhattan Project to build an A-bomb, the intelligence section of the British Ministry of Economic Warfare came through with electrifying information: The Nazis had ordered the Norwegian electrochemical plant, Norsk Hydro—largest of its kind in the world—to increase its production of deuterium oxide (so-called heavy water) from three thousand to ten thousand pounds a year.

That seemed to mean only one frightening fact: The Kaiser Wilhelm Institut was well along in its experiments to split the atom. The Norsk Hydro plant and its stock of heavy water had to be wiped out, so Colonel Frederick and his Forcemen were being readied to parachute into Norway and do the job—a classic "suicide mission."

The Forcemen's equipment included a specially designed and revolutionary new vehicle developed by U.S. Army Ordnance—the first effective over-the-snow vehicle. It was propelled by conveyor-type treads, much like those on a tank, could carry men, supplies or ammunition, yet was light enough to be dropped by a huge parachute. This top-secret vehicle was dubbed the Weasel.

Developer of the prototype of the Weasel was Geoffrey Pyke, a British civilian, who was not a scientist, but a man of vivid imagination who worked for Lord Louis Mountbatten, chief of Combined Operations, England's commando units. Pyke gave an entirely new meaning to the expression "eccentric behavior."

When Pyke was in Canada in 1942 working on what he called the Plough (later the Weasel), he was in the company of high-ranking military officers, and was walking about in deep snow in a shabby suit, thin overcoat, slippers, and no socks—with his trousers rolled up to his knees.

Because of his undeniably creative bent, Pyke's bosses, on another occasion, arranged for him to meet with Mackenzie King, the Canadian prime minister. For this audience, Pyke had been encouraged to buy a new suit to replace the shabby one he had been wearing steadily for months. The trousers of the new suit were fitted with a zipper, then a newfangled contraption, instead of the usual fly buttons.

Minutes before seeing Prime Minister King, Pyke took the precaution of going to the lavatory, and his zipper stuck. Tugging and pulling, Pyke failed to close his fly. Deciding not to waste any more time, he walked into King's office and drew attention to his trousers.

He exclaimed: "Prime Minister, I would not have to present myself to you in this state were it not for the fact that Canadian engineers are totally inefficient."

While being used in training at Fort Harrison, the Weasels were carefully watched, and at night, most of them were under armed guards. One Friday in December 1942, after the Forcemen had been working with the vehicles in chest-deep snow, one Weasel disappeared.

A great flap erupted. Colonel Frederick was irate. Where had it gone? Who had taken it? Nazi spies? How could a vehicle as heavy and unique as a Weasel simply disappear?

Frederick launched a search, including probes and inquiries in nearby Helena and elsewhere in the locale. Since the Weasel was top-secret, it was difficult to describe to the natives the type of vehicle that was missing without giving away the fact that it was a specially designed conveyance that ran on treads.

As it developed, the Weasel was not needed. The Forcemen were taken off the mission of wiping out the Norwegian plant; because of the urgency involved, British commandos were assigned the task. Nevertheless, the American-Canadian force in Montana conjectured long and hard about the Weasel that had gone on the lam.[9]

Who Tried to Murder de Gaulle?

EVER SINCE the British secret service spirited Charles de Gaulle out of France after the German Wehrmacht crushed the once vaunted French army in only six weeks in mid-1940, the Frenchman had been a royal pain in the neck to the British and to the Americans. On reaching London, de Gaulle, France's youngest two-star general, broadcast to the French people: "France has lost a battle, but France has not lost the war."

Haughty and aloof, the forty-nine-year-old de Gaulle hated the British and the Americans with a passion. In a secret speech to French paratroopers on February 4, 1943, he was said to have remarked: "Although it is now necessary for the French to make pro-English propaganda, the British, like the Germans, are hereditary enemies of the French. It is the Russians who will win the war. . . . After gaining control of France, I will not stand in the way of allowing the Russians to occupy Germany."

Seeking a scapegoat, de Gaulle blamed President Franklin Roosevelt for the humiliating defeat of the French army, although the United States was weak militarily and not even a participant in the conflict. De Gaulle was surrounded by anti-American advisers, who constantly reminded *le grand Charlie* that Roosevelt was conspiring against him.

General Charles de Gaulle.
(National Archives)

General de Gaulle's first action on arriving in England was to proclaim a Free French government with himself as its head. He set up his own radio stations and established his own newspapers, all of which spewed out incessant criticism of the British and Americans.

Winston Churchill, long a master of political infighting, was furious with de Gaulle and knew that the gangling Frenchman (six-feet, seven inches tall) was playing havoc with the war effort against the Third Reich. In early 1943, in a face-to-face confrontation, Churchill told de Gaulle that the British didn't regard the Frenchman as being indispensable.

On the morning of April 21, 1943, a few weeks after that tension-packed encounter, de Gaulle arrived at Hendon airfield, a short distance outside London, to fly to Scotland to inspect members of the Free French navy. The trip would be made in his personal plane, a four-engine Wellington bomber, which had been put at his disposal and maintained by the British.

Taking off at Hendon was a tricky endeavor. The runway was short and there was an embankment at one end. So a pilot had to rev up his engines to full speed, keep his wheel brakes on, and raise the plane's tail by using the elevator controls. Then he would release the brakes and zip down the runway, much like a rocket being fired out of a bazooka.

When RAF Flight Lieutenant Peter Loat, pilot of de Gaulle's plane, began the normal routine and headed down the runway, the tail suddenly dropped. Loat could not adjust it, for the elevator control was loose in his hands. Skilled pilot that he was, Loat managed to halt the aircraft shortly before it would have crashed head-on into the embankment.

General de Gaulle was assigned a lighter aircraft, and Loat flew the Frenchman and his party to Glasgow. Presumably suspecting British treachery and feeling that discretion was the better part of valor, de Gaulle returned to London by train.

In the meantime, de Gaulle's Wellington bomber was inspected by mechanics at Hendon and it was found that the elevator control rod had separated. The damaged crucial piece of equipment was sent to a laboratory for examination. Back came the report: The metal rod had been cut through with acid.

Flight Lieutenant Loat was informed by British authorities that German saboteurs had committed the sabotage. Loat didn't buy that explanation. Early in the war and during it, the British secret service had apprehended nearly every Nazi spy in Great Britain, and, through "turned" enemy agents, learned of the arrival of new spies in time to greet them when they landed.

Moreover, since the Hendon aircraft maintenance crew was a close-knit outfit, it would have been almost impossible for a Nazi saboteur to even reach de Gaulle's Wellington, much less pour acid on a critical piece of equipment, without being observed.

Not unexpectedly, halfhearted efforts by the British secret service to discover the identity of the Wellington bomber saboteur bore no fruit, and soon the investigation was quietly dropped.

There seemed to be no doubt in Charles de Gaulle's mind about who had tried to murder him. A month later, the French leader told an amazed colleague that he no longer had confidence in the British and Americans. From then on, he declared, he would base his policies on Germany and Russia.

For their part, de Gaulle's hated enemies, Winston Churchill and Franklin Roosevelt, were fed up with the pompous French general who was supposed to be an ally. Churchill told the American president that de Gaulle could no longer be trusted. On June 17, 1943, Roosevelt wrote to Churchill: "I am absolutely convinced that [de Gaulle] is injuring our war effort and that he is a very dangerous threat to us."[10]

The Strange Death of Joe Kennedy

IN THE FALL OF 1943, members of a French underground unit, code-named Century, reported on feverish and curious activities near the hamlet of Mimoyecques, a short distance inland from the English Channel port of Calais, the continental city nearest Great Britain. Mimoyecques is only ninety miles, as the crow flies, from London. Century's disclosure sent shock waves through the high councils of the British government.

From the cautious questioning of workers in villages around Mimoyecques, the French underground found that five thousand engineers, technicians, and excavators had been sent to the site to build elaborate underground installations for one of the potentially most incredible weapons of the war—the London Gun.

At first, British intelligence thought the earthworks were connected to long-range missiles, which, it was known, Adolf Hitler was preparing to unleash on England. But other evidence, including that received from the remote Baltic Sea region where the London Gun had been test fired, revealed no doubt that the installations were for London Guns.

Hitler had approved the weapon in July 1943. Consequently, the London Gun project had been given the highest priority in concrete, steel, and skilled manpower. There were to be built and installed along the English Channel coast in France fifty London Guns, each with a barrel 416 feet long (almost an American football field and a half in length). Through the ignition of explosives placed at intervals along the barrel, the weapon would hurl huge shells for a distance of more than one hundred miles.

While grim British intelligence officers kept close watch on the Mimoyecques development, they learned, through French agents, that the subterranean facilities for the fifty London Guns eventually would have concrete and steel roofs eighteen feet thick. Only the ends of the gun muzzles would protrude above ground. As a hedge against Allied bomber fleets, eight-inch-thick steel doors would slide across the muzzles.

One hundred feet below the surface would be a maze of dumps to hold the thousands of tons of shells to be brought in by a special railroad line. Each of the monster weapons would have its own elevator and electrical hoists. When all the London Guns were firing, they could deluge London with shells at the rate of about six hundred per hour.

In November 1943, a U.S. bomber force lifted off from airfields in southeastern England to pound the earthworks at Mimoyecques. Among the participants was Lieutenant Joseph P. Kennedy, Jr., the eldest son of the former ambassador to Great Britain, Joseph Kennedy, Sr. A long-time crony and political supporter of Franklin D. Roosevelt, the senior Kennedy hoped to groom Joe, Jr., for high political office after the war—perhaps one day he would even be president of the United States.

Lieutenant Kennedy's B-24 Liberator bomber was crammed with twenty-two thousand pounds of high explosives. Within seconds of his takeoff, a second Liberator rose into the sky. The plan—grotesque and highly dangerous—called for Kennedy to fly to a point close to the earthworks. Then he and his copilot would bail out—which meant they were likely candidates for capture by the Germans. That left the Kennedy bomber under the radio control of the second Liberator, which would direct the abandoned aircraft to crash into the deep installation at Mimoyecques.

Soon after both Liberators were airborne, something went awry. Kennedy's Liberator blew up with a tremendous roar that could be heard for many miles. None of the remains of Joe Kennedy and his copilot were ever found.

Other bombers, challenged every mile by Luftwaffe fighter planes, plastered the target with conventional explosives, causing such extensive damage that work on one twenty-five-gun battery had to be abandoned. German efforts were then concentrated on the completion of installations for the second battery. However, technical difficulties for the London Gun were never resolved, and a few months later, a delegation of some fifty scientists and engineers who had been working on the project called on Adolf Hitler in Berlin to break the bad news.

Meanwhile, circumstances surrounding the deaths of Lieutenant Joe Kennedy and his copilot remained cloaked in mystery. The cause of the premature explosion of twenty-two thousand pounds of high explosives was never determined by investigators. Or if it had been determined, the results of the inquiry have been kept secret.[11]

A Shining Beacon in Normandy

WHEN NIGHT pulled its cloak over the English Channel on June 5, 1944, the eve of D-Day, U.S. Navy Lieutenant Commander John D. Bulkeley and a swarm of his PT boats were shepherding a flock of nearly one hundred minesweepers toward Utah Beach in Normandy, where elements of the U.S. 4th Infantry Division would storm ashore in about ten hours. Bulkeley's flotilla was the vanguard of Neptune, the assault phase of the invasion.

The slow, ugly duckling minesweepers, the unsung heroes of earlier American invasions around the globe, had to sweep channels clear of mines all the way from the Isle of Wight, off southern England, almost up to the sands of Utah Beach. Similar operations were taking place at the other four Allied landing beaches.

Commander Bulkeley, who had been awarded the Congressional Medal of Honor and a chestful of other top decorations for his exploits in the Philippines during the early months of American involvement in the war, was confronted with a tremendously difficult and hazardous task. Thousands of contact and antenna mines had been sown by the German navy in recent weeks along the central English Channel. If Bulkeley's minesweeping task force were to fail, perhaps scores of the hundreds of vessels that would soon be bearing down on Utah Beach might be blown up, thereby disrupting the entire invasion.

As Bulkeley's spearhead flotilla churned through the dark swells toward Normandy, the commander was both alarmed and mystified to see that the lighthouse at Pointe Barfleur, at the northeastern tip of the Cherbourg

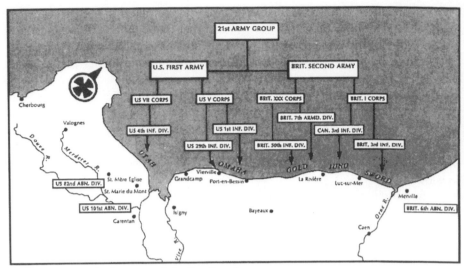

Cross points to the location of the Barfleur beacon.

Peninsula, was shining its powerful light beam. Bulkeley knew that German commanders had long before issued strict orders that troops manning the coastal defenses at night were forbidden to light even a cigarette in the open for fear that the tiny glow might be seen by approaching Allied ships. So why, Bulkeley puzzled, was this beam shining at a time when thousands of Allied ships were crossing the channel? Was the beam a prearranged signal by the Germans to alert the Normandy coast defenders that der Grossinvasion was about to strike? Neither John Bulkeley nor anyone else would ever learn the reason behind this incredible mystery.

All night Bulkeley's PT boats and minesweepers crept up and down the nine-mile length of Utah Beach, exploding mines. Each detonation would trigger a brilliant orange explosion. With dawn and H-Hour for the Utah Beach assault fast approaching, the minesweeping job was completed.

John Bulkeley and others in his task force were confronted by the second tantalizing puzzle of the night. Why hadn't German shore batteries fired a single shell at the minesweepers and PT boats, which were creating a tremendous racket and were sitting ducks perched under the enemy's nose?[12]

Ghost Voice in the Ardennes

HALF-FROZEN MEN of Company B of the U.S. 87th Mortar Battalion, veterans of the D-Day assault at Utah Beach, were holed up in old, wood and stone houses in the hamlet of Sadzot, Belgium, on the northern shoulder of what became known as the Battle of the Bulge. Five days earlier, on December 16,

1944, the outfit had been pulled from the Aachen sector twenty-five miles to the north and rushed to Sadzot, which was directly in the path of German spearheads that were charging toward their initial objective, Liège.

It was an eerie situation in Sadzot. All hell had broken loose throughout Belgium, but the GI mortarmen had been sitting on a powder keg in Sadzot for three days and nights without seeing a sign of a German soldier or hearing a shot fired. Where was the enemy spearhead that was supposed to be coming toward them?

An hour before midnight on December 27, Corporal John Snyder was hunched over his communications radio and heard an alarming report. The wireless set remained "open" at all times and its frequency connected it with the infantry battalion that was being supported by the eight mortars dug in at Sadzot.

"A large formation of Krauts are headed through the woods directly for your village!" the voice on the radio warned.

Captain James J. Marshall, the company commander, alerted the entire unit, whose members rushed to defensive positions along the front of the village. Clutching their weapons in the subzero cold, the GIs waited tensely for the looming German assault. But there was no enemy activity in the thick, pine forests surrounding Sadzot. So, after two hours, the alert was cancelled and those not assigned to outpost duty returned to their old houses and bedded down on the floors.

Back at the company command post, Captain Marshall asked his radio operator who at battalion headquarters had sounded the alert.

"I don't know," young corporal Snyder replied. "The guy simply came on the air and started talking."

An inquiry was made at battalion. No, the call had not come from there. Then where had it come from, Marshall reflected. The radio wavelength connected only the mortar company and the rifle battalion. If the caller had been an American from some other unit, how had he known the radio frequency? How had he been aware that there was a mortar unit in Sadzot? And how had he known that the German force was heading for that particular hamlet?

On the other hand, if the mystery caller had been an English-speaking German, how had he known B Company's wavelength? And would such a person have been likely to warn the Americans that they were about to be struck by a major assault?

Captain Marshall contacted other higher-level headquarters in the region. None of them had made the warning call.

An hour later at about 1:25 A.M., all was tranquil in Sadzot. Most of the mortar company's sixty-five men were sleeping soundly. Suddenly, pandemonium reigned. From out of the forest on three sides of the village charged hordes of wildly yelling figures: foot soldiers of the crack 2nd SS Panzer Division. There was a cacophony of grating noises: explosions, small-arms fire, and bursting grenades. Grabbing their weapons, the GIs dashed outside to do battle against the overwhelming force of an estimated four hundred SS men.

Flames from burning houses cast eerie, dancing shadows. Such was the confusion of the savage nighttime hand-to-hand fight that it was as though all of the combatants on both sides had been dumped into a gigantic tumbler by some supernatural force, then been thoroughly mixed and redeposited at random throughout Sadzot.

The death struggle lasted only about a half hour. Seventeen GIs managed to get out of the village; the remainder of the company was killed, wounded, or captured. Among the survivors was Captain Jim Marshall, who still pondered over the ghost voice. Who had made the call would forever remain a mystery.[13]

Who Concealed Soviet Butchery?

IN THE SUMMER OF 1945, the victorious Allies were drawing up charges of war crimes against leaders of the vanquished Third Reich, including the massacre of 11,000 Polish military officers, government leaders, clergymen, and intellectuals. Piled up twelve deep in seven mass graves near Katyn, six miles west of the Russian city of Smolensk, the victims had been felled by pistol shots in the back of the neck.

Although the grisly discovery of the Polish victims had been made known to the world by the Germans in April 1943, Soviet dictator Josef Stalin promptly blamed the Nazis for the "frightful butchery." President Franklin Roosevelt apparently went along with this Soviet verdict.

News of the mass murder of the Polish leaders touched off widespread indignation in the free world, which, in turn, led the Third Reich to invite twelve prominent forensic experts to visit the Katyn slaughterhouse and to conduct postmortems freely on whichever bodies they chose. With the exception of Professor Naville of the University of Geneva, the experts belonged to occupied or German satellite countries.

After having examined the mummified Polish bodies, their clothing, and the documents found on them, the forensic specialists concluded unanimously that the mass slaughter at Katyn could not have occurred any later than early 1940, at which time the Soviet army had controlled the area.

On the other hand, the Russians claimed that the massacre had been perpetrated during August 1941, just after the German army had overrun the entire Smolensk region. Government leaders and the media in the Allied camp chose to believe the Josef Stalin version and trumpeted it throughout the world.

Shortly after the Katyn discovery in 1943, U.S. Army Colonel John van Vliet and a number of other prisoners of war were taken to the massacre site by the Germans. At that time, the colonel secretly wrote down his observations,

Major General Clayton Bissell allegedly stifled a report blaming the Russians for the murder of 11,000 Poles. Had Roosevelt given him that order? (U.S. Army)

but kept them to himself until his release from German captivity in early May 1945.

Colonel van Vliet's report stated, in part: "The bodies wore winter uniforms. . . . If the Germans had been responsible for the murders, they would have taken place at the time the Germans invaded the Smolensk region [in the hot months of July and August 1944]. . . . I was convinced without any doubt of Soviet guilt."

Major General Clayton Bissell, an honorable officer who headed the United States Information Services, allegedly stifled van Vliet's revealing report, and was said to have ordered the colonel to make no mention to anyone about his observations at the Katyn slaughterhouse.

Had General Bissell, a relatively low-ranking official on the Allied totem-pole of power, taken it upon himself to gag Colonel van Vliet, presumably basing his action on reasons of major national interests about which he was not competent to judge? Or had Bissell been acting under direct orders handed down from on high—from the White House?

Curiously, at the war crimes trials held by the International Military Tribunal at Nuremberg in the months after the war in Europe, all mention of German guilt for the Katyn butchery was dropped.[14]

Part Five

People Who Vanished

The Polish Genius

SYDNEY COTTON, a squadron leader in the British Royal Air Force, was winging across the English Channel, bound for Orly airfield in Paris. His Lockheed 12-A was being escorted by four Spitfires, for Luftwaffe fighter planes were marauding the skies over the channel and France. Cotton may not have been privy to the secret, but he was on one of the most significant intelligence missions of World War II. It was May 18, 1940.

Nine days earlier, Adolf Hitler's legions had poured across the French border and spearheads were racing toward Paris. Now, anxiously awaiting Cotton's arrival at Orly was a mystery man, Richard Lewinski, a Jewish refugee from Poland, and his wife.

Cotton reached Orly, taxied to a side terminal where Lewinski (not his real name) and his wife were huddled. The couple climbed aboard and minutes later, the Lockheed was racing through the clear, blue sky for London.

A month later, on June 21, Adolf Hitler delivered his armistice terms to the French in a railroad car at the Forêt de Compiègne—the same car in which Germany had surrendered twenty-two years earlier in World War I.

The Lewinski scenario had its origins in 1938, when Major Francis Foley, a British secret agent stationed in Berlin, learned that the rapidly expanding German army was using a revolutionary cipher machine code-named Enigma. Further probing by the British disclosed that Enigma was actually the invention of a Dutch citizen, Hugo Koch, who had patented a Geheimschrij-machine (secret-writing machine) at The Hague in 1919. Koch had hoped to build the machine and market it to corporations but did not have the finances to achieve his goal. So he sold the patents to Artur Scherbius, a German engineer in Berlin. Using Koch's plans, Scherbius built a cipher machine and called it Enigma.

Scherbius's commercial venture fell flat on its face, so he sold his Enigma patents to another German company. Adolf Hitler was by now rapidly rearming the Third Reich, so his generals and admirals were searching laboratories for some sort of new cipher machine with which to protect their secrets and plans for war in Europe. The military leaders took control of Enigma.

Under the Wehrmacht's chief signals officer, Colonel Erich Fellgiebel, experiments were begun on Enigma—and the German high command was delighted. The machine was inexpensive to manufacture, compact, portable,

German Enigma encoding machine. (National Archives)

sturdy, and simple to operate. Most of all, Enigma was pronounced secure from even the most advanced cryptanalytical probing by an enemy.

But what if an Enigma is captured by the enemy, the Nazi leaders wanted to know. Colonel Fellgiebel explained that an Enigma in the hands of an enemy would be quite useless, for he would have to know the keying procedure, which would be changed almost daily.

Meanwhile, Major Harold L. Gibson, the British MI-6 (counterintelligence) agent posted in Prague, Czechoslovakia, learned that Polish intelligence, which was collaborating with MI-6 in spying on the Germans and the Russians, had acquired the commercial version of Enigma. Leading Polish mathematicians had resolved some of the mathematical problems involved in deciphering its transmission messages. However, the Polish experiments had penetrated only Enigma's mathematical problems, not mechanical ones.

In June 1938, Stewart Graham Menzies, a World War I battlefield hero and the number two man at MI-6, received another startling message from Major Gibson in Prague. Gibson reported that he had just returned from Warsaw, where he had encountered a Pole named Richard Lewinski, who had worked as an engineer and mathematician at the Berlin factory where Enigma was manufactured. Lewinski had returned to Warsaw after being expelled from Germany because of his religion.

On a dark street corner in Warsaw at about 9:00 P.M., Lewinski had met Gibson and had offered to sell his knowledge of Enigma: His price was ten thousand pounds sterling (about fifty thousand U.S. dollars at the time), plus a resident's permit for France for himself and his wife. The Pole claimed he had sufficient knowledge about Enigma to draw exact diagrams of the guts of the machine and to build a precise replica.

Back in London, Stewart Menzies was highly elated—and suspicious. Why would the Nazis allow an engineer with such intimate knowledge of a top-secret military item to leave the Third Reich? Was Lewinski and his proposal a German ploy to lead British intelligence down an endless path, while Nazi scientists continued to refine Enigma without having to worry about enemy surveillance?

Menzies brought in some of Britain's top cryptanalysts, and they examined a batch of technical data that Lewinski had drawn and which had been shuttled to London by Major Gibson. The experts told Menzies the data appeared to be genuine.

With war clouds gathering over Europe, Menzies dispatched two British experts to Warsaw to interview Lewinski. They were Alfred Dilwyn Knox, who was regarded as England's foremost cryptanalyst, and Alan Mathison Turing, a young man with a reputation as a genius in mathematical logistics. Both men were as eccentric as they were brilliant.

Forty-eight hours after leaving London, Knox and Turing made secret contact with Richard Lewinski, a thin, black-haired man in his early forties. As the trio strolled aimlessly around Warsaw, the British experts probed Lewinski with questions about Enigma, particularly about its keying procedures. It was clear that Lewinski had the answers to these highly complicated technical questions.

Knox and Turing returned to London and recommended to Menzies that Lewinski's proposal be accepted. So Major Gibson spirited the Pole and his wife out of Warsaw and escorted them to Paris, where they were placed under the charge of the resident MI-6 agent, Navy Commander Wilfred Dunderdale.

Under Dunderdale's supervision, Lewinski began to build an Enigma, working covertly in a modest apartment and guarded by MI-6 men in civilian clothes. Within months, the Pole had recreated Enigma, a machine about eighteen inches high and twenty-four inches square, which sat in a wooden boxlike enclosure. Previously, enciphering had been a slow and tedious task, done by human hand. But with Enigma, one could produce an infinite number of different cipher alphabets merely by changing the keying procedures.

This was the same Enigma, the ultimate secret-writing machine, that the German army, navy, and air force had adopted for enciphering messages from the high command down through the ranks. Adolf Hitler had been advised that the Enigma code was unbreakable. But unbeknown to the führer, the Poles and the French had penetrated Enigma's ciphers, and the British had obtained a duplicate of the machine. Adolf Hitler's blind trust in the "unbreakable" Enigma ciphers would play an enormous role in Allied victory in the war that was looming on the horizon.

On May 18, 1940, after building the duplicate Enigma and with war raging in western Europe, Richard Lewinski and his wife reached London from Paris in Squadron Leader Cotton's plane and were assigned a comfortable apartment and a police guard. A few days later, Lewinski vanished.

Intense investigation revealed that the Pole had made no effort to contact the Polish embassy in London nor any of the numerous Poles who were in exile in the British capital. How had he managed to disappear without a trace?

His around-the-clock police guard was to have both protected him and kept him from eluding British surveillance. Why, then, did none of the guards have any knowledge of the circumstances surrounding his disappearance? How had the genius slipped out of the apartment without being seen? Could a Nazi agent have learned of Lewinski's presence in London and murdered him? If so, where was the corpse?

Lewinski had no British passport, spoke hardly any English, and had never been in London before. How could he have fled the island on an air or sea commercial conveyance with those handicaps?

No doubt the baffling Richard Lewinski affair will forever remain an enigma.[1]

The Mysterious Countess

CAPTAIN HERBERT WICHMANN, a low-key, cunning, and dedicated navy officer, was in charge of the Hamburg post of the Abwehr, Germany's secret service agency. His job was to sneak spies and saboteurs into England, then receive and analyze their reports, usually sent back by radio. Wichmann possessed a key trait for a successful spymaster: an intense passion for anonymity.

In September 1940, Wichmann dispatched a three-person espionage team led by thirty-four-year-old Theo Druecke, a sophisticated intellectual and the son of a prominent Berlin lawyer. With him were a shadowy character named Waelti and a mystery-shrouded, well-proportioned woman known variously to her Abwehr associates as Vera, Viola, and the Countess.

Even Wichmann did not know the woman's family name, but he did know that she had been involved periodically in the world's oldest profession. Actually, the Countess was Vera de Witte, the daughter of a White Russian naval officer who had been killed while fighting the Bolsheviks.[2]

Bright, vivacious, and beautiful, the Countess was considered by Wichmann to possess the necessary qualities to become one of his ace operatives.

He expected big things from her once she merged into England's population and began radioing intelligence back to Hamburg.

The Countess and her partners (Theo Druecke was also her current lover) climbed aboard a seaplane at Stavenger, Norway, on September 30, and flew to a point off Banff in Scotland. They transferred to a rubber dinghy and paddled ashore. Reaching land, the Countess and her boyfriend Druecke went in one direction, Waelti in another.

When the two lovers tried to buy tickets to London at a small railroad station, the clerk grew suspicious and telephoned the constabulary. Minutes later, the police arrived and arrested the Countess and Druecke. A search of Druecke's suitcase revealed a German Mauser pistol, a cardboard-disk coding device, a list of Royal Air Force bases in southeastern England (his destination), and an Afu radio set.

Meanwhile in Edinburgh, Waelti had gone to a movie theater while waiting for the train that would carry him to London. Earlier, a clerk at the station where Waelti had stored his suitcase had become suspicious and called the police. The spy's luggage was opened and was found to be filled with espionage apparatus. When he returned, the police arrested him.

Druecke and Waelti were hanged at a British prison—unmourned by either side. The Countess became a mystery woman. Although she was as guilty as her two companions and had been caught red-handed, she avoided the gallows. Even though in British custody, she eventually disappeared, never to be heard from again.[2]

A Propagandist's Blunder

OVER ONE of Germany's powerful Zeesen transmitters, in February 1942, a plump, middle-aged, American-born (Atlanta, Georgia) woman named Jane Anderson began broadcasting four times each week. She was one of propaganda minister Josef Goebbels's prize tub-thumpers, and her pro-Nazi harangues were targeted at the shortwave radio audience in the United States.

Jane Anderson was shrouded in mystery. She had once been a respected journalist, and during World War I had written about the conflict for the London *Daily Express* and *Daily Mail*. In 1938, she was a correspondent reporting on the Spanish civil war, and in the United States was hailed by some as "a great champion in the fight against Communism."

Anderson (then married to the Marquis Alvarez de Cienfuegos) had been accused of spying for the anti-Communist Francisco Franco and had been pitched into a Spanish jail for six weeks by rebel forces. She was released through the intervention of the U.S. government. How she got to Germany remains a mystery.

Suddenly, she surfaced on Goebbels's radio broadcasts, working against her own country. In March 1942, Anderson was setting her United States audience straight on the reported German food shortages by describing her visit to a Berlin cocktail bar: "On silver platters were sweets and cookies, a delicacy I am very fond of. My friend ordered great goblets full of champagne, into which he put shots of cognac to make it more lively. Sweets, cookies, and champagne! Not bad!"

British propaganda experts rubbed their hands in glee. Her bacchanalian bombast was translated into German and radioed back to Germany, where the Herrenvolk had begun to feel food pinches and most knew champagne only as a vague memory.

The impact of the turnaround broadcast was considerable, British agents in Germany reported. People were furious that some privileged persons, such as Anderson and Nazi leaders, were gorging themselves while the plain people were scrounging.

Anderson, American turncoat, was never heard over the German radio again. She simply vanished.[3]

The *Lady Be Good*

A FIREBALL SUN had been beating down on northeast Libya on the Mediterranean coast of North Africa on April 4, 1943, when a four-engine B-24 Liberator piloted by Lieutenant William J. Hatton lifted off from an airstrip near Benghazi. On the Liberator's nose was painted "Lady Be Good," a name selected by Hatton and his eight crew members who were on their first combat mission.

Lady Be Good was one of twenty-five U.S. bombers involved in a strike on enemy airfields around Naples, Italy, some 750 miles to the north. Takeoff had been scheduled for 1:30 P.M., so that the bombers would arrive over the target region about dusk and would make the return flight across the Mediterranean at night, which would provide a cover against any pursuing Luftwaffe fighter planes.

Eleven bombers had blasted the primary targets, and the remainder had hit the secondary targets. Although some planes had received flak damage and others had developed engine trouble, all of the bombers had returned safely back to their home base—except for the *Lady Be Good*.

Just past midnight, the airfield's control tower received a radio call from the *Lady Be Good*. Lieutenant Hatton reported that he was unable to find the base because of the dense cloud that had blanketed the North African coast. He added that he was growing concerned about his low fuel supply, and asked for a radio fix so that he could home in on the airfield.

Hatton was given the fix—but dawn came and the *Lady Be Good* never returned. A search over the Mediterranean was launched but there was no sign of the missing bomber. Presumably, the plane crashed and its crew perished at sea.

"X" marks the crash site of the Lady Be Good. *The arrow indicates the location of the U.S. air base.*

In 1959, more than sixteen years later, an oil survey team reported to the U.S. Air Force's Wheelus Field, Libya, that it had sighted the wreckage of a large World War II airplane some 440 miles south of Benghazi, deep in the torrid wasteland of the Libyan Desert.

A C-47 transport plane carrying an air force search crew was dispatched from Wheelus, and it landed near the wreckage. The investigators promptly identified it as a Liberator. They were amazed by the sight that greeted their eyes. The torrid desert air had preserved the airplane. It was as though the Liberator had been plucked out of a timeless void and had been placed there that same day.

Expecting to find the ghastly skeletons of crew members, the investigators peered inside the fuselage. There were no skeletons. Climbing inside, the search team tested the radio receiver and, remarkably, found that it was in working order. Vacuum flasks had warm coffee, still drinkable.

A daunting question puzzled the investigators: The *Lady Be Good* had no battle damage; what was it doing in the desert, hundreds of miles from where it should have been? And what had become of the crew members?

Piecing together the puzzle of the flight of the *Lady Be Good*, the Air Force investigators concluded that when Lieutenant Hatton had called for a radio fix, the control tower had placed the bomber northwest of its home base, out over the Mediterranean, and all the pilot had had to do was to compensate for wind speed, velocity, and magnetic variation to bring the *Lady Be Good* over the air base. Then it could have been "talked down" through the thick clouds to a safe landing on the airfield runway.

Direction-finding equipment was relatively primitive in 1943, so the control tower apparently had been unaware that the *Lady Be Good* was already southeast of its airfield when the radio fix was sent. Consequently, Hatton kept flying ever deeper into the desolate Libyan Desert.

More than four hundred miles southeast of Benghazi, Hatton must have realized his fuel was virtually exhausted. Crash-landing in the darkness would have been suicidal. So he presumably had ordered all crew members to bail out.

Many months after the original discovery in 1959, the Air Force conducted a land search for any clue as to the fate of the crew members. Covering many miles around the crash site, the searchers found bits and pieces of discarded clothing and an ammunition clip from a .45-caliber pistol. No skeletons or other signs of the *Lady Be Good*'s crew have ever been detected.[4]

A General's Final Mission

ON HIS BLACKED-OUT COMMAND SHIP lying off southern Sicily on the night of July 8–9, 1943, Lieutenant General George S. Patton, Jr., was grim-faced, trying to conceal his deep concern over the fate of Colonel James M. Gavin's 505th Parachute Infantry Regiment. A component of the U.S. 82nd Airborne Division, Gavin's outfit had spearheaded Operation Husky, the Anglo-American invasion of Axis-held Sicily, earlier that night by jumping inland behind enemy coastal defenses. Since then, no word had been heard from the parachutists.

Patton need not have been unduly worried. Gale force winds, enemy gunfire, and the inexperience of C-47 pilots had resulted in Gavin's 3,406 men being scattered helter-skelter along a sixty-mile stretch of coastline. Undaunted, the paratroopers, faces blackened with charcoal, alone and in tiny groups, had begun stalking through the darkness, raising merry hell with unsuspecting German and Italian soldiers and installations.

On the morning of July 11 — D-Day Plus 1 — Brigadier General Charles L. "Bull" Keerans, assistant commander of the 82nd Airborne, who was in Tunisia, North Africa, across the Mediterranean from Sicily, received a coded message: "Mackall tonight. Wear white pajamas." It meant that the 82nd Airborne's other parachute regiment, Colonel Reuben H. Tucker's 504th, was to make a routine reinforcement jump that night on Farello, a Sicilian airfield three miles east of Gela, where amphibious troops had stormed ashore on D-Day. Farello was already in American hands.

General Keerans, who had been a daredevil motorcycle rider in his youth, had been ordered to remain behind in Tunisia to supervise the movement of 82nd Airborne men and supplies to Sicily. But then he succumbed to an overpowering urge to participate in the first major U.S. parachute operation.

The Bull, as the troopers called him, would ride in a C-47 copiloted by Lieutenant Ray O. Rousch. Since the reinforcement flight was regarded as a "milk run," the general expected to be back in Tunisia before dawn. Neither Keerans nor any others in the shuttle operation read any danger into the fact that the sky armada carrying the 504th Regiment to Farello would have to fly over hundreds of American ships lying off Sicily and a thirty-five-mile stretch of American-held beachhead—in the blackness of night.

Late on the night of July 11, an eerie silence blanketed the American beachhead and the Gulf of Gela. Junker bombers had just flown away after pounding the region for the fourth time that day. Tension was thick. Ears were cocked for the sound of approaching Luftwaffe planes. Jittery fingers were on triggers.

At 10:32 P.M., on the heels of the departing German bombers, the first flight of C-47s carrying Rube Tucker's combat team knifed over the coast on target, near Cape Passero, turned northwest and flew for thirty-five miles over the bridgehead to the drop zone at Farello. There the first paratroopers bailed out and landed routinely.

Just as the second serial winged over the shore at about seven-hundred feet, a lone American machine-gun spit a stream of tracers skyward. Almost immediately, a second gun followed suit. Then another. And another. Soon, a wide sweep of the Gela coast was aglow with a kaleidoscope of color: yellow flares, geometric patterns of red tracers, and black puffs of exploding antiaircraft shells. Directly into this hailstorm of "friendly fire" the C-47s flew.

Some planes, with troopers and aircrews still inside, burst into flames and plummeted crazily to earth. Other aircraft received direct hits, exploding in midair. Like a covey of quail suddenly fired on by concealed hunters, the sky armada scattered.

Some troopers, their C-47s ablaze, leaped without their static lines hooked up, and they plunged to their deaths. Others, their parachutes already hooked to static lines, bailed out pell-mell and descended into sectors held by American troops. Nervous ground soldiers thought the dark figures were German paratroopers and shot them in midair or after they had landed and were struggling to get out of their harnesses.

At Farello airfield General George Patton had joined Major General Matthew B. Ridgway, the 82nd Airborne commander, to greet the parachutists. The two men stood side by side and looked on in shocked disbelief as plane after plane tumbled out of the sky like fiery torches. Two of the United States Army's toughest generals were nearly overcome with grief and frustration, powerless to intervene.

"My God! My God!" Patton muttered repeatedly.

In the firestorm of friendly fire over southern Sicily, the C-47 carrying General Bull Keerans was rocked by shell explosions, and tracers ripped through the floor. Sergeant Ray Butler, the radio operator, reflected: "God, this is it!"

Suddenly, Sergeant Fielding Armstrong, the crew chief, called out: "The port engine's on fire!" Skillfully handling the controls of the disabled craft, Lieutenant John Gibson ditched about four hundred yards offshore.

Sergeant Butler edged along to the back of the dark cabin and could discern limp bodies draped over the bucket seats. Concluding that the paratroopers were beyond help, Butler scrambled out of the partially submerged door. Frightened because he could not swim, the airman grabbed onto a piece of floating debris and tried to paddle toward shore, but the current kept pushing him back under the tail section. In extricating himself, Butler gulped down a mixture of salt water, gasoline, and oil.

Now, American machine-gunners on shore opened fire on the barely floating plane and the men floundering in the water. Butler saw a couple of heads go under. Finally he and a few paratroopers crawled, exhausted and gasping, onto the beach. Moments later, the same machine gun sent bursts of fire at the little knot of soaked survivors.

In the skies over Gela and Scogletti, eighty-one paratroopers were killed, sixteen were missing and presumed dead, and one hundred thirty-two were wounded. Brigadier General Hal Clark's troop carriers had suffered sixty men killed and thirty wounded. Twenty-three airplanes had been shot down and many others had been badly damaged but limped back to Tunisia. It had been one of the great disasters in American military history.

Shortly after dawn, Sergeant Armstrong was traipsing along the shore looking for survivors of his ditched craft. Soon, he ran into Keerans, who, although dishevelled from the dunking in the Mediterranean, appeared to be in good shape. The general chatted briefly, said that he had swum ashore, greeted a few passersby that he knew, said he was "going inland" and walked away.

Then, Bull Keerans vanished. Later, he was officially listed as "missing in action." Headquarters down to battalion level all over Sicily were contacted, but none had seen the one-star general. Graves registration units, whose grim task was to pick up corpses from the battlefield once the violence had moved on, had no knowledge of having handled Keerans's remains.

Nearly two years later, when prisoner of war camps in the Third Reich were being overrun by American and British forces, word was flashed to be on the lookout for a brigadier general. This search proved to be in vain.

Keerans is the only American general in the war whose whereabouts and fate remain unknown.[5]

Churchill's Kin Freddy

PARIS'S 4 MILLION RESIDENTS, under the Nazi jackboot for nearly four years, were both excited and fearful. It appeared that the German Soldaten were pulling out of the sprawling, once beautiful, French capital, and rumors were rampant that Allied forces were knocking at the gates of the city. It was August 25, 1944.

Late that morning, Major General Jacques LeClerc's French 2nd Armored Division slammed into Paris from the west and Major General Raymond O. Barton's U.S. 4th "Ivy" Infantry Division, veterans of the D-Day assault at Utah Beach, charged into the city from the south.

Parisians went wild with joy. Throngs poured into the streets to welcome the American and French liberators. Among those cheering were twenty-seven-year-old Jacqueline Marguerite Princess de Broglie, scion of the Singer Sewing Machine fortune and a leading light in the European society scene before the war, and her husband, a handsome, dashing thirty-year-old Austrian named Alfred Kraus.

Jacqueline's mother, the sewing-machine king's granddaughter, Marguerite, was widowed in 1918, the same year that Princess de Broglie was born. The mother then wed a wealthy British banker, Reginald Fellowes, and she spent years commuting between her palace on the Seine near Paris, her spacious villa on the Riviera, and Donnington Hall in Britain, once the home of Beau Brummel.

In the 1930s, Marguerite Fellowes de Broglie Ducasez had been proclaimed the world's best-dressed woman and the foremost hostess of her era. Her cousin, Winston Churchill, had gone yachting several times aboard her 260-foot luxury ship, *Sister Anne*.

When the German army marched into Paris in mid-1940, daughter Jacqueline, the princess, was stranded in the city. Almost at once she had a new set of guests at parties in her ornate Paris town house and elegant château in the countryside—impeccably groomed German army officers whose boots were shined to a high gloss. Jacqueline met her new Teutonic friends through Freddy Kraus, who was one of her numerous beaux at the time. Lighthearted and witty, Kraus posed as an Austrian aristocrat of great wealth. Actually, he had been born into poverty to an Austrian father and a Hungarian mother.

Jacqueline's seeming coziness with the hated Boche (Germans) drew angry outbursts from patriotic Parisians. But they did not know that she had made contact with the British secret service and was providing it intelligence picked up from German officers at her parties and worked in the French underground.

Meanwhile, Jacqueline's role in the Resistance came to the attention of Lieutenant Colonel Hermann Giskes, a cagey Abwehr official in Paris. Giskes promptly sensed an opportunity to infiltrate the princess's underground network and wipe it out. For her boyfriend, avowed anti-Nazi Freddy Kraus, had long been one of Giskes's Abwehr agents.

Giskes encouraged Freddy to deepen his relationship with Jacqueline and try to worm his way into her confidence. A few weeks later, in early 1941, much to the astonishment of what remained of French society, the princess wed the dashing Freddy. France's upper crust considered the playboy to be far below her station.

After Paris was liberated in August 1944 and Hermann Giskes fled eastward with the retreating Wehrmacht, Freddy, as charming and loquacious as ever, began cultivating Allied officers who replaced the departed Germans at the couple's gala parties. Curiously, Kraus began dashing about Paris wearing the uniform of a British army captain.

Meanwhile, the aging but still attractive dowager, Mrs. Fellowes, who had spent the war in London's posh Dorchester Hotel, managed to contact her daughter, Princess Jacqueline, and was stunned to hear that she had married an Austrian. However, she invited both of them to visit her in England, and allegedly intervened with her cousin Winston (Churchill) to smooth the way for her daughter and son-in-law to enter England.

By secret communication, Freddy Kraus advised Giskes, who apparently was in Holland at the time of the couple's planned trip across the channel. Giskes was delighted: Here was a golden opportunity to infiltrate an agent right into the Winston Churchill family.

Princess Jacqueline became ill and could not make the trip. So Freddy convinced her that he should go alone. Wearing his British captain's uniform, he crossed the channel by ship. In London, Mrs. Fellowes greeted her son-in-law with open arms, and at the first opportunity, introduced him to Winston Churchill and his wife at Chartwell, the couple's country estate. Charming Freddy was lionized in London social circles: a French underground warrior, a wealthy Austrian, a decorated British army captain, husband of a continental society luminary.

When the war ended in May 1945, Kraus was still in England; his wife, the princess, had remained in Paris with the couple's three-year-old daughter. Soon British intelligence in France began picking up clues indicating that Freddy had betrayed a number of Resistance men and women to the Gestapo.

Prime Minister Churchill reputedly was informed of the serious evidence accruing against the husband of his second cousin, and he agreed that Kraus should be detained pending the clarification of his situation. So Kraus was taken to Ham Common, a prison used by the British secret service. There Freddy vehemently denied any wrongdoing.

Then one day in early June 1945—about a month after Victory in Europe Day had been proclaimed—a long black limousine, its blinds drawn, whisked Freddy away from Ham Common. He vanished. In the euphoric mood of the British people at war's end, few, if any, citizens cared about the mysterious fate of Winston Churchill's kin by marriage. No one has ever answered the puzzling question: What really became of Alfred Ignatz Maria Kraus?[6]

Into the "Devil's Triangle"

ON THE MORNING of October 21, 1944, a U.S. Navy blimp patrolling about thirty miles off the coast of Florida sighted the cargo ship *Rubicon* drifting aimlessly. The *Rubicon*, it would be learned, had sailed from Havana, Cuba, a

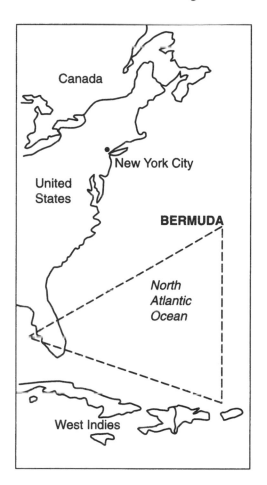

The Devil's Triangle, graveyard for many airplanes and ships.

day earlier, bound for New York City with a load of raw materials for U.S. war production.

The blimp's crewmen had radioed the Coast Guard in Miami and two boats were sent to investigate the drifting cargo vessel. It was in an area of ocean off the southeastern coast of Florida known as the Bermuda Triangle, or the Devil's Triangle. Since 1854, more than fifty ships and aircraft had vanished in or near the area.

Most of these ships and airplanes had disappeared under mysterious circumstances. Only a few captains or pilots had radioed distress messages. Searchers seldom found bodies or bits of wreckage. Some scientists believe that violent, unexpected storms or downward air currents destroyed the ships and planes. None could explain why these natural phenomena occurred in that particular locale.

Be that as it may, Coast Guard members were not prepared for what they discovered when they reached the *Rubicon*. The drifting ship, far from having been battered by "violent, unexpected storms," was totally seaworthy and in excellent condition.

Much to the astonishment of the Coast Guardsmen, there were no human beings on board. The only living creature on the *Rubicon* was a dog of undetermined ancestry. There was evidence that a meal had just begun.

Eighteen hours after her discovery, the *Rubicon* was towed into a Florida port. No indication of the fate of the vessel's crew was found in a study of the ship's log.[7]

Search for a German General

IN THE SPRING OF 1945, while Allied armies were overrunning Germany, British counterintelligence officers launched an extensive search for SS General Hans Kammler, who had been in charge of the mammoth V-2 rocket assault that had inflicted widespread death and destruction on London and other cities during the previous eight months. Word was out that the British wanted to give Kammler "a fair trial and a hanging."

The Hans Kammler affair had begun on August 22, 1943, at Wolfsschanze, Adolf Hitler's battle headquarters nestled in a thick forest behind the Russian front in Prussia, where a solemn führer was discussing a recent disaster at Peenemünde, the Third Reich's top-secret rocket research center on the Baltic Sea. Two nights earlier, a force of nearly 525 British bombers had nearly wiped out the key facility, killing a few scientists and engineers in the process.

Among those present at the führer's conference were Dr. Albert Speer, minister of war production; Reichsführer Heinrich Himmler, chief of the elite SS and the Gestapo; and Himmler's protègé, forty-year-old Brigadeführer (SS Brigadier General) Hans Kammler, a scientist who had the traits his boss demanded—a keen brain and a total lack of scruples.

Heinrich Himmler, forever lusting for greater personal power, had a proposal for the führer: The missile-development program, which was under the direction of the Heer (army), had been threatened because someone had betrayed Peenemünde to the British; therefore, the entire rocket organization—research, development, production, and firing—should be put in his (Himmler's) hands.

Just before dawn, which was the führer's customary time to go to bed after all-night rounds of conferences, Hitler reached a crucial decision: Reichsführer Himmler would be put in charge of the rocket program on which Hitler was banking to alter the course of the war and to bring victory to the Third Reich.

As soon as the new power was in his hands, Himmler promoted the ambitious Dr. Hans Kammler to SS major general and gave him direct control of the entire missile project, from research to firing. Kammler's new title was special commissioner.

"[Kammler's] directions are to be obeyed without question," Himmler's order declared.

One month later, in September 1943, the Harz Mountains of central Germany had become a beehive of activity under the guidance of Hans Kammler, an architect by profession. V-2 missiles, which had been researched and developed at Peenemünde, would be mass-produced there in what would become the largest underground factory in the world. Already the initial target of these huge (sixty feet long) rockets was known in the German high command—London.

On January 2, 1944, the underground factory shipped out the first three long-range missiles, whose speed was so enormous there would be no defense against them. General Kammler hatched a scheme to make his V-2 launching sites nearly invulnerable to Allied bombing attacks. The missiles would be fired by mobile batteries from the heart of Holland urban centers, mainly The Hague. If the Allies carpet bombed the V-2 launching site (in the hope that an occasional bomb might hit the intended target), they would massacre thousands of Dutch civilians.

What's more, there would be no military target for Allied bombers to hit. Once a mobile V-2 battery had fired all of its missiles, which would take less than a half hour, it would pack up and move to another locale for the next firing.

By early September 1944, Hans Kammler was ready for the signal to commence raining death and destruction on London, two hundred miles from Holland. The rocket would require about six minutes from liftoff to soar to a height of about fifty miles before plunging earthward.

At 6:48 P.M. on September 8, an enormous blast rocked suburban London. It sounded like a thunderclap, but the sky was blue and cloudless. So speedy was the V-2—it traveled faster than sound—that the explosion was heard first and then the rustling sound of the missile's approach.

Almost incessantly for six months, V-2s exploded on London. The final missile crashed into the teeming metropolis on March 27, 1945, killing 127 civilians and wounding 423. Altogether in the German aerial bombardment (including V-1s—robot bombs—and V-2s), 1.5 million houses were destroyed or damaged, 6,200 people were killed, and 18,000 were seriously injured.

In April 1945, Allied investigators got word that Hans Kammler was holed up in a large house near Garmisch-Partenkirchen, where the 1936 winter Olympic games had been held. They rushed to the site, but Kammler was nowhere to be found. German civilians in the neighborhood were questioned, but they professed that they knew nothing about a General Kammler.

Meanwhile, in the closing days of the war, the Americans launched Operation Hermes, a widespread search for the rocket geniuses who had developed the V-2 at Peenemünde. Eventually, some 350 engineers and technicians were rounded up (most of whom were soon invited to come to the United

States to continue with their rocket research). Although Kammler had been in overall command, none of the rocket men knew of his whereabouts.

In the weeks that followed, those operating scores of Allied POW camps in western Germany were asked to be on the lookout for a man answering Kammler's description. British investigators kept a watch on his hometown. Soviet authorities were contacted and asked to turn over Kammler in the event the Russians captured him.

As time went by, the ardor for finding Kammler began to cool in Great Britain, especially after a few reports in the world's press that said, in essence, if the British tried the German general for his role in bombarding London with rockets, British and American air generals would also have to be tried for the gigantic aerial bombing of cities in the Third Reich.

In any event, Hans Kammler has never been found—not even a clue has been uncovered as to his fate. He may have been the only German general engaged against the Anglo-Americans who had disappeared without a trace.[8]

Bormann: The Führer's Watchdog

REVENGE-BENT RUSSIAN TROOPS were swarming all over the ruins of Berlin, once a proud and beautiful capital, now a mass of rubble. On April 30, 1945, the leading Soviet tanks were two blocks from the Reich Chancellery, a massive, once magnificent structure that Adolf Hitler had built years earlier as the seat of power for Gross Deutschland (greater Germany).

Huddled in the Führerbunker under the chancellery were Hitler, a dim shadow of his once vibrant self; his mistress, Eva Braun; Propaganda Minister Paul Josef Goebbels and his family; Martin Bormann, whose bland title of secretary to the führer belied his enormous clout in the Third Reich; and a bevy of generals and Nazi Party functionaries.

Martin Bormann, pudgy, bullish, unscrupulous, and highly ambitious, was loathed and feared by almost everyone in the führer's inner circle, including Bormann's brother Alfred, who was one of Hitler's personal adjutants. While other Nazi nabobs—Hermann Goering, Heinrich Himmler, Josef Goebbels, among others—were fond of strutting about with the trappings of power, Martin Bormann operated almost silently behind the scenes in the shadows.

However, Bormann knew where the real power lay. He placed his own desk in an anteroom to the führer's office so that he controlled access to Hitler. This arrangement infuriated the high rollers of officialdom. Even such luminaries as Reischsmarschall Goering complained bitterly that it was often difficult, sometimes impossible, to see Hitler unless the führer's watchdog gave his prior approval.

Bormann, during the two years he had been in his key post, also had connived an arrangement whereby he would personally process all papers of a nonmilitary nature before they reached the führer's desk. This meant that he was

Reichsleiter Martin Bormann. (National Archives)

privy to nearly everything going on in the Reich and its various agencies. And Bormann could keep the führer from seeing certain papers if the watchdog so chose for whatever reason.

Martin Bormann also schemed to place in his hands another source of tremendous personal power—the Friends of the Führer Fund, to which industrialists and other wealthy Germans contributed "voluntarily." However, it wasn't likely that anyone would decline to kick in money and therefore, by inference, be labeled as an enemy of the führer. Since Adolf Hitler didn't like to be bothered by money matters, Bormann had at his disposal a huge slush fund with which he could bribe Nazi officials or anyone else without accounting to the führer for the expenditures.

So dependent on Bormann had the führer become that he, Bormann, even handled Hitler's personal finances. This resulted in a tricky situation whereby Eva Braun, the führer's girlfriend, had to cozy up to Bormann, whom she loathed, and beg him for pocket money.

Eva made no pretenses of her fervent dislike of Bormann. She told the führer, a nonsmoker and teetotaler, of Bormann's pretending to have those same traits, although, she pointed out huffily, he was a chain smoker, a heavy boozer, and "the girls all tell me he is an oversexed toad." Hitler merely shrugged. Martin Bormann was vital in the führer's scheme of things.

Now, on the night of April 30, the Black Angel of Death was hovering over the Führerbunker. With the crash of Russian artillery shells plainly heard only a short distance up the street, Adolf Hitler put a Luger pistol to his own head and squeezed the trigger. Eva Braun took poison and was dead within three minutes.

Acting in accordance with strict orders the führer had given prior to his lethal act, a few faithful SS men carried the two corpses outside the bunker, poured gasoline over them, set them ablaze, gave the Nazi salute over the flaming remains, and returned to the bunker.

Inside the bombproof shelter, Josef Goebbels, who had been at Hitler's side for two decades, poisoned his six young children, killed his beautiful wife Magda with a shot from a Luger, and then turned the weapon upon himself.

Meanwhile in the bunker, Martin Bormann was not being nearly as Führertreu (faithful to the führer) as had been Josef Goebbels. Bormann had no intention of joining the suicide rituals. With the Russians closing in on the bunker, he plotted to escape from Berlin. General Hans Baur, the führer's personal pilot, was also ensconced in the bunker. In preceding days, Bormann had talked at length with young Baur, who, it developed, had a plan for evacuating Hitler.

At an airport a short distance from Berlin, Baur had a hot new aircraft, a Junker-390, filled with gasoline and on standby. Although still in the prototype stage, a Luftwaffe pilot, two months earlier, had flown the speedy, ultramodern transport nonstop from Berlin to Japan over the polar route. So Baur was convinced that he could wing the führer to some distant locale, such as Manchukuo, almost halfway around the planet.

Twenty-four hours after Adolf Hitler's death, the denizens of the Führerbunker, in small groups, stole away into the night at twenty-minute intervals. In Martin Bormann's band was Hans Baur, Hitler's pilot. Presumably, Bormann had substituted himself for the führer in the planned escape flight to Manchukuo. Bormann was now the highest Nazi Party official in the new Reich government that Hitler had spelled out on paper before his death. The führer had bestowed upon Bormann the exalted title of Reichsleiter (German leader).

In the blackness, confusion, and fighting that was still raging on all sides, Martin Bormann became separated from Hans Baur and the others in his group. There would later be vague reports from those who said they saw the Reichsleiter "blown up" or riding on a Tiger tank that was engaged in a shootout with a Soviet tank.

Whatever may have been the case, Martin Bormann vanished. When the Soviets overran Berlin, the Reichsleiter was nowhere to be found.

In the American and British camps, it was presumed that Bormann was in Soviet hands. During the closing months of the war, intelligence officers at General Dwight Eisenhower's headquarters had become convinced that the shifty Bormann, without the führer's knowledge, had adopted a "foreign policy" of his own—he had secretly climbed into bed with the Russians and was, in essence, a Soviet spy at the highest level of the Nazi government.

General Richard Gehlen, head of Fremde Heere Ost (the German intelligence evaluation agency on the Russian Front) and later chief of the postwar German offensive intelligence branch, the DNB, swore that Bormann was indeed a Communist agent.

For three decades, the British and Americans presumed that the former Reichsleiter was either dead or in Moscow, serving the Soviet state in the ongoing cold war with the West. Then, in 1975, Artur Axmann, who had been the Reichsjugendführer (Nazi youth leader) and who had been with the Martin Bormann group trying to escape Berlin, told of coming across the dead bodies of Bormann and Dr. Ludwig Stumpfegger, who had been Hitler's personal physician during the last days in the Führerbunker.

"I leaned over and could see the moonlight playing on their faces," Axmann recalled. "They were lying very close together. There was no visible sign that they had been shot or struck by gunfire. . . . I assumed that they had taken poison."

No trace of Martin Bormann or his corpse had been found for twenty-seven years, although in the immediate postwar era both the Soviets and the Anglo-Americans had conducted exhaustive searches. Then on a cold day in late November 1972, German construction workers at the site of a new park uncovered two skeletons, lying side by side. One was that of a short man (Bormann had been five feet, seven inches tall) and an exceptionally tall man (Dr. Stumpfegger had been six feet, six inches tall).

Berlin police were called, and subsequent medical examination reportedly disclosed slivers of cyanide capsules tucked into the jawbones of each skeleton. Reportedly, German police also tentatively identified Martin Bormann's remains from dental diagrams drawn from memory by his dentist.

However, the enigma involving the fate of Reichsleiter Bormann endures. It had long been known in Adolf Hitler's inner circle that Artur Axmann hated Bormann with a passion. Had Axmann truly seen a dead Bormann on that black, chaotic night in Berlin thirty years earlier? Confused fighting had been raging throughout the sprawling, battered metropolis. Thousands of corpses—those of Soviet and German soldiers as well as civilians—were strewn about the city. Why had Axmann stopped to examine the Bormann and Stumpfegger corpses?

There are those who claimed that Bormann fled to South America and lived in comfort for three decades. Whatever may be the case, Martin Bormann's ultimate fate remains a conundrum.[9]

A Bell Tolls for a Sailor

In OCTOBER 1945, Coast Guard Yeoman Philip C. Ford returned to his home in New York City. A few days later, he called at the district Coast Guard office, then disappeared. His stepfather, Edwin Booth, offered a five-thousand-dollar reward for information leading to the discovery of his whereabouts. There were no takers.

Ford's mother purchased an eighteen-hundred-dollar bell and had it installed in the steeple of the Village Presbyterian Church in New York City. The gift was not in her son's memory, she explained, "but rather in the thought that Philip will hear a church bell ringing somewhere and remember who he is."

Young Ford apparently never heard the bell.[10]

Doomsday for Flight 19

ON THE AFTERNOON of December 5, 1945, five Avenger torpedo bombers lifted off from Fort Lauderdale, Florida, on a 320-mile navigation training mission. They were scheduled to fly east, then north, over Grand Bahama Island, then southwest back to their base. Leading Flight 19 was U.S. Navy Lieutenant Charles C. Taylor, one of two experienced airmen aboard the planes. The other twelve—pilots, radio engineers, and gunners—were all still in training.

Less than two hours after the 2:10 P.M. takeoff, radio messages were received back at the Fort Lauderdale base indicating that Lieutenant Taylor, a veteran of countless flights, had become disoriented.

"Both my compasses are out," he said. "I'm over land, but I'm sure I'm in the Keys [on the southern tip of Florida], but I don't know how far down and I don't know how to get [back] to Fort Lauderdale."

Actually, the flight plan should have had Taylor's group near Great Sale Cay, two hundred miles northeast of the Florida Keys.

For the next two hours, bits and pieces of radio messages reached Flight 19's base. Then the home base heard Charles Taylor's final orders radioed to his five craft: "All planes close up tight. We will have to ditch unless landfall. When the first man gets down to ten gallons we will all land in the water together."

Then there was silence.

An exhaustive search by air and by sea over 250,000 square miles of ocean failed to find any trace of Flight 19, yet another tragic and mysterious victim of the ill-famed Bermuda Triangle.

A U.S. Navy board of inquiry produced a four-hundred-page report on the fate of Flight 19—and failed to cast any logical light on the episode. Significantly, the board could not explain why a planned two-hour training flight had became a meandering five-hour journey to nowhere.[11]

Part Six

Peculiar Premonitions

Churchill's Sudden Impulse

BEGINNING WITH the Battle of Britain in 1940, German air attacks on England (particularly London) were so frequent that most of the sturdy British became adjusted to them, if not indifferent toward the deadly bombardments. Air raids became a way of life.

Among those who endured the Luftwaffe's heavy assaults was Prime Minister Winston S. Churchill, known widely as the British Bulldog. On May 10, 1940, King George VI summoned the cherubic, cigar-chomping Churchill to Buckingham Palace and asked him to take over the reins of government. He would succeed seventy-year-old Neville Chamberlain, who for two years had been trying to appease Adolf Hitler, the Nazi warlord.

Churchill, then the First Lord of the Admiralty, accepted eagerly, and when Chamberlain "resigned" the next day, Churchill took over as prime minister and began directing the British war effort. With Hitler's mighty juggernaut poised across the English Channel and preparing to pounce on England, a nation at bay, and with the powerful Luftwaffe pounding the British Isles, Churchill felt that as a leader, it was his job to be seen by his beleaguered people and fighting men.

Widely known for his courage, Winston Churchill left the relative safety of his bomb shelter, deep underground, and traveled at night to various anti-aircraft batteries to inspire the crews. One night, during an especially heavy Luftwaffe bombing, he had just visited a battery whose gun barrels were red hot from almost constant firing, and he was strolling back to his waiting black limousine. An aide opened the right rear door, and the prime minister started to climb in to take his customary seat in the vehicle—just as he had done hundreds of times before.

Suddenly, Churchill had a change of heart. Walking around the back of the limo, he opened the door on the other side and got in, seating himself on the left. Accustomed to the prime minister's periodic fits of impetuousness, the aide made no inquiries about Churchill's sudden decision.

Picking its way through the blacked-out streets, the limo had driven for about ten minutes when there was an ear-splitting blast. A bomb had exploded nearby, jolting the automobile and causing it to career on its two right wheels for perhaps a hundred yards before righting itself.

"I must say, that was some ride!" Churchill grumbled tongue in cheek.

Prime Minister Winston S. Churchill. (National Archives)

Later, he explained that "my beef on the left-hand side of the limo had caused it to pull down [instead of turning over]."

When Lady Churchill asked her husband about his close call with death or serious injury, he replied: "Something said 'Stop!' just as I started to climb into the car. It then appeared to me that I was told I was meant to get in the door on the other side and sit there. That's what I did."

Later, Churchill told a miners' group: "I sometimes have a feeling—in fact, I have had it very strongly—a feeling of interference. I want to stress it. I have a feeling sometimes that some guiding hand has interfered."[1]

Mamie Eisenhower's Prediction

LIKE COUNTLESS OTHER WIVES in wartime America, Mamie Eisenhower was both proud and sad. "Ike," her doting husband of twenty-three years, was ready to ship out to a foreign land—England. There, as a two-star general, Dwight Eisenhower would be the commander of ETOUSA (European Theater of Operations, United States Army). His job was to prepare Britain as a gargantuan base for an eventual cross-channel attack against Nazi-held France. It was late June 1942.

Ike Eisenhower would fly to England with a handpicked aide, forty-six-year-old, gangling Major General Mark Clark (who later would gain fame as a four-star general), with whom Eisenhower had previously served in a staff assignment.

Before bidding farewell to her husband, Mamie Geneva Doud Eisenhower took Clark aside and said: "Mark, I've had a premonition. Ike is going to be the General Pershing of this war." Five-star General John J. "Blackjack" Pershing had commanded the American Expeditionary Force (AEF) in World War I, during which he became a national idol.

Clark, taken aback by the seeming absurdity of that prediction, tactfully replied, "Yes, ma'am."

Indeed, it did seem to be a far-fetched notion. Only fourteen months earlier, Ike had been an obscure lieutenant colonel manning a desk and shuffling papers at Fort Sam Houston, Texas. Now, after a meteoric rise up the rank totem-pole, he was wearing two stars on his shoulders—and was still obscure. Besides, Mark Clark and nearly all other professional officers knew that Ike's assignment in England was temporary in nature. He would be a sort of super administrator and housekeeper until a qualified combat general would take over the task of one day leading American troops across the English Channel.

However, Mamie's prediction became a reality: Ike did become "the General Pershing of this war"—and then some. In World War I, Pershing's AEF had far fewer troops and but a fraction of the awesome firepower that Ike had at his beck and call. At the time of the Normandy invasion in June 1944, Eisenhower was the most powerful man that history had known. Held in his hands was total control over the massive land, sea, and air forces of several Allied nations.

Unlike Pershing, Ike also had enormous political clout. He could and often did bypass Washington to deal directly with heads of state on matters of far-reaching implication.[2]

General Patton's "Previous Life"

GEORGE SMITH PATTON, JR., was in his element—leading a large force of fighting men in a desperate battle. Tall, ramrod straight, and immaculately tailored, the fifty-seven-year-old Californian was flamboyant and profane, but at the same time, deeply devout. The silver-haired major general had been one of the army's best known figures since his days at West Point, where he had been the center of conversation among fellow cadets since the day when he had stood up between targets as his comrades blasted away on the rifle range. "Wanted to know what it feels like to be under fire," young George had explained.

Now, in early May 1943, Patton was heading for the front in a staff car with two aides, in the vicinity of Tunis, Tunisia, in North Africa. His II Corps was joining with the British in a northward drive to trap the remnants of German Field Marshal Erwin Rommel's Afrika Korps in the northeastern tip of Tunisia.

General George S. Patton.
(U.S. Army)

Three miles from Tunis, Carthage, one of the greatest cities of its time, had stood. Founded in 846 B.C., Carthage had gained fame for its size and wealth and the great empire it ruled. As Carthage rose in power and influence, the other powerful city of the era, Rome, came to look upon Carthage as a dangerous rival. So the two rivals went to war in 246 B.C. and bloody battles were fought in the region through which George Patton was now traveling.

When Patton's driver reached a fork in the road, he halted the vehicle, uncertain of which branch to take. Major Charles Codman, the general's aide and a socially prominent wine distributor in peacetime, directed the driver to take the left branch. Patton spoke out: "No, take the other road."

"But, sir," Codman protested. "A reconnaissance of the route was made earlier today. I'm sure it's the left road."

Patton was adamant. "No, goddamn it, I happen to know it's that direction," pointing to the right branch. "You see, Codman, I've been here before. I fought with the Carthaginians against the Romans on this battlefield in 246 B.C."

Codman and the others knew that Patton was a strong believer in reincarnation. And he was the boss. So the driver took the right branch, and the party reached its destination safely.

Later, it would be learned that had Patton's vehicle continued on the left branch, as his aide had insisted was the correct course, the party would have collided head-on with dug-in German troops.[3]

"Captain Eddie" Senses Big Trouble

JUST PAST 1:30 A.M. on October 21, 1943, Captain William T. Cherry, Jr., was at the controls of a B-17 Flying Fortress as it zoomed down the runway at

Honolulu's Hickam Field, then soared off and set a course for Guadalcanal, eighteen hundred miles to the southwest. There were seven other men on board, including the famed World War I ace, Edward V. Rickenbacker.

Captain Eddie, as the popular figure was known in nearly every American household, was on a top-secret assignment that had been given to him directly by Secretary of War Henry L. Stimson. Since Eddie, a civilian, could not work free for the government, he had signed a one-dollar-per-year contract.

When daylight broke at about 6:30 A.M., Rickenbacker, who was seated directly behind pilot Cherry, was gripped by a strange sensation, a premonition he would later call it. Captain Eddie felt that the flight was in trouble. However, Bill Cherry said that the plane was to make landfall on a tiny island (where refueling would take place) in three hours, at 9:30 A.M.

An hour before that time, flying at one thousand feet, those on board began looking for the flyspeck piece of land. At 10:15 A.M., three-quarters of an hour beyond the expected arrival time, Captain Cherry was still holding to the original course.

"How much gas do we have?" a worried Rickenbacker asked.

"A little over four hours," came the reply.

Captain Eddie kept his qualms masked, but deep inside, he was convinced that the plane had overshot the mark and was moving ever farther away from it into the vast maw of the blue Pacific. A half hour later, all on board were gripped by the stark reality: The Flying Fortress was lost—and nearly out of fuel.

Soon those in the plane, like all others lost in the Pacific, got what airmen called "island eyes." There are tens of thousands of assorted-sized islands in that huge body of water. An airman in distress saw land because he wanted to see it. With those on Rickenbacker's craft, every cloud shadow momentarily held the promise of land.

Captain Eddie, who had turned age fifty-two three weeks earlier, looked at the man in the next seat, Colonel Hans C. Adamson, who was the same age. In his youth, Adamson had been an explorer, but he had become "too old to fight" and, in his words, was now a "desk jockey and paper shuffler."

Adamson flashed a grim smile and said, "Eddie, I hope you like the ocean. I think we're going to spend a long time on it!" Rickenbacker's premonition had been fulfilled.

Twenty-one days later, Lieutenant Frederick E. Woodward, pilot of a Navy Kingfisher scout plane, returned to his base on Funafuti Atoll and leaped excitedly to the ground, reporting that he had seen a yellow raft ten miles to the south of the atoll. Could this be carrying the famed Captain Eddie Rickenbacker and other survivors of the Flying Fortress that had been lost in the Southwest Pacific since October 21?

Navy men on Funafuti, some sixteen hundred miles northeast of Australia, would learn later that Rickenbacker and his companions had crash-landed into the Pacific and had clambered onto three small rafts. They had had

Captain Eddie Rickenbacker is transferred to a PT boat in midocean. (U.S. Air Force)

no time to get provisions before the B-17 sank, so they ate raw flying fish that occasionally fell into the rafts. A seagull that landed on Captain Eddie's head had provided a feast—he had grabbed it by its feet and wrung its neck.

All the while, a broiling Pacific sun scorched the men in the daytime. They had no fresh water to drink. One man gulped the ocean seawater, became delirious, and died in agony.

Rickenbacker encouraged his companions not to give up hope. One man had a pocket New Testament, so the men spent a great deal of time reading aloud from it and praying. Captain Eddie kept his thoughts to himself, but he had calculated that the odds of the rafts being found were, perhaps, one million to one.

Now at Funafuti Atoll, upon receipt of Lieutenant Woodward's stunning news, Lieutenant Alvin P. Cluster, a PT-boat skipper, and his crew raced to the reported raft sighting. There they found one exhausted and half-conscious survivor, Captain William Cherry, pilot of the Flying Fortress. Bearded, gaunt, and near death, Cherry spoke through lips parched and cracked by the merciless sun. He said that other survivors were on two rafts that had become separated from his a few days earlier.

Four PT boats based at Funafuti, the PT-boat tender *Hilo*, and four navy patrol planes scoured hundreds of square miles of trackless ocean. The day dragged on—with no results. Then, at sunset, the *Hilo* received a message from a patrolling Kingfisher: Another raft was spotted northeast of the atoll. *Hilo* relayed the news to the closest boat, PT-26, skippered by Ensign John M. Weeks, and the speedy craft began racing for the reported sighting. Night was drawing its veil across the Southwest Pacific when PT-26 reached the raft.

As Captain Eddie was being brought aboard on the fantail of the PT, crewmen jockeyed for the honor of being the first to help the American idol aboard. These youngsters were calling him Mr. Rickenbacker, and he exclaimed, "Just call me Eddie, boys, but get me on this damned boat!" Other survivors followed.

As the PT boat set a course for the forty-mile run to Funafuti atoll, Rickenbacker was taken below and sat down on a bunk as the sailors gathered around him, staring in wide-eyed awe.

"Well, boys," Captain Eddie remarked casually, "this has sure been my lucky day!" Then he glanced at a calendar pinned to the bulkhead: It was *Friday, the thirteenth.*[4]

"I'll See You Someday!"

THE MIGHTY AMERICAN invasion fleet stood off the central Pacific atoll of Tarawa in the early morning darkness of November 20, 1943. Sixteen shadowy shapes—troop transports—stole into position off the islet of Betio. On board were thousands of grim marines, one of whom was Lieutenant William D. Hawkins, leader of the Scout-Sniper Platoon that would hit the beach at Betio five minutes ahead of the first wave.

Known to his thirty-four marines simply as "Hawk," the lieutenant was as convinced of ultimate victory as he was of his own death. Without a trace of fear or emotion, he confided to his closest friend: "I'll see you someday, Mac— but not on this earth."

At dawn, Bill Hawkins and his platoon headed for the shore in two landing crafts. Hawk felt the situation was well in hand: He had always boasted that his thirty-four men could lick any Japanese battalion. Like Hector in his chariot, the lieutenant stood erect in his boat as it churned through the Pacific swells for the enemy-held shore. His platoon's mission was to seize the pier that extended five hundred yards into the lagoon off Betio. The pier split the marines' landing beaches, and from it, Japanese machine gunners and riflemen could pour devastating fire into the marine amtracs (amphibious tractors) that would pass to either side.

Hawk and his men hit the reef near the pier. Betio was aglow, a mass of flames, from the heavy pre-H-hour naval bombardment. Enormous smoke and dust clouds hovered over the islet. No longer visible under that pall, Betio had been torn apart.

Suddenly, Japanese mortar shells began exploding on and around Bill Hawkins and his platoon. Gasoline drums, stacked on the pier, began to burn briskly. Machine-gun bursts ripped into the stalled marines. Hawkins waved his men forward. They fought with flamethrowers, grenades, and bayonets. It was death at close quarters—for both sides. Yard by yard, the marines battled along the pier, killing and being killed.

Hawkins was hit by shell fragments and lost blood. But when corpsmen (medics) started to carry him away, he became angry. "I came here to kill Japs, not to be evacuated!" he barked. Hawk remained in the fight.

All day, the invading 2nd Marine Division battled the entrenched Japanese. Early the next morning, Lieutenant Hawkins and his platoon (or what remained of it) were ordered to wipe out five Japanese machine guns that barred the way to an advance inland on Betio.

Growing weaker from loss of blood, Hawk led his men forward. One by one, the spitting machine-guns were wiped out, but not before Bill Hawkins took an enemy slug in the chest. This time he was carried to the rear and died soon afterward. He would never know that "impregnable" Betio was conquered by marine guts and blood in four days.[5]

"I've Got a Gut Feeling!"

PT BOAT 156 (nicknamed Cowboy) sailed from its base on primitive Bougainville Island on a mission to scour the eastern side of that large South Pacific island for Japanese shipping. Many of these patrols were routine, with no action involved. However, on that night in December 1943, Lieutenant Frank H. Jones, a twenty-seven-year-old Virginian, was gripped by a haunting sensation. Turning to the man standing with him in the cockpit, Boatswain Mate 2nd Class Charles O'Neil, Jones remarked: "You know, I've got a gut feeling we're going to get the shit shot out of us tonight!"

A short time later, PT-156 was stealing through the water between two islands, relying mainly on the inky blackness for protection. Suddenly, loud roars echoed across the sea and orange flashes illuminated the sky. Japanese eight-inch guns on both sides had caught PT-156 in a vicious cross fire.

Shell fragments riddled the Cowboy, and several wounded men were sprawled on deck in pools of their own blood. However, the battered little boat finally was able to limp away from the lethal ambush. Lieutenant Jones's "gut feeling" had become a reality.

From that point on, Frank Jones was regarded as Squadron 9's resident psychic. Each time PT-156 was assigned a patrol, crewmen would slip up to him and ask: "Mr. Jones, are we going to run into any hot action tonight?"[6]

An Old Colonel's
Luck Runs Out

REDOUBTABLE COLONEL Harry A. "Paddy" Flint customarily went into action with a black silk scarf knotted around his neck and carrying an ancient Springfield bolt-action rifle. Paddy was the leader of the 39th Infantry Regiment of the U.S. 9th Infantry Division.

There was no doubt about it: At age 56, the cavalry-trained Flint, a poker-playing, drinking buddy of General George Patton, was far overage to command an infantry regiment in battle. Yet, there he was during fierce fighting in Normandy under the hot summer sun, a happy, dust-caked fugitive from a dozen cushy—and safe—liaison jobs. When the army didn't know what to do with an overage member, he usually was made a liaison officer.

Profane, gruff-voiced, fearless, and revered by his warriors, Paddy Flint had begged his now high-ranking West Point classmates to "get me away from all those goddamned paper shufflers." So he was given the 39th Regiment. It was soldier talk that his pal General Eisenhower, a West Point plebe (freshman) when Flint was a first classman (senior), had personally seen to it that Paddy got the up-front command—and had kept him there.

In Normandy, as in North Africa and Sicily, Paddy's short, aging, horse-bowed legs sometimes were not as sturdy as his fighting heart. When they let him down, the "Old Colonel" would simply take a seat, even at an outpost in view of the Germans, to get back his strength.

"Ya know," he quipped to an aide on one of those occasions, "I can't figure out why I'm not always able to keep up with these nineteen-year-old kids!"

Paddy never worried about enemy marksmen picking him off. When they would shoot at him he would merely spit contemptuously in their direction. "Those goddamn Krauts couldn't hit a bull in the ass with a boat oar!" he would bark.

The Old Colonel was delighted to be in the thick of things. "Normandy," he declared, "is my graduation exercise as a foot-slogger!"

Now, on July 24, 1944, Paddy Flint was about to receive his diploma. His regiment's mission was to drive the Germans back across the east-west St. Lô-Perriers Road and dig in before charging on southward at dawn.

Earlier that morning at his command post in a ramshackle Norman farmhouse, a few members of his staff heard Paddy remark matter of factly: "Fellows, old soldiers run out of luck sooner or later. You have just so many chances, and I've about used up my share."

His officers cast grim glances at one another. They had never heard Paddy talk like that; they had come to believe that he was indestructible.

Just past 1:00 P.M., the 39th Regiment jumped off and struck a buzz saw almost at once. Tenacious Feldgrau, dug into the thick earthen hedgerows and armed with an array of Schmeisser machine pistols and other automatic weapons, refused to budge. Dogfaces, as the GI foot soldiers called themselves, were falling like flies. Then mortar rounds began exploding among the stalled regiment, taking a heavy toll.

"I'm going to see what'n hell's holding up our boys," Paddy Flint told an aide. Stripped to the waist, he took a rifle platoon forward. Said the Old Colonel over a walkie-talkie, "I've found the goddamned bottleneck. Some dug-in Krauts with Schmeissers. We'll start those bastards cooking!"

Flint called to a nearby Sherman tank, hopped aboard it on his creaking legs, and dodged a hail of bullets aimed at him as the tracked monster sprayed the hedgerows. "Goddamn Krauts never could hit anything!" Paddy spit out.

The tank driver was wounded. So Flint crawled off the Sherman and stalked forward alone on foot. A sharp crack rang out from a hedgerow, and the seemingly immortal Paddy Flint went down, hit in the head by a bullet—"a goddamned lucky shot," the Old Colonel would have called it.

Medics rushed up and loaded Paddy onto a stretcher. Said a private as the party started for the rear, "Remember, Colonel Flint, they can't kill an Irishman—they can only make him mad!" It was an expression that Flint had used countless times.

Paddy smiled weakly. Perhaps he realized that his death, forecast by him earlier that day, was looming. Twelve hours later, the Old Colonel entered Valhalla.[7]

"Friendly Fire" off Anzio

AT DAWN on January 28, 1944, Lieutenant General Mark Clark, the lanky leader of the Fifth Army, boarded a swift PT boat at the mouth of the Volturno River in western Italy. With Clark were several army officers and Frank Cervasi, an American war correspondent.

Three days earlier, an American and British force of sixty thousand men had stormed ashore at the small port of Anzio, sixty miles behind the Germans' heavily fortified Gustav Line, which ran generally east and west across the narrow waist of Italy. Now, Mark Clark was making a seaborne end run around the western flank of the Gustav Line to visit his Anzio force.

As Clark's craft and another PT boat roared off, there was a thinly masked veil of tension between the crews. Luftwaffe air raids and shelling at and around the Anzio beachhead had become increasingly heavy, and reports were that enemy Schnellboote (small, fast craft similar to American PT boats) were roaming the coast to shoot up and torpedo Allied vessels.

While slashing through the heavy swells of the Tyrrhenian Sea seven miles south of Anzio, the two PT boats were challenged by an American minesweeper. One PT-boat skipper ordered green and yellow flares to be fired and the designated signal to be flashed on the blinker to identify the craft as friendly.

General Mark Clark on his favorite
PT-boat seat. (U.S. Army)

Up until that moment, General Clark had been seated in his customary
place on deck, a stool located where the bridge of the boat furnished some protection against the chilling, wet blasts of air. Then, Clark would assert later,
"something told me" to rise from the stool and move toward the front of the
boat. Moments later, a shell fired by the American minesweeper exploded directly where Clark had been sitting, smashing his wooden stool into kindling.

The PT-boat skipper was wounded in both legs and writhed in agony on
the deck. Two other navy crewmen were killed and three others were
wounded. Strangely, all the casualties were navy: Not a single army man was
as much as scratched.

Nearly everyone on board had been knocked off his feet. In the confusion, a Very pistol was dropped to the deck. General Clark picked it up and
fired the correct flare to once again identify the PT boat as friendly. This act
brought another round of shelling from the minesweeper.

Then, a young ensign, painfully wounded in both legs and bleeding profusely, dragged himself to the wheel, swung the PT boat around and, with
Mark Clark holding him upright, headed back toward the Volturno River. With
the badly damaged craft was the other PT boat, which had not been hit. All
the while, the gunners on the minesweeper kept firing shells at the fleeing PT
boats.

About thirty minutes into their trek southward, the PT boat transferred
the five dead and wounded navy men to the British minesweeper *Acute*, which

happened to have a doctor aboard. Then, General Clark told the remaining naval crew, "Okay, head back for Anzio." At the wheel was the skipper of the undamaged PT boat.

Reaching the point seven miles south of Anzio from which the PT boats had been shelled earlier, Clark and the others on board were concerned when they sighted the same American minesweeper—presumably with its itchy gunners ready to fire again. This time, the identification signals were recognized. All on board the PT boat exhaled collective sighs of relief.

Grabbing a megaphone, the PT-boat skipper hailed the captain of the minesweeper and shouted, "You goddamned sons of bitches fired on General Mark Clark and killed and wounded five of our boys!"

"Please accept our apologies," the embarrassed minesweeper captain called back through his megaphone. "The rays of the early morning sun made it impossible for us to recognize your signals."

Still boiling from the "friendly fire" encounter, the ensign responded, "It's a wonder you ignorant bastards didn't shoot at the sun!"

Thirty minutes later, Mark Clark climbed off the PT boat at Anzio, perhaps reflecting that he was alive because of an urgent impulse to move from his customary stool on deck.[8]

No Need for a Lighter

MAJOR JULIAN COOK and his battalion of paratroopers of the U.S. 82nd Airborne Division, veterans of Sicily and Italy, were convinced that they had been handed a classic "suicide mission." Cook's men were to paddle across the five-hundred-yard-wide Waal River in broad daylight and proceed into the teeth of a formidable line of defenses on the German-held bank—machine-guns, pill-boxes, and a wicked-looking old Dutch fort that loomed ominously over the landscape.

"We've got two chances to reach the other side," one grim paratrooper remarked to comrades, "slim and none."

Major Cook's men huddled tensely behind an embankment on the south side of the Waal (an extension of the Rhine River) and waited for the imminent arrival of small British boats. It was 1:00 P.M. on September 20, 1944.

Three days earlier, in history's largest airborne operation, Allied troops had leaped and glided to landings along a sixty-mile carpet extending deep into German-held Holland. Primary objectives were a series of crucial bridges, but some nine thousand men of the British 1st Airborne Division, who had been dropped near Arnhem, the farthest bridge in the operation, were trapped there.

At the same time, Major General James Gavin's 82nd Airborne had seized the south edge of the big bridge at Nijmegen, nine miles to the south of Arnhem. But British tank columns could not dash over the span and race on northward to link up with the British paratroopers until the Nijmegen bridge was completely in Allied hands.

Therefore, Julian Cook and his troopers were to cross the swift-flowing Waal and capture the north end of the bridge.

As the minutes ticked past and the British boats failed to show, the American paratroopers grew more tense and angry. Let's get it over with! was the mood. They waited . . . and waited some more. Still no boats. Nerves were taut to the breaking point.

Lieutenant Harry F. "Pappy" Busby pulled out a pack of Chesterfields, lit one of the cigarettes, then tossed the nearly full pack away. "I won't need those anymore," Busby said calmly. Then he pitched away his Zippo lighter. "Won't be needing that either," he told a comrade, Lieutenant Virgil F. Carmichael.

Finally, the boats arrived. Grimly, the GIs tumbled into them and began paddling furiously for the far bank. A torrent of machine-gun fire raked the craft. Survivors of the crossing charged onward and took control of the north end of the bridge. Pappy Busby was not with them. He was lying on the north bank of the Waal—dead.[9]

Ernest Hemingway Changes Chairs

ERNEST "PAPA" HEMINGWAY, tough, jovial, and possessing a disdain for anything intellectual, was not only a widely known author, but was also a personality almost in a class with baseball superstars and Hollywood silver-screen luminaries. Now, in October 1944, the forty-five-year-old, hulking, bearded Hemingway was a war correspondent covering the American onslaught against Adolf Hitler's vaunted Siegfried Line, the gun-studded, steel-and-concrete barrier along the western border of the Third Reich.

Hard-drinking, hard-driving Papa was loved by the GIs with whom he often shared frontline dangers and hardships. In his correspondent's uniform, they thought he looked like "a khaki teddy bear," as one infantryman put it.

Hemingway, wearing a German combat jacket and clutching a Tommy gun, entered a house in the Hueitgenwald (Hueitgen Forest), just inside Germany. It was the command post for Colonel Charles T. "Buck" Lanham, the wiry, scrappy leader of the 22nd Regiment of the 4th "Ivy" Infantry Division, Hemingway's favorite outfit.

Papa burst into the CP in his typical flamboyant style. "Ernest Hemorrhoid is my name," the visitor declared, holding out his hand. "The Poor Man's Ernie Pyle."

When it was time for a meal to be served, Colonel Lanham, an old friend, suggested that Hemingway sit in a certain chair among those drawn up around a large, oblong-shaped table. The author started to lower himself into the designated seat, then (he would later declare) "something told me not to

Famed author Ernest Hemingway was with U.S. troops in Huertgen Forest. (National Archives)

sit there." So he moved to an adjoining chair, and the first one was left unoccupied.

Minutes later, a high-velocity German shell tore through the wall Hemingway was facing and went out the wall behind him without exploding. After it became clear that this had been a random round, two officers extended a taut rope from where the shell had entered the room to where it emerged on the other side. They concluded that, had Hemingway not suddenly decided to switch to an adjoining chair, the shell would have torn off his head.

Six weeks later, after Hemingway had returned to Paris for a few days to "replenish my booze supply," he was again visiting Buck Lanham in the "Green Hell of Bloody Huertgen," as it came to be known. Shortly after dawn, the colonel went forward to inspect his 1st Battalion, which had suffered grievous casualties in recent days; its commander had been killed and it was bracing for an expected German attack. Hemingway tagged along.

At the battalion CP (which consisted of a log-covered hole) Buck Lanham discussed the situation with a young major, who had succeeded the deceased commander. On the way back, Lanham told Hemingway that the major was "not doing too good a job" and might have to be replaced.

Hemingway replied thoughtfully, "Buck, you won't ever have to relieve him."

Puzzled, the colonel asked, "What in the hell do you mean?"

"He won't make it. He's going to be killed—and soon."

When the two men reached the regimental CP, they were met by Lanham's executive officer. "Colonel, who takes over at 1st Battalion? The major there has just been killed."

"How the hell did you know that was going to happen?" an amazed Colonel Lanham asked Hemingway.

Papa merely shrugged.[10]

A Bride's Haunting Nightmare

EARLY IN DECEMBER 1944, Sergeant Richard D. Fisco, a member of the U.S. 509th Parachute Infantry Battalion, received the required permission from American authorities and married a beautiful young French woman, Louise. His unit was in reserve after having spearheaded the invasion of southern France the previous August and then fighting in the Maritime Alps on the Italian border.

In an occupation known for its venturesome and often quirky members, paratrooper Dick Fisco was regarded as a free spirit of the first order. Comrades told of how Fisco, during the savage fighting on the Anzio beachhead of Italy in early 1944, had stood up in his foxhole and, with bullets hissing past his head, thumbed his nose at hordes of German soldiers charging toward his company's foxhole line.

Now, while the newlywed Fiscos were enjoying a brief honeymoon in France, Louise awakened abruptly in the middle of the night. She told of a frightening dream in which Dick was back in action and was seriously wounded in the left arm, which had to be amputated.

"I know I dreamed it would be your left arm, because you were wearing your wedding ring on that hand," the distraught Louise sobbed.

Fisco tried to console her. "Our battalion won't see any more action in this war," he assured her. "The Krauts are as good as kaput."

Twenty-four hours later, the honeymoon was cut short. Fisco and his 509th Parachute Infantry were rousted out in the middle of the night and rushed in trucks to Belgium. At the tiny village of Sadzot, on December 28, the battalion clashed with elements of the 2nd SS Panzer Division, which was trying to break through American lines and race northward to seize Liege, the initial German objective in what came to be known as the Battle of the Bulge.

Liège was crammed with thousands of tons of gasoline, weapons, ammunitions, and other supplies, which the surging Wehrmacht spearheads desperately needed in order to drive onward to the main objective, the port of

Sergeant Richard Fisco (left) and a comrade. (Courtesy Nick de Gaeta)

Antwerp. If the Germans were to break through at Sadzot, the road to Liège would be wide open.

Bitter, no-holds-barred fighting raged for three days and nights in and around Sadzot. Scores on both sides were killed or wounded. Conditions were brutal—the coldest winter in Europe in a quarter century. At night, the temperature plunged to thirty degrees below zero. Snow was often waist-deep. Men froze to death.

On the fourth morning, Sergeant Fisco's company was attacking through the thick forest, where visibility was often only a few feet. Typically, Fisco had volunteered to be the scout and was out in front of his comrades. Suddenly, he paused, much like a hunting dog on the point. His comrades had always sworn that Fisco could "smell Germans at fifty yards."

Now his sense of "smell" told him that deadly danger lurked just ahead in the murky woods. Moments later, staccato bursts from several German machine-guns, firing at point-blank range, raked Fisco and his fellow paratroopers, who were behind him.

An intense firefight erupted. Streams of bullets zipped past Fisco like swarms of angry hornets. However, he wriggled forward through the deep snow and could see that there were three German machine-guns. Then a loud noise jolted Fisco: A mortar shell had exploded next to him. White-hot fragments tore into his *left* arm—just as his wife Louise had "seen" in her nocturnal nightmare.

Dazed, bleeding profusely and in excruciating pain, the sergeant refused to abandon the fight. Inching forward, he and a few comrades, with rifles, Tommy guns, and grenades, wiped out the three, spitting machine-guns. Only then did Dick Fisco stagger to the rear, his left arm hanging in shreds and dripping a trail of blood in the snow.

One facet of Louise Fisco's nightmare proved to be wrong. Through the skills of army surgeons, her husband's mangled left arm was saved.[11]

"Old Blood and Guts" Awakens

DURING THE Battle of the Bulge in late December 1944, Lieutenant General George S. "Old Blood and Guts" Patton awakened abruptly for no apparent reason at three o'clock in the morning. The colorful and profane commander of the U.S. Third Army telephoned his longtime secretary, Sergeant Joseph D. Rosevich. "Get over here right away!" Patton thundered. When Rosevich arrived at the general's Luxembourg quarters, he found Patton partly dressed, wearing a combination of his stylish, custom-made uniform and his pajamas. The sergeant guessed rightly that the general had jumped out of bed and wanted to dictate.

Nothing his mercurial boss did had ever surprised Rosevich. However, now he was slightly taken aback when Patton told him that he was expecting the Germans to mount a major attack at a certain point along Third Army's line on Christmas Day. Acting on a "sudden inspiration that struck me right in the ass in the middle of the night," as he would explain it later to his staff, he decided to thwart the Germans by launching an attack of his own just before the enemy force was to jump off.

Patton began dictating orders for his attack to Joe Rosevich. When the dictation was concluded, he told the sergeant to type up the transcript, make copies, and have them distributed to his staff. Then Patton went back to bed.

On Christmas morning, the Americans attacked, catching the Germans off guard at the very moment they were preparing to assault American lines— just as Patton had envisioned. The enemy was stopped cold in their tracks.[12]

Ernie Pyle's Last Battle

FAME AND FORTUNE had engulfed timid, wiry Ernie Pyle. His name was a household word. Millions loved him and prayed for his safety. He might well have rested on that pedestal. Yet, in March 1945, he found himself bidding goodbye to his beloved wife Geraldine, at the couple's modest home in their adopted city of Albuquerque, New Mexico. Once again, forty-four-year-old Ernie Pyle was off to war.

As a correspondent for United Features Syndicate, the Indiana native had been covering American GIs in the crucible of battle since the invasion of North Africa in November 1942. There the Pyle legend had burst into full bloom. In simple, gripping pieces, many done in foxholes, often under fire, Ernie had brought home all the fear, pain, horror, loneliness, and homesickness that every GI felt. Those articles were the perfect supplement to the soldiers' own letters to loved ones.

Although he wrote of his own feelings and his own emotions as he saw boys killed and as he saw wounded boys die, he was merely interpreting the scene for the GI doing the fighting and bearing the brunt of the war. Ernie got people on the home front to understand that life in battle "works itself into an emotional tapestry of one dull, deadly pattern—yesterday is tomorrow and, O God, I'm so tired."

Ernie Pyle never made war look glamorous. He hated it. Rather he wrote of the nobility of young men fighting for their country. When asked why he was there, his standard reply was: "A small voice came in the night and said go."

Ernie's first love was the infantry dogfaces—those who suffered the most and who took 90 percent of the casualties—and he shared their hardships in the front line and beyond. He was always on their side, putting into words in his columns what the GIs could not quite write. Ernie was the first to suggest that the combat soldier deserved extra pay, not as a reward—because there was no reward big enough—but as a sign of appreciation and recognition that the foot soldier was something special.

Blown from a ditch by a German dive-bomber in North Africa, blasted out of a building at Anzio, almost killed by strafing planes at St. Lô in Normandy, Pyle told of the death, heartache, and agony around him and always he named names of the boys and got their home addresses. Hundreds of thousands of combat troops, from star-spangled generals to infantry privates, knew him by sight, and called, "Hi ya, Ernie!" when he passed.

In Europe, by late 1944, Ernie was a thin, sad-eyed man gone gray at the temples, his face lined, his reddish hair thinned. "I don't think I can go on and keep sane," he told his millions of readers. He started back home, with abject apologies to the GIs.

"You get to feeling that you can't go on forever without being hit," he would tell close pals. "I feel that I've about used up all my chances."

Meanwhile, Pyle's books, *Here Is Your War* and *Brave Men*, a collection of his columns, hit the best-seller lists. He was wildly acclaimed whenever he dared show himself in public, and reluctantly journeyed to Hollywood to watch Burgess Meredith impersonate him in the film version of his books.

Ernie loafed a while in his humble white clapboard cottage in Albuquerque. For hours, he would sit there on the veranda with Geraldine and stare

White-haired Ernie Pyle with marines on Okinawa a few days before he was killed on Ie Shima. (U.S. Marine Corps)

silently across the lonely mesa. The front lines haunted him, beckoned to him; in January 1945, he felt that he had to go back. But this time, it would be to the Pacific.

"I'm going simply because there's a war on, and I'm part of it," he told Geraldine. "I've known all the time I had to go back. And I hate it."

So he went, winging out over the seemingly endless Pacific to embattled Okinawa, a final stepping-stone to Japan. He stalked the enemy with marine patrols and huddled with them under fire in foxholes. On April 8, a three-column photo in *The New York Times* showed Ernie, clad in full combat gear but carrying a batch of writing pads instead of a weapon, second man in a squad of marines probing ahead of the lines.

A week later, Pyle was on Ie Shima, an obscure flyspeck of an island west of Okinawa. There two army divisions were locked in a death struggle with tenacious Japanese defenders who contested every yard of the bleak, rocky landscape. Before going to the front, Ernie Pyle felt a strange sensation.

"This will be my last battle," he confided to a fellow correspondent. "Sooner or later, a man's luck is bound to run out. You have just so many chances." Then he wrote George A. Carlin, his boss back in the States: "The boys [GIs] are depending on me, so I'll have to stick it out."

On April 18, Pyle was jeeping to the front with Lieutenant Colonel Joseph B. Coolidge, commanding officer of a 77th Infantry Division regiment. Suddenly, a hidden Japanese machine-gun on a nearby ridge began chattering, and those in the jeep leaped for a roadside ditch as bullets hissed past them.

Two minutes later, Coolidge and Pyle raised up to look around. Another fusillade struck. Ernie fell over dead, a bullet in his head. A chaplain and four litter bearers edged up to the side and brought the correspondent's body behind the front lines.

In his command post, the hard-bitten combat veteran, Colonel Coolidge, fought to hold back tears as he told newsmen of Ernie's death. "The GI has lost his best friend," Coolidge declared.

America was shocked by Pyle's death in battle. President Harry S. Truman said: "Nobody knows how many individuals in our forces and at home Ernie helped by his writings. But all Americans understand how wisely, how warmheartedly, how honestly he served his country and his profession."

Taps were sounded for Ernie Pyle at 11:00 A.M. on April 20 near the scene of the battle that was still raging on remote Ie Shima. He was laid to rest alongside fallen soldiers such as those who loved him the world over because he had made himself one of them. The simple ceremony was characteristic of the life of the man who had confronted the Black Angel of Death in North Africa, Europe, and in the Pacific.

The simple headstone on his grave read:

At This Spot

The

77th Infantry Division

Lost A Buddy

Ernie Pyle

18 April 1945

Ernie Pyle's forecast that he would be killed in Ie Shima had become a reality.[13]

Patton Tells His Family Good-bye

ON JUNE 7, 1945—precisely one month after Victory in Europe Day—General George Patton returned to Boston and a reception that dwarfed anything the city had known. Massachusetts was his home state by marriage only, but nearly a million shoving, jostling, cheering natives proclaimed him as their own.

Patton, who had once told his staff that he was a "goddamned natural born ham," didn't disappoint the multitudes: He looked every inch the conquering hero. Standing in an open car during the parade, the general was agleam with 24 stars—four on each shoulder, four on each collar tab, four on his cap, and four on the handle of the pistol at his hip. On one bare hand were three immense rings, and a riding crop was gripped in the other white-gloved hand.

Underneath his jovial posture, however, George Patton was suffering from a broken heart. Nearly all the big-name American generals in Europe were receiving new assignments to go to the Pacific for the invasion of Japan. Patton, who lived to fight, was wanted by no one. The Pentagon didn't know what to do with the army's fightingest and, many held, most successful general, who had a penchant for getting himself into hot water.

A few weeks later, Patton, now sixty years of age, his hair white but his ramrod posture still intact, made ready to return to his Third Army, now an occupying force in southern Germany.

"They're turning me into a goddamned paper shuffler," he remarked ruefully to a close friend. Before departing for Europe, Patton, a loving father, startled his two daughters by telling them, "Well, girls, goodbye. I won't be seeing you again."

Puzzled, the young women conjectured over the meaning of his strange comment. They had never heard him talk in such a pessimistic tone. And, since he was not going to the fighting in the Pacific, why was he in such a macabre mood?

Back in Europe, the general was inundated by an avalanche of awards from France, Luxembourg, Belgium, and other countries. However, his pessimistic outlook remained. "Sometimes I feel that I may be nearing the end of this life," he wrote in his diary.

In his job of "denazifying" the crushed Third Reich, George Patton was the classic fish out of water. In his frustration, he casually remarked to a group of reporters that the Nazi Party was much like the Democrats and Republicans back home. Back in the States, a tornado of criticism was heaped on the general, one so intense that he was removed as commander of Third Army, which he had led to scintillating victories across Europe only a few months earlier.

Now he was named head of the new Fifteenth Army. It was a hollow post. The mission of his new command was to write the American army's history during the war in Europe. Wags said the Fifteenth designation came from the fact that the total number of persons in that organization was fifteen.

Patton's outlook became steadily more morose. Again he predicted, this time to his longtime friend Lieutenant General Hobert R. "Hap" Gay, that his life was nearing the end. Gay shrugged off the remark with a joke.

Early on the morning of December 9, 1945, Patton and Gay climbed into a 1938 Cadillac limousine at Bad Nauheim, Germany, and drove off for a pheasant-hunting trip and brief vacation. At the wheel was a young private, Horace Woodring, who had been a sergeant but was busted when caught "fraternizing," as the army termed such actions, with a German woman. Trailing Patton's seven-passenger limo was a GI quarter-ton truck driven by Sergeant Joseph Spruce. In the rear of the vehicle was a hunting dog.

George Patton, who claimed psychic powers on occasion, no doubt was unaware that Dame Fate was conspiring against him by cooking up a curious set of circumstances for the trip.

The weather was cold, and snow flurries began to pelt the two-vehicle convoy. About an hour from Bad Nauheim, Patton emerged from his limo to inspect some ruins. As he stomped around, his boots and socks became soaked, and on returning to the Cadillac, he got into the front seat next to the driver to thaw his feet with the heater while continuing the trip.

A short time later, the tiny caravan halted at an American roadblock, where MPs were checking credentials. Then came another unexpected turn. Patton got out of the limo and yelled at Sergeant Spruce in the truck: "Bring up that goddamned dog before he freezes to death and put him next to Woodring [in the front seat of the limo]." Then Patton, who had been riding in front, got into the back next to Hap Gay once more and the limo drove off.

Horace Woodring whipped onto a ten-mile stretch of the autobahn just outside Mannheim. Traffic was light. At about 11:45 A.M., the limo stopped at a railroad crossing as the red crossing-lights flashed and the gates lowered. A mile-long freight train passed by.

Waiting on the far side was a large army GMC truck, driven by Corporal Robert L. Thompson. With him in the cabin were two buddies, a violation of strict rules. Only two GIs were allowed in a truck cabin. Now the train had gone, the gates came up, and the traffic started to move. Just as the limo crossed the tracks, it collided with the GMC truck.

Since the vehicles were just starting up, neither was going in excess of twenty miles per hour. At first, the crash seemed to be minor: The GMC truck was barely damaged, and the Cadillac's radiator was dented, but not a single window was broken. No one in the truck was injured, nor was General Gay and Horace Woodring in the limo. But George Patton was slouched back, having difficulty breathing. And he could not move his fingers.

At his post a short distance away, Captain Ned Snyder, a medical officer, was notified of the collision. He hurried to the scene and found Patton in the back seat. In a barely audible voice, the general said, "I think I'm paralyzed."

A young military police officer, Lieutenant Peter K. Babalas, had arrived before Captain Snyder. "How bad is it, Doc?" he asked.

"His neck is broken," Snyder replied in a whisper.

An ambulance rushed the injured general twenty-five miles to an Army hospital outside Heidelberg. Although conscious, he did not speak a word throughout the trip.

General Patton was admitted to the 130th Station Hospital ninety minutes after the crash. Lying on the operating table, paralyzed from the neck down, bleeding from head wounds, pale from shock, punctured by an array of needles, blood plasma dripping into his veins, the general was moving his lips. An attending army doctor leaned down to catch his words. With a wan smile, Patton whispered, "Captain, I merely said, 'Jesus Christ, what a way to start a vacation!' "

Enlisted-men pallbearers carry General George Patton's remains to a halftrack on the way to the funeral service. (U.S. Army)

Twelve days later, an attending physician, Captain William Duane, Jr., wrote a final entry in his progress notes: "[General Patton] died at 1745 [5:45 P.M.], 21 December 1945, with sudden stopping of the heart."

General Patton's last premonition had been fulfilled. "Old Blood and Guts" entered Valhalla, the great hall of the dead heroes in Norse mythology. Valhalla has walls of gold and a roof of battle shields. Each morning, the hero warriors ride out to the battlefield to fight. George Smith Patton would be in his element.[14]

Part Seven

Strange Encounters

Roosevelt Meets a Nazi Agent

JUST TWO WEEKS after Adolf Hitler's war juggernaut plunged into neighboring Poland and triggered a bloody conflict in Europe on September 1, 1939, William Rhodes Davis, a wealthy American businessman, was ushered into the Oval Office in the White House for a meeting with President Franklin Roosevelt. A day earlier, on September 14, an influential public figure had telephoned Roosevelt and asked the chief executive to receive Davis "on a matter that might be of the highest importance to the United States and to humanity."

Roosevelt knew that Davis, a freewheeling private international oil speculator, had long been playing footsie with Nazi Germany, for the State Department had been building a dossier on the fifty-four-year-old Montgomery, Alabama, native since 1927. So the president asked Assistant Secretary of State Adolf A. Berle, Jr., his most trusted adviser on espionage and security matters, to be present for the meeting.

Davis had a rags-to-riches background. As a youth, he had been a hobo of sorts, and in 1913, he had started his own oil company in Muskogee, Oklahoma. By 1938, he had extensive oil holdings in Texas, Louisiana, and Mexico. Overseas, he owned terminals and distribution facilities throughout Sweden and Norway. His vast oil empire was directed from a plush suite on the thirty-fourth floor of a building in New York's Rockefeller Center.

Now, in the White House, William Davis received a cool reception from solemn-faced President Roosevelt, who listened without comment as the oil baron reeled off his plan for "world peace." Three days earlier, Davis explained, he had received an urgent cable from General Hermann Goering, with whom he had been "doing business in Germany." Goering had suggested that Davis try to determine if Roosevelt would either act as a peace arbitrator himself or assist in securing the leader of another neutral nation to perform that role.

"The Germans desire to make peace," Davis said, "providing that certain of their conditions are met."

No doubt Roosevelt was galled to find himself holding court for an American citizen who had furnished huge amounts of precious oil for Adolf Hitler's armed forces, which at that precise moment were brutalizing a nearly defenseless Poland. The president would have been even more irked had he known that Davis was included on the roster of the Abwehr (the German espionage agency) in Berlin as Agent C-80.

President Franklin D. Roosevelt conferred in the White House Oval Office with William R. Davis (right), Nazi secret agent C-80. (FBI)

Back in 1936, Davis, aware that Nazi Germany was desperate for oil, had concocted a scheme that would both relieve the acute fuel pinch in the Third Reich and line his own pockets. Davis proposed building his own refinery in Germany. In his scheme, the facility would be paid for with funds that Hitler would confiscate from Boston's First National Bank under a trumped-up pretext and deposit in the Reichsbank.

No shrinking violet, Davis had sent his plan directly to Hitler. A few days later, the American entrepreneur was seated in a Berlin boardroom, explaining his oil scheme to Dr. Hjalmar Schacht, president of the Reichsbank, and twenty-one other high-level German financiers. Davis could sense by the stone faces that his proposal to steal the Boston bank's money was falling on deaf ears. Just then, a door opened and Adolf Hitler strode into the room.

"Gentlemen," the führer said evenly, "I have reviewed Mr. Davis's proposition and find it feasible. I want the Reichsbank to finance it."

The führer had spoken. There was not a dissenting vote. Soon work began on Davis's huge refinery, called Eurotank, at Hamburg. Now what Hitler needed was oil to refine. Davis had a scheme to achieve that goal. He negotiated a complex barter deal with Mexican President Lazaro Cardenas in which Mexico agreed to furnish oil to Hitler in return for German industrial products. Between September 1938, when the first tanker left Vera Cruz for Germany, and until war broke out in Europe a year later, more than four hundred thousand tons of Mexican oil flowed into storage tanks of the Wehrmacht. In the process, William Davis was becoming even richer.

Suddenly, the wheeler-and-dealer's oil bonanza was cut off. Great Britain had declared war on Germany, and the British navy had thrown up a blockade and was intercepting any shipment that would aid the führer's war effort. Davis was desperate: His goose that had been laying golden eggs for a year had ceased producing. So the oil tycoon's fertile mind hatched a bizarre plot. Poland was doomed, so if the shooting could be halted in Europe, his oil shipments from Mexico to Germany could be resumed. The goose would begin laying once more. But the entire scheme hinged on restoring peace. By cable from Mexico, Davis outlined his proposal for obtaining peace to Hermann Goering in Berlin: The oil baron would visit President Roosevelt and ask him to arbitrate a cease-fire in Europe.

Like many persons in power, Goering had a penchant for dabbling in machinations. So he gave Davis's "peace plan" the green light and asked the Abwehr to coordinate arrangements. For the clandestine operation aimed at President Roosevelt, Davis was designated Abwehr Agent C-80; Goering's "cover" was "Harold."

Now, seated in the Oval Office of the White House, Davis anxiously awaited Roosevelt's response to his "peace plan." Despite his loathing of Davis, the president remained noncommittal and did not reject the plan outright. Like any shrewd politician, Roosevelt was keeping his options open.

A few days later, Davis was in Berlin and Goering was eager to hear the details of the Roosevelt meeting firsthand. The Nazi bigwig urged his American confederate to follow up on the White House peace initiative, so on October 9, Davis landed by Pan American airplane at Port Washington, Long Island. Early the next day, he telephoned the White House and tried to make an appointment with the president.

In the meantime, Roosevelt had had a change of heart about Davis's "peace plan." After the earlier meeting in the Oval Office, Adolf Berle had told the president that he considered the oil tycoon to be "almost a Nazi agent." Roosevelt had agreed, but said he didn't see how he could do anything about it. Davis had broken no American laws, as far as the president knew.

Thus ended the personal relationship between Roosevelt and Davis. No doubt it had been the first—and only—time in history that a president of the United States had played host to an enemy secret agent.[1]

A Pipeline to the Führer

WHEN ADOLF HITLER began preparing for war in the early 1930s, he concluded that the United States, with its gigantic industrial potential, would be the "decisive factor" in the looming global conflict. Because the United States had no single agency charged with fighting subversive operations, Hitler's spymasters were able to field a formidable army of spies and saboteurs into the United

States. They penetrated nearly every major defense contractor, military estab-lishment, and branch of the federal government.

By 1939, with a few hundred Nazi agents roaming the United States at will, President Franklin Roosevelt finally designated the Federal Bureau of In-vestigation as the organization that would combat subversive forces.

One of those involved in Nazi espionage activities in the United States was William Sebold, who had fought in the German army as a corporal in World War I. Soon after hostilities ceased, he came to the United States, changed his name from Wilhelm Georg Debowski to William Sebold, married an American woman, and became a citizen.

Early in 1939, Sebold grew nostalgic to see Germany again. So he saved his money and took a leave from his job as a draftsman with Consolidated Air-craft Company in San Diego. Crossing the Atlantic on the SS *Deutschland*, he landed in Hamburg, where he was approached by two Gestapo men.

"So you plan to return to America," one Gestapo man said to Sebold. "That corresponds exactly with our plans. We can use men like you in America."

Sebold was hustled into an automobile and driven to a large, brownstone building where he was ushered into a cavernous office and greeted by a smil-ing, black-uniformed SS officer.

"My name is Colonel Paul Kraus, chief of the Hamburg Gestapo," he said graciously, shaking hands with the newcomer.

As the American puffed nervously on a cigarette and licked his lips, Colonel Kraus reeled off a lengthy recital of Sebold's background from his boy-hood days at Mülheim-on-Ruhr to his work at Consolidated Aircraft. The Gestapo officer ominously said that Sebold's aging mother, two brothers, and a sister were in Germany.

Now the velvet gloves were off. "Your kin live in Mülheim, Sebold, not in the United States," the colonel snarled. "If you refuse to cooperate, we can-not guarantee their safety." Kraus's voice trailed off, casting an even more sin-ister connotation to the threat. "You will spy in the United States for the fatherland."

Sebold was trapped. He had no choice. Either he spied for the Nazis in the United States or his mother, sister, and brothers were doomed, and it would be unlikely that he would get out of Germany alive. Colonel Kraus was de-lighted to hear Sebold's decision and told the spy recruit that he would live in Hamburg for three months while taking training at the Abwehr's espionage academy.

On January 10, 1940, Sebold was aboard when the SS *Washington* sailed into New York harbor. Suddenly, his cabin door flew open and two grim-faced men in civilian clothes entered. One flashed a badge and called out, "FBI!" Sebold was taken to a shabby Manhattan hotel where he could be interrogated without interruption.

Sebold turned over to the FBI agents four microfilms which had been concealed in the back of his watchcase by the Abwehr in Hamburg. These

William Sebold (alias William G. Sawyer) talks with a top Nazi spy (facing camera) in Sebold's phony New York City office. The photo was taken through a two-way mirror by FBI men who were concealed in the adjoining room. (FBI)

microfilms contained a list of twelve priority espionage missions for Sebold to carry out.

There was good reason for Sebold's cooperation. Before leaving Hamburg, and at great personal risk, Sebold had traveled to Cologne, slipped into the U.S. consulate there, and told his story to Vice Consul Dale W. Maher. The consulate then radioed Washington and advised the FBI, which ran a background check on Sebold. Only when the G-men barged into his ship cabin had he known the FBI had been advised that he was coming, and that he had volunteered to be a counterspy

Before leaving Hamburg, Sebold had been instructed to set up a shortwave radio station to send intelligence to Germany. He was told that "a large sum of money" had been deposited in an account of William G. Sawyer (the name the Abwehr had assigned to him) with the Chase National Bank to pay for the radio parts and a house for the station.

Hamburg officials had been fearful that the secret radio station would be detected if a parade of Nazi agents traipsed in and out of the house. So Sebold had been told that five thousand dollars would be deposited for him in another New York City bank. These funds were to be used for opening an office in midtown Manhattan, where he could receive German spies and collect their materials for transmission or transport to Germany.

Abwehr officials had given him the names of four Nazi agents, who, in turn, advised other subversives about William G. Sawyer, the phony firm (Diesel Research Company) he used as a front, and the location of his office suite in the Knickerbocker Building on Forty-Second Street.

Meanwhile, FBI Director J. Edgar Hoover had taken a personal interest in Sebold's shortwave radio project. His men picked out the transmission site, a small, frame house in a sparsely populated area in Centerport, Long Island, a short drive from Manhattan. Operating the station would be two G-men, J. C. Ellsworth and M. H. Price. One of them had been a "ham" (licensed amateur radio operator) for several years, the other had once lived in Germany and spoke like a native Berliner.

The Centerport radio connection would be used primarily for *sehr sehr dringend* (very, very urgent) reports from the Nazi agents who brought their information to Sebold in his Manhattan office. Large items—maps, blueprints, photographs, and charts—were carried to Hamburg on ocean liners by Abwehr couriers posing as stewards—after the materials had been "doctored" by the FBI.

Hoover formed a team of "scriptwriters," clever and devious-minded G-men. They inspected all the materials as Sebold collected them from the Abwehr spies who came to his office. Often, accurate, but largely unimportant information was permitted to be sent, to give the subversive agents a degree of credibility with Hamburg. Genuine military secrets were twisted or garbled. The scriptwriters also came up with their own messages—outdated information or true facts that were relatively harmless. U.S. Air Corps planes that had been secretly declared obsolete were described in accurate detail.

As the weeks passed, the Abwehr spymasters in Hamburg and Berlin grew ecstatic with the torrent of intelligence coming in from the Centerport station. Then one day, Hamburg learned, accurately, that one of their spies had been arrested in New York by the FBI. Price and Ellsworth received an urgent inquiry from Hamburg: Could the arrest result in the radio station being unmasked?

Price and Ellsworth replied: "No danger. FBI too stupid."

Centerport was one of the most bizarre encounters of the war. FBI agents, in essence, were whispering into Adolf Hitler's ear, for the contents of most of the messages sent over the shortwave radio no doubt reached his desk and may have influenced some operations of his armed forces. And J. Edgar Hoover took impish glee from the knowledge that the führer was financing the entire machination.[2]

Unlikely Reunion on the Rhine

BY LATE MARCH 1945, five powerful Allied armies had crossed the majestic Rhine River, Germany's historic barrier to invasion from the west, and were charging hell-bent into the Third Reich. The entire Wehrmacht defense had begun to crumble like a piece of dry bread.

Private First Class William Bohlenberger, a member of an American artillery battalion, was riding in a truck going through one little German town after the other. His convoy finally halted to permit the GIs to relieve themselves. Suddenly, Bohlenberger felt that he recognized the place, as though he were in a dream. As his comrades looked on in amazement, he ran all out toward a little, white house just off the road, calling out, "Mom! Mom!"

It was a scenario that would have been rejected by a Hollywood filmmaker as implausible. Bohlenberger bolted through the front door and found his mother washing dishes in the kitchen. Seated in the living room was his brother, still wearing his Wehrmacht uniform, although he had deserted and had come home a few days earlier, when it was clear to every German except Adolf Hitler that the Third Reich was kaput.

It had been fifteen years since the Bohlenbergers had seen one another, and the GI, a naturalized American, and his German mother were incoherently crying and laughing at the unexpected reunion. But the American and his German soldier-brother didn't speak a word to each other.

All too soon, Bill Bohlenberger's comrades came in. It was time to go. They had to all but drag the youth away from his weeping mother.[3]

A Publisher Visits the Front

EARLY IN MAY 1945, with the once-vaunted German Wehrmacht crumbling into chaos and peace in Europe only days away, Amon Carter, Sr., the publisher of the *Fort Worth Star-Telegram* in Texas, was among a group of sixteen leading U.S. newspaper executives who had been asked by Secretary of War Henry Stimson to come to Europe especially to view the concentration camps.

Publisher Carter had a deep personal interest in the outcome of the war: His son, Lieutenant Amon Carter, Jr., had been a German prisoner of war since the day General (later Field Marshal) Erwin Rommel's famed Afrika Korps overran young Carter's 1st Armored Division battalion at Faid Pass in North Africa in February 1943. In common with many American parents whose sons had been captured during the war, Carter, Sr., had long had to bear a gnawing anguish: Was his POW son dead or alive?

One stop in the tour for publisher Carter and the other media executives was lunch with Lieutenant General William "Big Bill" Simpson's U.S. Ninth Army. Simpson's outfit was dug in north to south, along the Elbe River, the geographical landmark ninety miles west of Berlin which had been chosen by SHAEF as the stop line for the American advance into the battered Third Reich.

Just as the luncheon, held at the headquarters of Major General Robert C. Macon's 83rd "Thunderbolt" Infantry Division, broke up and the media executives walked out the door, a vehicle carrying a small group of just-liberated American POWs came to a halt in front of the building. One of those who climbed out was Lieutenant Amon Carter, Jr., who, in disbelief, came face-to-face with his father.

As the Texas publisher stood rooted in astonishment, the young lieutenant strolled up to him and said quietly: "Well, here I am, Dad."

Choking with emotion, the elder Carter silently embraced his son and held him tightly, patting the back of his son's head.[4]

A Chance Homecoming in Italy

AMERICAN SERGEANT Carl Longo parked his jeep at the bottom of a hill up which a cobblestoned street ran through the village of Panni, in southern Italy. When he started walking up the incline, crowds began to line either side of the street, shouting, "Bravo! Bravo!"

It seemed to the GI that he had seen it all before. And, indeed he had. Fourteen years earlier, he had moved from his hometown of Panni to Barrington, Rhode Island, where he played third base for a town baseball team called the Barrington Townies.

A few weeks earlier, Sergeant Longo had landed in Italy with the Fifth Army. Now, by chance, he had returned home. Since nearly everyone in Panni was a cousin of someone else in town, Longo presumed that those doing the cheering were relatives of his. It was November 1943.

Still on foot, the American headed for the house in which he had lived for many years, thinking that it might have been destroyed in the war. Much to his amazement, the homestead was standing—and it looked precisely as it had when he had departed as a boy in 1930.

It was merely a two-room house, and the large hole over the front door was still there, an opening designed to let fresh air in and smoke out. It succeeded in doing neither. The same picture was hanging over the bed, and the small, old fireplace was laboring to produce a few degrees of heat. Peppers were hanging from the ceiling, just as he had remembered.

Later, Sergeant Longo regaled his GI comrades with the story of his Panni homecoming. "The only thing different about the house was the pig who lived with us in a corner of the room—it was a different pig!"[5]

Truce in an Irish Pub

ONE NIGHT in late August 1944, Royal Air Force Flight Officer John H. Allix and his six crewmen lifted off in a Wellington bomber from their base near Lough Foyle in Northern Ireland, a part of the United Kingdom. Their mission was to seek out and sink German submarines that might surface off the coast to run their diesels and vent their exhausts.

Allix and his men were frustrated. At a time when most RAF bombers were pounding military and industrial targets in Germany, their Wellington was assigned an almost impossible task. Two months earlier, the U-boats had been fitted with a *Schnorchel,* a device consisting of a retractable pipe through which, so long as they stayed at a depth of some twenty-five feet, could recharge their batteries and vent their exhausts. So the U-boats could go for weeks without surfacing.

Knifing through the blackness some ten miles out to sea, Flight Officer Allix and his crew saw several brilliant flashes, one after another, followed by the red glow of four torpedoed ships. For two hours, the Wellington crisscrossed the dark waters but never sighted the marauding U-boat which had just taken a deadly toll. However, a Royal Navy ship picked up the submarine's echo and chased the enemy craft until it took refuge in the Lough Swilly, an arm of the sea that stretches deep into neutral Ireland, just south of the border with Northern Ireland.

For several days, the Wellington searched in vain for the U-boat, which apparently was remaining below the surface. Then, Flight Officer Allix received a two-day furlough, changed into civilian clothes, and headed southward for Buncrana, a small town on the shore of Lough Swilly just across the border in Ireland.

Food and liquor were plentiful in Ireland and were unrationed, so it had became the custom of the RAF men to change into civies and cross the border into Ireland. On these occasions, guards on both sides of the frontier conveniently looked the other way.

Reaching Buncrana, Allix strolled into a pub, ordered a beer, and noticed a lone customer, also drinking a beer, seated at a table. The RAF officer struck up a conversation with the young, tall, blond man who was wearing a tweed jacket and flannel trousers. Allix introduced himself as John Stewart, thinking it prudent not to reveal his true surname while in a neutral country. Hesitating for a moment, the other man, who spoke in fluent English, offered his hand and said his name was Charles Hamilton.

Allix felt that his new acquaintance was also a British officer. However, as the evening wore on and the men drank and dined together, the Briton began to grow suspicious of his friendly companion. Although the man's knowledge of London appeared to be extensive, when wartime changes were discussed, Hamilton seemed to be uninformed.

Suddenly, Allix was struck by a weird notion: The man was a German! Acting on an inspiration, the RAF officer addressed his acquaintance as Karl, a German variation of Charles. The other looked startled. Both men stared for a long moment. Each had been gripped by the peculiarity of the situation: Charles (or Karl) was a German officer, Allix now knew, and Karl now was aware that "John Stewart" was a British officer.

Then the impasse was broken. "We could both be interned!" Allix declared. Both men broke out laughing.

As the evening wore on and the beer continued to flow, Karl said he had spent several years in London where his father had been head of a German firm before the war. Karl had attended British public schools and graduated from Oxford. Then the German dropped a blockbuster: He was the skipper of the U-boat that had taken refuge in nearby Lough (Lake) Swilly two nights earlier and had became exhausted from constant tension. So he had changed into the civilian clothes that he had bought years before while in London, his U-boat surfaced, and two of his men paddled him ashore in a rubber dinghy for his short walk to Buncrana and an evening of relaxation.

John Allix then revealed that he was in command of the Wellington that had been trying to locate and blow up Karl's U-boat. Allix remarked that just because, a short distance away, the two men had been trying to kill one another and no doubt would be doing the same thing in twenty-four hours, there was no reason why they could not call their private truce for the time being. Karl readily agreed.

Four hours later, near to midnight, Karl said he had to leave. Together, the two men strolled to the end of the village where they solemnly shook hands. Then each walked off in different directions.[6]

Two Soldiers in a Foxhole

AT MIDAFTERNOON at two airstrips on southern Leyte Island in the Philippines, fourteen hundred men of the Japanese 2nd Parachute Brigade finished a feverish day of preparation for a do-or-die assault they would make at dusk on three key American airfields—San Pablo, Buri, and Bayug. These keenly trained and dedicated paratroopers were part of Operation Wa, code name for an airborne and ground offensive designed to seize the initiative on Leyte. It was December 6, 1944.

A few hours later, Captain Kenneth A. Murphy of the U.S. 11th Airborne Division, a tall, solidly built former football player at the University of Minnesota, was standing in a chow line at San Pablo airfield and was casually watching the approach of two flights of transport planes. Suddenly, Murphy became alert. The planes were lighted and a man was standing in the door of each one.

When the two flights were directly overhead, the grayish sky filled with parachutes. Cries of "They're Japs!" rang out.

Since San Pablo was far behind the active front, the 11th Airborne men on duty there were not carrying weapons. Now, there was a wild scramble as Captain Murphy and the others dashed for their tents to retrieve their weapons. The descending Japanese paratroopers came down right on top of the 11th Airborne command post and on the nearby Buri airstrip.

On both San Pablo and Buri, some of the invaders went about systematically blowing up light aircraft, gasoline dumps, and buildings. But most seemed to be confused, drunk—or both. In the shadows cast by the flickering blazes, Japanese paratroopers ran madly about San Pablo screaming "Banzai!" and shooting off flares at random and sounding their horns, clappers, whistles, and gongs.

Pandemonium reigned, as confused Americans and equally confused Japanese paratroopers, alone, in pairs, and in tiny groups, became entangled in a lethal cat-and-mouse game as they stole through the blackness. Shouts erupted continually; streams of tracer bullets zipped through the night sky; orange grenade blasts pierced the air; wild shoot-outs broke out. No one could be certain if a shadowy figure was friend or foe.

Captain Ken Murphy was stalking the enemy and being stalked in turn. Then, a bright chain of tracer bullets erupted to his front and he leaped into a deep, two-man foxhole that was already occupied by a dark, dim figure. Murphy was glad to have a comrade. Neither man spoke a word for the enemy was all around and any sound could result in an incoming shower of grenades.

After what seemed an eternity of tense, silent vigilance, gray tinges in the sky to the east heralded the approach of dawn. Glancing at the dim figure beside him, the captain noticed that the silhouette of his helmet had a curious configuration. Suddenly, he felt a surge of concern; his foxhole "friend" was an enemy—a Japanese paratrooper.

At virtually the same moment, the Japanese had apparently arrived at a similar conclusion with regard to Captain Murphy, because he quickly raised his rifle with its fixed bayonet and gave the American a vicious hack on the side of the neck. Murphy tried to raise his carbine, but a split-second later, another blow of the razor-sharp bayonet sliced into the captain's shoulder.

The bayonet was raised for another, possibly fatal, slash when Murphy squeezed the trigger on his carbine. The bullet caught the Japanese in the head, and he crumpled in a bloody heap to the bottom of the hole. Captain Murphy took a silk battle flag and pistol from the dead enemy paratrooper. Then, bleeding and dazed, Murphy managed to pull himself from the hole and join others in organizing a defense until relief arrived later that morning.[*]

Getting an Old Friend Hanged

IN THE SPRING OF 1944, powerful Allied armies in England were preparing to launch Operation Overlord, the cross-channel assault against northwest Europe. The fate of the Third Reich, which Adolf Hitler had boasted a decade earlier would last for one thousand years, rested to a considerable degree in the hands of two of the Nazi regime's quaintest figures, Brigadeführer (SS Major General) Walther Schellenberg and Admiral Wilhelm Canaris. Each headed a competing intelligence agency, and it was their crucial task to pinpoint the time and place of der Grossinvasion.

Canaris, fifty-six years old, a small, nervous, intense, white-haired man, was chief of the Abwehr, with sixteen thousand agents scattered around the world. Thirty-three-year-old Schellenberg, bright, energetic, ambitious, and ruthless, was head of the SD, the political intelligence branch of the SS, an elite army within an army.

Spymasters Wilhelm Canaris and Walther Schellenberg could have been a father and son, for they seemed to be devoted to one another. Early every morning, Schellenberg left his Berlin home near the Kurfurstendam to meet Canaris at the riding stable in the Tiergarten, where they mounted sleek thoroughbreds and, impeccably clad in riding outfits, cantered along the tree-shrouded paths.

Actually, the two men were mortal enemies, and the morning horseback rides were merely a means for them to feel out one another to try to get clues as to what kind of attack the SD planned to launch against the Abwehr, and vice versa. Above all, Schellenberg hungered to be the hero who could go to the führer and tell him the true secrets of the Allies' D-Day, an intelligence bonanza that would skyrocket the young general into a post as head of all German intelligence agencies—including Canaris's Abwehr, which would then be absorbed into the SD.

Schellenberg had long suspected that his "good friend" Canaris had been and still was passing German secrets to British intelligence agents, which was indeed the case. The little admiral was a key leader in the Schwarze Kapelle, a tightly knit secret group of prominent German leaders who, for several years, had been conspiring to get rid of Adolf Hitler and his Nazi regime.

In the eyes of Schellenberg and his young SD officers, Canaris and his elderly Abwehr aides were traitors and should be hanged. But proof was still lacking. Even a more serious offense, in Schellenberg's view, was that the Abwehr leaders were rivals with the SD for power—an unforgivable crime.

Thanks to an extraordinary deception scheme, Plan Bodyguard, Allied forces stormed ashore in Normandy on June 6, 1944, taking the Germans by total surprise.

Six weeks later on July 20, Adolf Hitler was conducting his daily military briefing at his battle headquarters at Wolfsschanze, a sprawling complex of wooden buildings and underground bunkers set among gloomy woods in East Prussia behind the Russian Front. While the führer and his generals and colonels were standing around the conference table, a thunderous blast rocked Wolfsschanze. The explosion killed two generals and the stenographer, seriously wounded one general and one colonel, and inflicted lesser injuries on four more generals. Miraculously, the target of the time bomb, Adolf Hitler, survived with relatively minor cuts, burns, and bruises.

A revolution that the Schwarze Kapelle had planned to launch following Hitler's assassination was nipped in the bud. The Gestapo arrested hundreds of those suspected of being involved in the bomb plot, and scores were shot or hanged. Under intense torture, some of those arrested disclosed Schwarze Kapelle secrets.

Shortly after noon on July 23, three days after the blast, the doorbell rang at the home of Admiral Canaris at Schlachtensee, a pristine, lake resort outside Berlin. The little admiral had been living alone with two servants since, a few months earlier, the SD had connived to get him booted from the Abwehr post he had held since 1933.

When Canaris opened his door and saw the caller, he said quietly, "Somehow I felt that it would be you."

It was a peculiar confrontation indeed. The caller was Canaris's old friend and longtime riding partner, Walther Schellenberg, who had come to arrest the admiral on treason charges. A few months later, Canaris was hanged.[8]

An Oil Baron Calls on Himmler

IN OCTOBER 1944, Swedish oil baron Eric Erickson boarded a plane in Stockholm and winged over the waters of the Baltic Sea and over the drab plains of northern Germany to Templehof Airdrome in Berlin. Erickson had an appointment with Nazi Germany's second most powerful man, Reichsführer Heinrich Himmler, head of the SS army and the Gestapo.

The war had reached a crucial stage for the Third Reich. Powerful Allied armies in the west were charging toward the Rhine River, Germany's traditional barrier to invasion, and the Third Reich was desperate for oil. Erickson intended to brief Himmler on a grandiose plan the Swede had concocted to relieve that critical shortage.

Sweden was officially neutral, but nearly the entire population was pro-Allies. Although he was a Swedish citizen, Erickson had been born and brought up in Brooklyn, New York, and had graduated from Cornell University. Returning to Sweden in the late 1920s, he had started his own company to import American oil products.

In the 1930s, Erickson became a leading figure in the international "oil crowd," in which he might be competing vigorously against an individual in London, Teheran, Berlin, or Hong Kong one year, then be in league with the same individual to cut some big deal the next.

Soon after the war began in Europe, Erickson saw a glowing opportunity to do business with the Nazis, thereby reaping huge profits for himself. He drew away from his longtime friends, joined the German Chamber of Commerce in Stockholm, hobnobbed at plush clubs with German business-men, and let it be known that he was in sympathy with Adolf Hitler and the Nazis.

Soon, the western Allies announced publicly that Eric Erickson had been put on their blacklist for trading with Germany and aiding its war effort. Allied intelligence reported that he was making regular trips to Germany, dealing in oil, and that he was on friendly terms with high-ranking Gestapo officials.

Erickson's old friends in Stockholm crossed the street when they saw him coming. His wife was also ostracized when it became known that she and her husband hosted Gestapo officials in their home.

Although U.S. and British bombers had been pounding German oil refineries and storage depots in the first half of 1944, much of the industry was still functioning. Reacting with typical resilience, the Germans quickly repaired bombed facilities. And many refineries had been so well concealed or camouflaged that Allied air intelligence knew nothing of their existence.

Knowing that oil was the lifeblood of modern military machines, Erickson's plan proposed the construction of a huge oil refinery in Sweden to produce oil for Germany. It would cost $5 million and be financed by both Swedish and German funds. The oil magnate calculated that his proposal would appeal to Berlin because it would establish a source for oil in a neutral country, outside the reach of Allied bombers.

Through his contacts with the Gestapo in Stockholm, Erickson arranged the appointment with Heinrich Himmler, who had the authority to "buy" the Swede's deal.

After landing at Templehof in October 1944, Gestapo agents escorted the Swedish wheeler-dealer to Himmler's posh office, where he was greeted cordially by the Reichsführer. They discussed Erickson's oil plan at great length, and Himmler was impressed. But, Erickson said, before the plan could be implemented, he would have to make a firsthand inspection of German oil refineries and other facilities.

Desperate for new sources for oil, Himmler provided the Swede with a letter authorizing him to go anywhere and see anything he wanted in the oil industry. He was assigned a car, a driver, and unlimited rations of gasoline.

Erickson set out on a tour that covered much of central Europe. He inspected the big plants, talked with executives about what they planned to do, what steps they were taking to conceal their facilities or to keep bomb damage to a minimum. Having collected a wealth of information, Erickson returned to Stockholm.

In the weeks ahead, Luftwaffe headquarters in Berlin was mystified. As the Allies accelerated their air offensive against German oil, the bomber streams seemed to know the exact locations of all refineries, as well as the antiaircraft batteries and the smoke-screen facilities that defended each plant. Even more puzzling to the Germans, the Allies knew how long repairs would take after a refinery had been bombed. On the day the facility was ready to resume production, Allied bombers hit it again. When the final great Allied ground offensive began in March 1945, large numbers of German tanks and airplanes sat immobilized because of a lack of oil.

It was not until after the war in Europe ended in May 1945, that the Allied high command disclosed that results of the meeting between Heinrich Himmler and the Swedish wheeler-dealer had helped to bring the Third Reich to its knees much earlier than might have otherwise been the case. "Red" Erickson had been an Allied spy almost from the beginning of the war. He had been contacted by British intelligence and had agreed to be a secret agent. Putting his name on the Allied blacklist had been Erickson's own idea.[9]

Notes and Sources

Part One—Puzzling Events

1. Author interview with Vice Admiral John D. Bulkeley (Ret.), October 1989, January 1993.

   Papers relating to the *Foreign Relations of the United States and Japan 1931–41*, Washington, D.C.: Government Printing Office.

   New York Times, December 10–11, 1937.

2. Author correspondence with Professor Reginald V. Jones of Aberdeen, Scotland, October 1991.

   Affadavit signed by Alfred Naujocks at Nuremberg, November 10, 1945.

   Illustrated Story of World War II (Pleasantville, NY: Reader's Digest Association, 1955), p. 66.

3. Intercepts of Japanese Diplomatic Messages, 1940–45, SRDJ series, National Archives, Washington, D.C.

4. *Saturday Evening Post*, April 3, 1942.

   Times (London), October 19, 1939.

5. Count Ciano Diaries in the *Chicago Daily News*, 1947.

   Anthony C. Brown, *Bodyguard of Lies* (New York: Harper & Row, 1975), pp. 200–03.

   Adolf Galland, *The First and the Last* (London: Metheun, 1955), pp. 112–14.

   Hitler's War Directives, 1939–45, National Archives, Washington, D.C.

6. Ladislas Farago, *The Game of the Foxes* (New York: McKay, 1970), pp. 557–60.

7. Intercepts of Japanese Diplomatic Messages, 1940–45, SRDJ series, National Archives, Washington, D.C.

8. Chronology of Principal Events Relating to the Soviet Union, Part II, June 22, 1941 to September 1945, National Archives, Washington, D.C.

   Illustrated Encyclopedia of World War II (London: Marshall Cavendish, 1966), vol. 4, pp. 528–31.

   Winston Churchill, *The Second World War* (London: Cassell, 1948), vol. 3, pp. 316–24.

9. Pierre Accoce and Pierre Quet, *A Man Called Lucy* (New York: Coward-McCann, 1965).

   Illustrated Encyclopedia of World War II, vol. 4, p. 531; vol. 10, pp. 1306, 1309; vol. 18, p. 2438.

   Dwight D. Eisenhower, *Crusade in Europe* (Garden City, NY: Doubleday, 1948), p. 227.

10. *The New Yorker*, November 22, 1941.

    Scientific American, October 1972.

    Lee Kennett, *For the Duration* (New York: Scribner's, 1984), pp. 68–69.

    New York Times, December 11–13, 1941.

11. *Secrets and Spies* (Pleasantville, NY: Reader's Digest Association, 1966), p. 208.

    Janusz Piekalkiewicz, *Secret Agents, Spies, and Saboteurs* (New York: Morrow, 1975), p. 282.

    Philippe Ganier-Raymond, *The Tangled Web* (New York: Pantheon, 1963), p. 72.

12. "German Espionage and Sabotage Against the United States, 1940–45," U.S. Naval Intelligence Review, January 1946.

    Time, February 23, 1942.

    John Maxtone-Graham, *The Only Way to Cross* (New York: Collier, 1972), p. 378.

    New York Times, February 10, 1942.

    A. A. Hoehling, *Home Front USA* (New York: Crowell, 1966), pp. 27–29.

13. S. W. Roskill in the *Daily Telegraph* (London), November 4, 1963.

14. *Illustrated Encyclopedia of World War II*, vol. 17, pp. 2242–44.

    Dwight D. Eisenhower, *Crusade in Europe*, p. 287.

    Ernest Dupuy, *Men of West Point* (New York: Sloan, 1952), p. 324.

    Ladislas Farago, *Patton: Ordeal and Triumph* (New York: Obelensky, 1964), p. 157.

15. *Illustrated Encyclopedia of World War II*, vol. 15, p. 2042.

16. Harry C. Butcher, *My Three Years With Eisenhower* (New York: Simon & Schuster, 1946), p. 187.

    Wallace Carroll, *Persuade or Perish* (New York: Houghton Mifflin, 1948), p. 201.

    Royal Air Force Bomber Command Intelligence Narrative of Operations No. 774, U.K. Public Record Office, London.

    Casualty Report, Nuremberg, Night 30/31 March 1944, U.K. Public Record Office, London.

    "Luftwaffe War Diary," U.S. Air Force Historical Branch, Maxwell Air Force Base, Montgomery, Ala.

    Cajus Bekker, *The Luftwaffe War Diaries* (New York: Doubleday, 1968), pp. 143–49.

    Wesley F. Craven and James L. Cate, *The Army Air Forces in World War II* (Chicago: University of Chicago Press, 1949), pp. 30–37.

    Anthony C. Brown, *Bodyguard of Lies*, p. 664.

17. Anthony C. Brown, *Bodyguard of Lies*, p. 918.

    John Wheeler-Bennett, *Nemisis of Power* (New York: MacMillan, 1964), p. 589.

    Karl Heinz Abshagen, *Canaris* (London: Hutchinson, 1956), pp. 238–43.

18. Otto Skorzeny, *Skorzeny's Secret Missions* (New York: Dutton, 1950), pp. 162–70.

    Kenneth Strong, *Intelligence at the Top* (New York: Doubleday, 1969), p. 236.

    Illustrated Encyclopedia of World War II, vol. 16, p. 2156.

    Author's archives.

Part Two—Odd Coincidences

1. *Reader's Digest*, January 1953.

   Basil Collier, *The Battle of Britain* (New York: Berkley, 1969), pp. 137–39.

   Hugh R. Trevor-Roper, *Blitzkrieg to Defeat* (New York: Rinehart and Winston, 1971), pp. 146–47.

2. Richard Deacon, *History of the British Secret Service* (London: Muller, 1968), pp. 272–73.
   David Kahn, *Hitler's Spies* (New York: MacMillan, 1974), pp. 205–09.
3. Author's archives.
4. *Times* (London), June 12, 1940.
5. *The Sunday Times* (London), May 5, 1974.
6. Blake Clark, *Remember Pearl Harbor* (New York: Arbor House, 1962), pp. 27–28.
7. Author's archives.
   Illustrated Encyclopedia of World War II, vol. 8, pp. 1045–46.
8. Author's archives.
9. Author's archives.
10. Ralph G. Martin, ed., *The GI War* (Boston: Little, Brown, 1966), pp. 88–89.
11. British Air Ministry, *By Air to Battle* (London: British Air Ministry, 1945), pp. 117–19.
12. Author correspondence with Colonel Vincent M. Lockhart (Ret.), September 1987.
13. Author interview with Lieutenant General William P. Yarborough (Ret.), June 1993.
14. *Yank, the Army Weekly*, December 2, 1943.
15. Author interview with Colonel Barney Oldfield (Ret.), May 1992.
16. Ibid.
17. Author interview with Lieutenant General James M. Gavin (Ret.), June 1987, May 1988.
18. Courtney Whitney, *MacArthur: His Rendezvous with History* (New York: Knopf, 1956), p. 144.
19. Author interview with Monsignor Francis L. Sampson, Major General (Ret.), April 1994.
20. Author's archives.
21. Author interview with Lieutenant General Richard J. Seitz (Ret.), August 1989.
22. Author interviews with Colonel Carlos C. Alden (Ret.), August 1993, and with Lieutenant Colonel Jack Darden (Ret.), June 1992.
23. Samuel Eliot Morison, *The Liberation of the Philippines* (Boston: Little, Brown, 1969), pp. 56–71.
24. Author interviews with Thomas Dellaca, August 1990, and with Richard D. Fisco, October 1990.
25. Author interview with Brigadier General George M. Jones (Ret.), August 1992.
26. *Stars and Stripes*, February 2, 1945.
27. Author correspondence with Lieutenant General James M. Gavin (Ret.), December 1987.
28. Author interviews with five 101st Airborne Division veterans, August, September 1990.

Part Three—Curious Happenings

1. *New York Times*, August 20, 1941.
2. Richard Gehlen, *The Service* (New York: World, 1971), pp. 97–112.
3. Walther Schellenberg, *The Labyrinth* (New York: Harper, 1955), pp. 117–18.

4. Ladislas Farago, *The Game of the Foxes*, p. 266.
5. P. R. Reid, *Colditz* (New York: St. Martin's, 1984), p. 6.
6. *Yank, the Army Weekly*, July 15, 1942.
7. Some details from Robert L. Scott, Jr., *Damned to Glory* (New York: Scribner's, 1944).
8. *Yank, the Army Weekly*, September 17, 1944.
9. Author interviews with John H. "Beaver" Thompson, April 1988, and Colonel John Berry (Ret.), May 1989.
10. Desmond Young, *Rommel* (New York: Harper, 1950), pp. 147–48.
    Anthony C. Brown, *Bodyguard of Lies*, p. 413.
    Author's archives.
11. *Picture History of World War II* (New York: American Heritage Publishing, 1966), pp. 348–49.
12. Ladislas Farago, *The Game of the Foxes*, pp. 282–83.
    Anthony C. Brown, *Bodyguard of Lies*, p. 811.
    J. C. Masterson, *The Double-Cross System* (New Haven: Yale University Press, 1972), p. 171.
13. Ralph G. Martin, ed., *The GI War*, p. 111.
14. Ibid., p. 109.
15. Author correspondence with Joseph M. Cline, Jr., August 1993, and with Alyce Mary Guthrie of PT Boats Association, September 1993.
16. Author interview with participant Charles H. Doyle, April 1991.
17. Solly Zuckerman, *From Apes to Warlords* (New York: Harper & Row, 1975), pp. 262–73.
18. Author interview with Doug Wilmer, April 1991.
19. Associated Press dispatches by Roger O. Greene, May 1945.
20. *New York Times*, March 13, 1974.
21. Author interview with participant Colonel Edward H. Lahti (Ret.), April 1994.
22. Author interview with General Maxwell D. Taylor (Ret.), June 1989.
23. Kenneth Hechler, *The Bridge at Remagan* (New York: Ballantine Books, 1957), pp. 88–89.
24. Ralph G. Martin, ed., *The GI War*, p. 331.
25. Samuel Eliot Morison, *The Liberation of the Philippines*, pp. 227–33.
    Author's archives.
26. Edwin P. Hoyt, *The U-Boat Wars* (New York: Arbor House, 1983), pp. 217–22.
27. Heinz Hoehne, *The General Was a Spy* (New York: Coward, McCann & Geoghegan, 1971), p. 13.
    David L. Gordon and R. J. Dangerfield, *The Hidden Weapon* (New York: Harper, 1947), pp. 13–14.
    James P. O'Donnell, *The Bunker* (Boston: Houghton Mifflin, 1947), pp. 176–77.
28. Jay Nash, *Among the Missing* (New York: Simon and Schuster, 1978), pp. 69–70.

Part Four—Uncanny Riddles

1. *Illustrated Encyclopedia of World War II*, vol. 4, pp. 432–34.
2. Author interview with participant Vice Admiral John D. Bulkeley (Ret.), November 1994.

Ellis M. Zacharias, *Secret Missions* (New York: Putnam, 1946), pp. 78–79.
3. Albert Speer, *Inside the Third Reich* (New York: MacMillan, 1951), p. 314.
   James P. O'Donnell, *The Bunker*, pp. 305–06.
   William L. Shirer, *The Rise and Fall of the Third Reich* (New York: Simon and Schuster, 1959), pp. 498–99.
   New York Times, May 12, 1945.
4. U.S. Army Intelligence Division, Correspondence 1917–1941, Record Group 165, Old Military Records, National Archives, Washington, D.C.
5. Walther Schellenberg, *The Labyrinth*, pp. 109–10.
   Richard Deacon, *History of the British Secret Service*, p. 112.
6. Harry C. Butcher, *My Three Years With Eisenhower*, pp. 213–15.
7. Affidavit signed by Captain Herbert Wichmann at Nuremberg, December 1945.
8. *Secrets and Spies* (Pleasantville, NY: Reader's Digest Association, 1964), pp. 72–74.
9. Author interview with William Story, who trained at Fort Harrison, Montana, in World War II, March 1994.
10. David Irving, *The War Between the Generals*, (New York: Congdon & Lattès, 1980), pp. 130–32.
    Author's archives.
11. *V-Weapons Campaign*, U.S. Air Force Historical Branch, Maxwell Air Force Base, Alabama, pp. 362–68.
    Manuscript, dated March 12, 1946, John F. Kennedy Library, Cambridge, Massachusetts.
12. Author interview with Vice Admiral John D. Bulkeley (Ret.), May 1992.
13. Author interviews with participants John C. Phalen, Alphonse J. Remillard, and Harold Popadick, between March and May 1982, James Groves, January 1996.
14. Author's archives.
    Illustrated Encyclopedia of World War II, pp. 1425–28.

Part Five—People Who Vanished

1. *Times* (London), June 16, 1954.
   Anthony C. Brown, *Bodyguard of Lies*, pp. 20–23.
   Author's archives.
2. Ladislas Farago, *The Game of the Foxes*, p. 215.
3. *Time* magazine, April 6, 1942.
4. Author's archives.
5. Author correspondence with participants John M. Gibson, Ray O. Rousch, October–November 1991.
6. Author's archives.
7. *New York Herald-Tribune*, October 25, 1944.
   Miami Herald, October 22, 1944.
8. *New York Times*, August 26, 1945.
   Philippe Ganier-Raymond, *The Tangled Web*, pp. 127–30.
   Author's archives.
9. Affidavit signed by Richard Gehlen, Nuremberg, November 2, 1945.
   James P. O'Donnell, *The Bunker*, pp. 272–74.
   Author's archives.

10. Jay Nash, *Among the Missing*, pp. 125–26.
11. *Miami Herald*, December 7–10, 1945.
    New York Times, December 9, 1945.
    Lawrence D. Kusche, *The Bermuda Triangle* (New York: Warner, 1975), pp. 104–07.

Part Six—Peculiar Premonitions

1. Brad Steiger, *Mysteries of Mind, Space, and Time* (Englewood Cliffs, NJ: Prentice-Hall, 1974), pp. 168–70.
   Author's archives.
2. Mark Clark, *Calculated Risk* (New York: Harper, 1950), p. 54.
3. Charles R. Codman, *Drive* (Boston: Little, Brown, 1956), p. 102.
4. Author interview with former PT-boat skipper L. Rumsey Ewing, March 1994.
   Author correspondence with former PT-boat officer Edward A. Green and with Alyce Mary Guthrie of the PT Boat Association, April-May 1993.
   Some details from Edward V. Rickenbacker, *Seven Came Through* (New York: Doubleday, Doran, 1943).
5. Author interview with participant Marine Gunnery Sergeant Dwight W. Mace (Ret.), August 1987.
   Illustrated Story of World War II (Pleasantville, NY: Reader's Digest Association, 1955), pp. 237–38.
6. Author interview with participant Frank H. Jones, July 1994.
7. Author's archives.
8. Author interview with Lieutenant General William P. Yarborough (Ret.), General Clark's aide at time, February 1994.
9. Author interview with participant Virgil F. Carmichael, March 1994.
10. Carlos Baker, *Ernest Hemingway* (New York: Scribner's, 1969), pp. 149–52.
    Author's archives.
11. Author interviews with participants Richard D. Fisco, Nicholas DeGaeta, and Kenneth Shaker, April 1990.
12. Ladislas Farago, *Patton: Ordeal and Triumph* (New York: Obelensky, 1964), p. 259.
13. Joseph P. Mittelman, *Eight Stars to Victory* (Washington, D.C.: privately printed, 1947), pp. 142–48.
    Author's archives.
14. *Stars and Stripes*, December 22, 25, 29, 1945.
    New York Times, December 24, 28, 1945.
    Boston Globe, December 23, 1945.
    Ladislas Farago, *The Last Days of Patton* (New York: McGraw-Hill, 1980), pp. 259–67.

Part Seven—Strange Encounters

1. Ladislas Farago, *The Game of the Foxes*, p. 356.
   Adolf Berle notes of Roosevelt-Davis conference, Yale University Library, New Haven, CT.
   Beatrice B. Berle and Travis Jacobs, eds., *Navigating the Rapids* (New York: Norton, 1961), p. 173.

2. Michael Sayers and Albert E. Kahn, *Sabotage!* (New York: McKay, 1971), p. 24.

   Secrets and Spies (Pleasantville, NY: Reader's Digest Association, 1964), p. 76.

   Alan Hynd, *Passport to Treason* (New York: McBride, 1943), p. 30.

   Author interview with W. Raymond Wannall, former assistant director of the FBI, December 1995.

3. *Stars and Stripes*, April 4, 1945.

4. Ibid., May 3, 1945.

5. Ralph G. Martin, ed., *The GI War*, p. 116.

6. *Illustrated Encyclopedia of World War II*, vol. 9, pp. 1245–50, vol. 12, pp. 1545, 1571.

   Reader's Digest, May 1958.

7. Author interviews with participants Colonel Kenneth Murphy (Ret.), and Colonel Henry Burgess (Ret.), April 1991.

8. Walther Schellenberg, *The Labyrinth*, p. 410.

9. Author's archives.

Selected Bibliography

Books

Abshagen, Karl Heinz. *Canaris*. London: Hutchinson, 1956.

Accoce, Pierre, and Pierre Quet. *A Man Called Lucy*. New York: Coward-McCann, 1965.

Baker, Carlos. *Ernest Hemingway*. New York: Scribner's, 1969.

Bekker, Cajus. *The Luftwaffe War Diaries*. New York: Doubleday, 1968.

Berlitz, Charles. *The Bermuda Triangle*. New York: Doubleday, 1973.

Blumenson, Martin. *Breakout and Pursuit*. Washington, D.C.: Office of Chief of Military History, 1961.

British Air Ministry. *By Air to Battle*. London: British Air Ministry, 1945.

Brooke, Field Marshal Alan. *Diaries*. London: Collins, 1956.

Brown, Anthony Cave. *Bodyguard of Lies*. New York: Harper & Row, 1975.

Bullock, Alan. *Hitler*. New York: Harper & Row, 1962.

Butcher, Harry C. *My Three Years With Eisenhower*. New York: Simon & Schuster, 1947.

Carell, Paul. *Invasion—They're Coming!* New York: Dutton, 1962.

Carroll, Wallace. *Persuade or Perish*. Boston: Houghton Mifflin, 1948.

Chatterton, George. *Wings of Pegasus*. London: McDonald, 1961.

Churchill, Winston. *The Great War*. London: Newnes, 1933.

———. *The Second World War*, vol. 3. London: Cassell, 1948.

Clark, Blake. *Remember Pearl Harbor*. New York: Arbor House, 1962.

Clark, Mark. *Calculated Risk*. New York: Harper, 1950.

Codman, Charles R. *Drive*. Boston: Little, Brown, 1956.

Cole, Hugh M. *The Ardennes*. Washington, D.C.: Office of the Chief of Military History, 1964.

Collier, Basil. *The Battle of Britain*. New York: Berkley, 1969.

Colvin, Ian. *Master Spy*. New York: McGraw-Hill, 1950.

Craven, Wesley F., and James L. Cate. eds. *The Army Air Forces in World War II*. Chicago: University of Chicago Press, 1949.

Deacon, Richard. *History of the British Secret Service*. London: Muller, 1968.

Delmer, Sefton. *Black Boomerang*. New York: Viking, 1961.

Dornberger, Walter. *V-2*. New York: Viking, 1958.

Dulles, Allen W. *The Craft of Intelligence*. New York: Harper & Row, 1962.

Eisenhower, Dwight D. *Crusade in Europe*. Garden City, NY: Doubleday, 1948.

Farago, Ladislas. *Patton: Ordeal and Triumph*. New York: Obelensky, 1964.

———. *The Game of the Foxes*. New York: McKay, 1970.

———. *The Last Days of Patton*. New York: McGraw-Hill, 1980.

Foot, M. R. D. *SOE in France*. London: HMSO, 1965.

Galland, Adolf. *The First and the Last*. London: Metheun, 1955.

Ganier-Raymond, Philippe. *The Tangled Web*. New York: Pantheon, 1963.

Gehlen, Richard. *The Service*. New York: World, 1971.

Gittleson, Bernard. *Intangible Evidence.* New York: Fireside Books, 1986.
Gordon, David L., and R. J. Dangerfield. *The Hidden Weapon.* New York: Harper, 1947.
Hall, Angus. *Signs of Things to Come.* Garden City, NY: Doubleday, 1974.
Hayman, LeRoy. *Thirteen Who Vanished.* New York: Messner, 1977.
Hechler, Kenneth. *The Bridge at Remagan.* New York: Ballantine Books, 1957.
Hemingway, Ernest. *The Way It Was.* New York: Scribner's, 1974.
Hoehling, A. A. *Home Front USA.* New York: Crowell, 1966.
Höhne, Heinz. *The General Was a Spy.* New York: Coward, McCann & Geoghegan, 1971.
Hoyt, Edwin, P. *The U-Boat Wars.* New York: Arbor House, 1983.
Hutton, J. Bernard. *Hess.* London: Baker, 1965.
Hynd, Alan. *Passport to Treason.* New York: McBride, 1943.
———. *Out of This World.* London: Baker, 1968.
Illustrated Encyclopedia of World War II. London: Marshall Cavendish, 1969.
Irving, David. *The Mare's Nest.* London: Kimber, 1963.
———. *The War Between the Generals.* New York: Congdon & Lattès, 1980.
Kahn, David. *Hitler's Spies.* New York: MacMillan, 1974.
Kennett, Lee. *For the Duration.* New York: Scribner's, 1984.
Kusche, Lawrence D. *The Bermuda Triangle.* New York: Warner, 1975.
Leahy, William D. *I Was There.* New York: McGraw-Hill, 1950.
Leasor, James. *Green Beach.* New York: Morrow, 1975.
Leckie, Robert. *Strong Men Armed.* New York: Random House, 1960.
Manchester, William R. *American Caesar.* Boston: Little, Brown, 1977.
Martin, Ralph G., ed. *The GI War.* Boston: Little, Brown, 1966.
Maxtone-Graham, John. *The Only Way to Cross.* New York: Collier, 1972.
Merriam, Robert. *Dark December.* Chicago: Ziff-David, 1947.
Mittelman, Joseph P. *Eight Stars to Victory.* Washington: Privately printed, 1947.
Moran, Lord Charles Wilson. *Diaries.* Boston: Houghton Mifflin, 1947.
———. *Churchill: The Struggle for Survival.* Boston: Houghton Mifflin, 1946.
Morison, Samuel Eliot. *The Liberation of the Philippines.* Boston: Little, Brown, 1969.
Nash, Jay. *Among the Missing.* New York: Simon and Schuster, 1977.
O'Donnell, James P. *The Bunker.* Boston: Houghton Mifflin, 1977.
Patton, George S., Jr. *War As I Knew It.* Boston: Houghton Mifflin, 1947.
Phillippi, Wendell C. *Dear Ike.* Nashville: Two-Star Press, 1988.
Picture History of World War II. New York: American Heritage Publishing, 1966.
Piekalkiewicz, Janusz. *Secret Agents, Spies, and Saboteurs.* New York: Morrow, 1975.
Reader's Digest Association, *Illustrated Story of World War II.* Pleasantville, NY: Reader's Digest Association, 1955.
———. *Mysteries of the Unexplained.* Pleasantville, NY: Reader's Digest Association, 1981.
———. *Secrets and Spies.* Pleasantville, NY: Reader's Digest Association, 1966.
Reid, P. R. *Colditz.* New York: St. Martin's, 1984.
Rickenbacker, Edward V. *Seven Came Through.* New York: Doubleday, Doran, 1943.
Sayers, Michael and Albert E. Kahn. *Sabotage!* New York: McKay, 1971.
Schellenberg, Walther. *The Labyrinth.* New York: Harper, 1955.
Scott, Robert L., Jr. *Damned to Glory.* New York: Scribner's, 1944.

Shirer, William L. *The Rise and Fall of the Third Reich.* New York: Simon and Schuster, 1959.

Skorzeny, Otto. *Skorzeny's Secret Missions.* New York: Dutton, 1950.

Speer, Albert. *Inside the Third Reich.* New York: MacMillan, 1951.

Steiger, Brad. *Mysteries of Mind, Space, and Time.* Englewood Cliffs, NJ: Prentice-Hall, 1974.

Strong, Kenneth. *Intelligence at the Top.* New York: Doubleday, 1969.

Summersby, Kay. *Eisenhower Was My Boss.* New York: Prentice-Hall, 1948.

Trever-Roper, Hugh R. *Blitzkrieg to Defeat* New York: Rinehart and Winston, 1971.

Weintraub, Stanley. *Long Day's Journey Into War.* New York: Dutton, 1990.

Wheeler-Bennett, John. *Nemisis of Power.* New York: MacMillan, 1964.

Whitehall, Walter M. *Fleet Admiral King.* New York: Norton, 1951.

Whitehead, Don. *The FBI Story.* New York: Random House, 1956.

Whitney, Courtney. *McArthur: His Rendezvous With History.* New York: Knopf, 1956.

Winterbotham, F. W. *The Ultra Secret.* New York: Harper & Row, 1973.

Young, Desmond. *Rommel.* New York: Harper, 1950.

Zacharias, Ellis M. *Secret Missions.* New York: Putnam, 1946.

Zuckerman, Solly. *From Apes to Warlords.* New York: Harper & Row, 1975.

Magazines
American History Illustrated, American Legion, Army, Collier's, Life, Parade, Reader's Digest, Saturday Evening Post, Scientific American, Time, VFW, Yank

Newspapers
Boston Globe, Chicago Daily News, Chicago Tribune, Daily Telegraph (London), *Denver Post, Los Angeles Times, Miami Herald, New York Herald-Tribune, New York Times, St. Louis Globe-Democrat, St. Louis Post-Dispatch, Stars and Stripes, Times* (London), *Washington Post, Washington Star.*

Index